MADAME TUSSAUD

A LIFE AND A TIME

MADAME TUSSAUD

A LIFE AND A TIME

TERESA RANSOM

SUTTON PUBLISHING

First published in 2003 by
Sutton Publishing Limited · Phoenix Mill
Thrupp · Stroud · Gloucestershire · GL5 2BU

British Library Cataloguing in Publication Data
A catalogue record for this book is available from the British Library.

ISBN 0-7509-2765-8

Typeset in 11/14.5 pt Sabon.
Typesetting and origination by
Sutton Publishing Limited.
Printed and bound in England by
J.H. Haynes & Co. Ltd, Sparkford.

For Gemma

On voit que l'histoire est une galerie de tableaux où il y a peu d'origineaux et beaucoup de copies.
One sees that history is a gallery of pictures in which there are few originals and many copies.

Alexis de Tocqueville, *L'Ancien Régime*, 1856

En effet, l'histoire n'est que le tableau des crimes et des malheurs.
Indeed history is nothing more than a tableau of crimes and misfortunes.

Voltaire, *L'Ingénu*, 1767

Contents

List of Illustrations

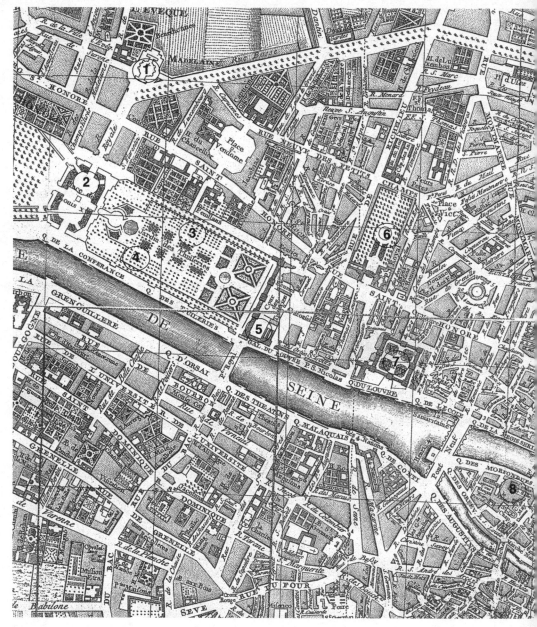

1. Madeleine Church and cemetery where Marie took death masks of Louis XVI and Marie Antoinette
2. Place Louis XV, later Place de la République and site for the guillotine
3. Location of the Ménage, where the Assembly met
4. The Tuileries gardens
5. The Tuileries palace
6. The Palais-Royal before conversion
7. The old Louvre

Paris 1777

8. The Conciergerie prison
9. Notre Dame
10. Place de Grève, here the guillotine was first used
11. Hôtel de Ville, the Town Hall
12. The Bastille, destroyed on 14 July 1789
13. The Temple in which the royal family were imprisoned
14. Boulevard du Temple. Curtius's *Salon de Cire* was at no. 20
15. 36 rue des Fosses du Temple where François Tussaud died in 1848

The Magnificent Group of the Royal Family, as it will appear at Madame Tussaud's, in a few years' time.

I DREAMT THAT I SLEPT AT MADAME TUSSAUD'S

I.

Madame Tussaud beside herself.

I dreamt that I sle-ept at Madame Tussaud's,
    With Cut-throats and Kings by my si-i-ide ;
And that all the Wax-figures in tho-ose abodes,
    At Midnight became vivifi i-ied.
I dreamt William the Four-urth sat dow-own to smoke
    With Collins, who aimed at his eye,
And I a-also dre-eamt King Hal—what a joke !—
    Danc'd the Polka with Mi-istress Fry,
    Danc'd the Polka—the Polka with Mi-istress Fry,
    Danc'd the Polka—the Polka with Mi-istress Fry.

II.

The Brigand of Windmill Street on the look-out down the Haymarket.

I dreamt that Napo-le-on Bo-onaparte
    Was waltzing with Madame T-e-ee ;
That O'Connell, to study the regicide art,
    Had a gossip with Fieschi-e-ee ;
And Penn making eyes with Queen Be-ess I saw,
    And Pitt taking gro-og with Fox.
And I a-also dreamt the Sun melted—oh la !
    The nose of Lord Brougham and Vaux—
    The nose of—the nose of Lord Brougham and Vaux—
    The nose of—the nose of Lord Brougham and Vaux

George IV., at Madame Tussaud's, without his grand Coronation Robes.

Napoleon, at Madame Tussaud's, melting before the Sun of England.

Preface

In the late 1780s the first rumblings of the French Revolution were heard in London, and after the fall of the Bastille in 1789 fleeing *émigrés* brought disturbing stories from the other side of the Channel. As the massacres in Paris intensified, the number of refugees increased dramatically, crowding the streets of London and swelling the purses of merchants. In 1802, during the transient Peace of Amiens, many of those refugees returned home, but their places were taken by others who had survived the Terror and were looking for fortune and security in London. One of these was Anne-Marie Tussaud, an unknown 41-year-old Frenchwoman, who came to London with a collection of wax figures of royals and revolutionaries. Most of these figures she had modelled herself; and it is her hands which tell the story of the time in which she lived.

Marie was trained as an artist by Doctor Curtius, a wax modeller of great renown in Paris and owner of the famous *Salon de Cire*. Before the Revolution Marie had lived for eight years at the court of Versailles as tutor in the art of wax modelling to Louis XVI's youngest sister, Madame Elisabeth. Forced to leave Versailles by the looming menace of the Revolution, Marie returned to live in the rackety, dangerous, show-business world of Paris. Although thrown into prison in July 1794, during the height of the Terror, unlike many others she escaped the guillotine. Then Curtius died, and left to Marie, his sole heir, his *Cabinet de Curiosités*, his collection of wax figures, his properties in Paris – and his debts. Not long afterwards, in 1795, she married François Tussaud.

In 1802 Marie took advantage of the brief moment of peace and left Paris for London, taking with her thirty-five full-sized figures, such materials as she needed to ply her trade and her four-year-old son Joseph. She left her husband in charge of the Paris wax museum, and entrusted him with the care of her mother, her aunt and her two-year-old son François. She spoke only French and German, but hoped to make enough money in the peaceful prosperity of England to pay off her mounting debts.

During the Revolution Marie had met and modelled most of the notables in the government, and had made numerous death-masks. Her display of figures from France was the first chance for many in England to actually see both the perpetrators and the victims of the Revolution. News was sparse: information was slow to arrive and often distorted by rumour. One way to catch a glimpse of another, tantalising world was to visit an exhibition of famous figures modelled in wax. Most exciting of all of Marie's exhibits was the group, 'modelled from life', of the French royal family, Louis XVI, Marie Antoinette, the dauphin and the princess, Madame Royale. The poignancy of the scene was emphasised by models of the decapitated heads of the king and queen. Visitors learned that these models had been made by the diminutive Frenchwoman herself, who had taken casts from the royal heads as they lay bundled in baskets, awaiting burial in a mass grave at the Madeleine cemetery. This was eyewitness news – and it was as near to history as most people wanted to get. This was almost as good as being there yourself.

Cut off from France by the resumption of hostilities in 1803, Marie was never to return. Over the next thirty-five years with dogged determination she toured with her exhibition, travelling the length and breadth of Britain. Slowly her fame grew, and in 1835, at the age of seventy-four, she found a permanent home for her figures at Baker Street in London.

Madame Tussaud's has now become a household name, a name which for over 160 years has been synonymous with the art of wax modelling. And yet, what of the woman behind the name, who rose from humble and obscure beginnings to international recognition? Who was Madame Tussaud?

ONE

'A great crowd of curious people'

Marie, born in Strasbourg, the principal town of Alsace, was the daughter of 18-year-old Anna Marie Waltner[1] and 45-year-old Johann Joseph Grosholtz of Frankfurt.[2] She was christened Anne Marie Grosholtz on 7 December 1761.[3] In her *Memoirs*, dictated to a family friend, Francis Hervé, and published when she was seventy-seven, Marie said that her father had served in the French army as adjutant to Major-General Count Dagobert Sigismund Würmser, and fought in the Seven Years War. He had been 'so mutilated with wounds, that his forehead was laid bare, and his lower jaw shot away, and supplied by a silver plate'. She never knew him: he died from his terrible injuries two months before she was born. Her soldier father was twenty-seven years older than her mother, and no record has yet been found of either their meeting or their marriage. However, in Marie's memoirs she tells how he 'espoused a widow named Marie Walter [sic], who had seven sons, the daughter of a Swiss clergyman, justly celebrated for her fine person, and who lived to the age of ninety, and whose family were remarkable for their longevity, her mother living to a hundred and four, and her grandmother to a hundred and eleven'.[4] Marie was looking back on her past from a distance of many years, which may account for the confusion here, as it seems unlikely that eighteen-year-old Marie Waltner had already produced seven sons by the time her daughter was born. Of these seven half-brothers, however, three became officers in the King's Swiss Guard in Paris and were massacred at the Tuileries on 10 August 1792. Members of the Grosholtz family had been public executioners in Zurich since 1473. Marie's grandfather was the executioner in Strasbourg, her great uncle, in Baden Baden.[5]

Within two years of the death of Joseph Grosholtz, when the

Seven Years War ended in 1763, Marie's mother had moved south to Berne with her daughter, and obtained a post as housekeeper to 26-year-old Philippe Guillaume Mathé Curtius, who had been born in Stockach in 1737. A medical doctor, Curtius used wax to model replicas of internal organs, and from that practical beginning went on to portraiture. Wax busts and heads were popular, as were the erotic miniatures Curtius modelled for his special clients. There can only be speculation as to the connection between Curtius and Marie's mother. Nothing has been found to show where or how they met, or to explain why he offered a home in Berne to her and her daughter. Curtius never married, and Marie and her mother shared his house with him until his death. Marie, who referred to him as her uncle, seems to have regarded him more as a father figure.

In 1763, the same year that Marie and her mother moved to Berne, the Prince de Conti, who was travelling incognito in Switzerland, called on his protégé, Jean-Jacques Rousseau. The prince, a cousin to Louis XV and a notorious libertine, had fallen out of favour at the French court because of his hostility to Madame de Pompadour. He lived in the north-east of Paris, where the Temple buildings housed a prison, many apartments and a luxuriously furnished palace. There he enjoyed semi-royal status, entertained lavishly and was patron to many artists.[6] Rousseau, who had achieved popular fame as a writer with the romance *Julie, ou La Nouvelle Héloïse*, had followed this in 1762 with *Émile*, widely viewed as an outright attack on the Church, and the *Contrat Social*, which was condemned by the court as anti-royalist. In imminent danger of arrest Rousseau had been advised by the Prince de Conti to leave France, and in 1763 he was in hiding in Switzerland on the island of Saint-Pierre in the Lake of Bienne.[7] There the prince visited him, then went on to nearby Berne, where he called on Rousseau's friend, Doctor Curtius. Impressed by Curtius's skill in wax modelling the prince invited him to Paris, and Curtius duly set off leaving Marie Waltner and her infant daughter in Berne. He was given rooms in an apartment in the Hôtel d'Allègre in the rue Saint-Honoré, a place where many artists lived, and for some time he was kept busy executing orders for his patron. To the west and north of rue Saint-Honoré were market gardens, but nearby was a gallery called the Académie de St Luc, where the paintings and sculptures of aspiring artists were shown. Curtius collected paintings, made pictures in enamel, created wax-relief portraits and also made popular erotic wax miniatures.[8] The Paris climate of excess and pleasure favoured his salon, and he opened a second showplace in boulevard Saint-Martin. By 1767 Curtius was doing well enough to send for Marie and her mother. He needed his housekeeper and he had hopes that Marie might become an apt apprentice. Six-year-old Marie and her mother spoke only German.

When young Marie Grosholtz arrived in Paris in 1767, she must have found her new surroundings very different from the orderly peace of Berne. Paris was noisy and dirty. Life on the streets was tough. There was an endless panorama of street theatre, peepshow vendors and freak shows, and the boulevards swarmed with mountebanks and prostitutes. The smell in the boulevards was nauseating, the noise unbelievable. Household waste was emptied straight into the undrained streets. Animals were slaughtered outside the butcher's shop, and down the centre of the mean and narrow streets ran a stream of sewage, mud, blood and offal. Carriages rumbled all day over the cobbled roads in the centre of the city, and the cries of street vendors echoed through the tall buildings, competing with the shouts of drivers, horsemen and servants trying to clear a passage. The journalist Mercier noted:

> Our poorer classes are naturally noisy, and shout with equal disregard for their own throats and their listener's ears. Cries make a Babel of our mean streets, cries raucous, or toneless, or shrill. . . . Men screaming like women, women shouting like men. The din never ceases; no words can give any idea of the abomination of this piteous vocal torment when all the cries meet and mingle, as they sometimes do, at a cross roads.

Passers-by were in constant danger of being splattered by the filthy runnel in the road, and in wet weather enterprising Parisians charged for the use of a plank to enable pedestrians to cross from

3

one side of the road to the other without wading through the muck. Mercier continued:

> There is no defence against our mud; you may walk delicately, you may cultivate eyes in the back of your head – all to no purpose; sometimes, even, the too-zealous broom of a street cleaner bespatters with its gleanings the white stockings of the passer-by. This is the signal for the brusher-down, who lies in wait at the street corner – ready for just such accidents with his officious brush.[9]

The inhabitants thrived in this competitive, filthy atmosphere, and the figures in Curtius's *Salon de Cire* gave them a glimpse into another world. Here the nobility came to be modelled in wax and the citizens happily paid two sous to gawp at the images. Curtius's *salon* became popular in court circles and he had many notable models, including Louis XV, Queen Marie Leczinska and her father, the ex-king of Poland, King Stanislas. In 1765, not long after his arrival, Curtius had modelled a recumbent portrait of Jeanne Beauvarnier (or Bécu), Jean du Barry's beautiful 22-year-old mistress, who had caught the roving eye of Louis XV. After making a judicious marriage to her lover's brother, Madame du Barry became the king's favourite. She was a beautiful but indolent woman who, unlike her predecessor Madame du Pompadour, had no wish to meddle in politics. Madame du Barry was one of Curtius's most memorable sitters, and her figure certainly went to England with Marie Tussaud in 1802. It seems very likely that she was also the much-acclaimed 'Sleeping Venus' of Sylvestre's London exhibition in 1785.

In 1770, when Marie was nine years old, Curtius moved from rue Saint-Honoré and opened his exhibition of wax figures at 20 boulevard du Temple, a tall building tucked in-between two theatres. It was a large rambling house, and there Marie lived with her mother, Madame Waltner; her aunt, Madame Allemann; her 'uncle', Doctor Curtius; and a number of assistants, including a doorman who acted as a barker, calling out the museum's attractions to the passers-by.

There is a letter to Curtius from his lawyer, Altenbourg, in Germany, dated March 1776 and addressed to: Palais-Royal – Cote de l'Avenue de l'Opera par la Cour Desfontaine.[10] This was thought by some earlier biographers to indicate that Curtius was established at the Duc d'Orléans's Palais-Royal. However, looking at contemporary maps of Paris this seems unlikely. The Duc d'Orléans gave the Palais-Royal to his son in 1776, but it was not until 1784 that the palace and gardens were converted into the arcades which contained cafés, shops and theatres and became a fashionable meeting place. It was then that Curtius rented arcades numbers seven and eight. In 1776, when the letter was written, the work had not been started.[11]

The boulevard du Temple near the Prince de Conti's palace was originally a sad and deserted place on the outskirts of Paris. Bounded by walls and deep ditches, the street was unpaved, muddy, criss-crossed by tracks and splattered with puddles of dirty rainwater. In 1760 Nicolet, a clown in a troupe run by M. Gaudon, rented a small room in the boulevard du Temple for use as a theatre; when this was destroyed by fire, his son rebuilt it as le Salle des Grands Danseurs. Because of mud, flooding and the rough uneven ground, there were many problems at the start. Nicolet's theatre presented a varied programme, including pantomime, rope dancers, tumblers and marionettes. These shows appealed to the labourers and artisans of Paris and the theatre was well patronised. In 1769 Audinot, a rival to Nicolet and another protégé of the Prince de Conti, built his *Ambigu Comique* in the boulevard. Initially he used marionettes but quickly changed to child actors and presented ribald and satirical plays. The show catered for all tastes with songs, burlesque, satire and sentimental drama. Prices were cheap and the theatre was always crowded.[12] As the showmen moved in, the boulevard du Temple began to come to life, and when Curtius went there in 1770 it was already one of the most popular meeting places in Paris. This was the raucous, entertainment centre of Paris, where every sort of spectacle could be found. Balladeers sang in the streets. Prostitutes mixed with ladies of rank. There were exhibitions of art, magic shows and Curtius's wax museum. Traditional theatre could be found in the more fashionable Opéra and the Comédie-Française, but popular street theatre where all classes and ranks mingled together in happy anonymity was found in the boulevard du Temple. Life in the boulevard, where Marie grew up, was noisy, uninhibited and vulgar.

The journalist Mayeur de Saint-Paul lived in the same district as Curtius, and wrote about the area between the rue de l'Ancri, just north of the rue du Temple, down as far as the Pont-aux-Choux on the west side of the boulevard du Temple. He described the boulevard before it reached the theatres of Nicolet and Audinot:

> There were barkers all along the road shouting out their attractions. One barker invites you in to look at a menagerie of animals; another a giant; another a concert of Musical Glasses, and another tells you the exact hour when a marionette comedy will commence. When you enter the animal menagerie the smell is so overpowering you have to resort to your smelling bottle to overcome it, but you go in anyway because you believe that you will be rewarded by the sight of rare animals. In fact all you see is three or four villainous monkeys, all very dirty, and a few dogs. When you go in to look at the giant, you expect to see someone enormous, and truly the woman is large, very large, but very ordinary. This colossus is created by wearing a pair of five-inch heels, and a gravity-defying hairstyle.

Curtius's wax museum was situated further along the road in-between the theatres of Nicolet and Audinot. Mayeur de Saint-Paul continued:

> This industrious German is able to model wax heads which, when coloured, appear to be living. He alone is both the modeller and painter. One can see these heads in his 'cabinet', boulevard du Temple, & at the Saint-Laurent & Saint-Germain Fairs, where, because they can obtain this pleasure for two sous, they attract a great crowd of curious people from all classes. Curtius also undertakes the making of wax portraits and makes them look

very realistic. Every unusual event gives him the opportunity to add to his collection. At present one can see the portraits of M. Destaing [d'Estaing], that of Voltaire, the royal family, etc. But it is the production of the little groups of Gaillards and Libertines [erotic lovers] that he sells to those interested in adorning their boudoirs, which brings him the best return.[13]

By this time Anne Marie Grosholtz was in her late teens, and was already a skilled wax modeller. She had learned her trade under the strict tuition of her uncle and modelled many of his visitors for the *salon*. Many of the figures attributed to Curtius were in reality made by her. Francis Hervé, who later transcribed her memoirs, commented that while she lived with her uncle:

> She had clearly imbibed the greatest taste for that art in which he so excelled, but in which his niece so closely imitated him, that it was impossible to distinguish as to the degrees of excellence between their performances. At that period, modelling in wax was much in vogue, in which representations of flowers, fruit and other subjects, were often most beautifully executed: and to such perfection had [Marie] arrived in giving character and accuracy to her portraits, that, whilst still very young, to her was confided the task of making casts from the heads of Voltaire, Rousseau, Franklin, Mirabeau, and the principal characters of that period . . . the house of M. Curtius had become the resort of many of the most talented men in France, particularly as regarded the literati and artists.[14]

These men dined frequently with Curtius. Marie, who was always present, made careful and professional note of their appearance, and has left detailed first-hand impressions of them in her memoirs. By the time she met Rousseau he had acquired a reputation as an unhappy and difficult man, who, although much admired, was tormented by his imagination. He had travelled widely, and in the first half of his life, until he was thirty-three, 'if he was known at all it was as an eccentric ragabond'. In 1758 he had written a pamphlet attacking Voltaire, as a result of which they became implacable enemies. Banished from Switzerland in 1766, he had journeyed to Britain where he lived under the patronage of David Hume, the metaphysician and historian. Once again Rousseau's bizarre behaviour made him quarrel with his benefactor and drove him back to France. In 1770 he returned to Paris where for eight years he lived in the rue Platière, becoming increasingly paranoid.[15] Marie found Rousseau to be:

> much below middle height, and inclined to be stout; he wore a short round wig with curls, something like that worn by George the Third, and what coachmen used to wear in the country, and which custom is still continued in some families of the old school; he generally dressed in a snuff-coloured suit, very plain, and much resembling the present garb of the Quakers; but at one period of his life he adopted the Armenian costume, wearing a long robe, trimmed with fur, and a cap of the same material. He was very fond of the Swiss mode of living; therefore found the table of M. Curtius to his taste.[16]

Rousseau's writings glorified a return to simple country living. He advocated that people should enjoy a rustic life and allow their children to be brought up to run free and wild. This was far from the doctrine he himself practised. His common-law wife Thérèse le Vasseur, a servant at the inn where he had once lodged, was treated harshly; his five children by her were all consigned to foundling hospitals; he betrayed his friends and failed to pay his debts.

In February 1778 the ailing Voltaire was given permission by the king to return to Paris from exile in Switzerland, and he stayed at the town house of the Marquis de Villette in the rue de Beaune. He was rapturously welcomed by his countrymen with fêtes and celebrations. That spring, Talleyrand, who had always admired Voltaire, was taken to meet him by an old school friend, Sebastien de Chamfort, whom Marie was later to know when he became employed as librarian to Madame Elisabeth. Voltaire was old and frail but he would sometimes dine at Curtius's house at

20 boulevard du Temple. There he would occasionally meet the unpredictable Rousseau. Marie, who was present, well remembered:

> . . . the acrimony displayed between Voltaire and Rousseau in their disputes in the support, perhaps, of some metaphysical theory, in which themselves alone could feel interested. . . . Bitter, indeed, was then the venom which was emitted by those two celebrated authors at each other; most rancorous were the reproaches which Rousseau would launch forth against Voltaire, while his replies were not less deficient in their gall. . . . When Voltaire retired, then would Rousseau give free vent to all his rage against his arch rival . . . until he was fatigued with the fury of his own eloquence. The latter was far more biting in his sarcasms than his competitor, who sometimes felt so irritated, that, losing his self-possession, the point of his satire often lost its keenness. Voltaire, also, was ever gay, whilst Rousseau was generally the reverse, and rather misanthropic.[17]

Rousseau died in the summer of 1778, probably by his own hand. Marie remembered Voltaire as:

> Tall and thin, with a very small face, which had a shrivelled appearance, and he wore a large flowing wig, like those which were the mode at the time of Louis the Fourteenth. [He] was mostly dressed in a brown coat with gold lace at the button-holes, and waistcoat the same, with large lappets reaching nearly to his knees, and small clothes of cloth of a similar description, a little cocked hat and large shoes, with a flap covering the instep, and generally striped silk stockings. He had a very long thin neck, and when full dressed, had ends to his neckcloth of rich lace, which hung as low as his waist; his ruffles were of the same material, and, according to the fashion of the day, he wore powder and sword.[18]

Marie modelled him only two months before his death, in the spring of 1778. This model is still on show at Madame Tussaud's in London.

In 1777, when Marie was sixteen, some improvements were made to the streets around Curtius's *salon*. The ditches, walls and escarpments were flattened to allow new houses to be constructed. The muddy rue Saint-Antoine and the boulevard du Temple were paved, which improved access, and Temple Gate was partly demolished so that faubourg du Temple and rue d'Angoulême could be opened. Theodore Faucheur remarked:

The boulevard became the place to find everything that was new and original. Its long avenue of centuries-old trees, and the small ditches that crossed at intervals beside the road of Filles du Calvaire became the rendezvous for Parisians of all classes and conditions. The artisans jostle the capitalists, the soldier, the onlooker, the courtesans and the grande dame; all classes of society are mixed together here, braving the rain, the cold and the heat. Each of them in their promenade, finding an emotion, a distraction, a pleasure in which they can forget for a moment their daily cares, and the evils of our poor miserable human life.[19]

Many of the shows in the boulevard took place in small wooden kiosks crammed into the spaces in front of the main buildings. Here could be seen performing fleas pulling tiny carriages, fire eaters, snake charmers, children swallowing boiling oil and trained dogs who could count 'as well as a minister of finance'. The shows generally started at midday, when the noise of singers, musicians and merchants was joined by the cries of street vendors selling oranges, sugar and hot or cold drinks. As evening approached the boulevard became more frantic, and when the theatres opened their doors the public were able to 'cry, rage, laugh, and share their emotions with their favourite actors'. Faucheur described the boulevard as 'a perpetual fair'.[20]

A feature of many of Curtius's fellow showmen-scientists was the ability to employ their knowledge of new discoveries, such as magnetism, gas and electricity, to baffle and amuse the public. One of these scientists was the famous physician Comus, whose real name was Nicolas-Philippe Ledru. He lived and worked in the building next door to Curtius, and both were interested in electricity and the properties of light. Comus had started as a conjuror, using mind-reading, magic tricks and phantasmagoria. He then became a master of science, interested in the use of scientific instruments, and lectured on many subjects including medicine, physic, chemistry, electricity, anatomy and natural history. He was a skilled teacher and attracted many followers. He did much research into the medical use of electricity, and pioneered electro-shock treatment for epileptics.[21] Although he achieved fame as a healer, he always remained an entertainer at heart and successfully combined science and showmanship with his performances on the boulevard du Temple. This was true of another showman, Friedrich Mesmer, who arrived in Paris in 1778, promising miraculous cures. According to the gossipy journalist Mercier, he conducted his healing sessions in a large, dimly lit room, where music played in the background. The 'patients' sat on chairs around a large circular copper bath in the centre of the room, and each held one of the handles projecting from the lid. A 'Current of Influence' passed from the handle to the patient, at which moment each patient released their handle and linked forefingers and thumbs around the table forming 'the chain', while Mesmer directed the current around the circle with an iron wand. He treated difficult cases personally by sitting directly in front of the patient with his feet and knees touching theirs, and stroking the more sensitive parts of their body. Mercier reports that this was especially efficacious with women.[22] Six years later, in 1784, Benjamin Franklin was a member of a committee which was ordered by the king to investigate mesmerism; their negative findings resulted in the disgrace and flight of Mesmer.

Doctor James Graham's 'Celestial Bed' was another piece of quackery reported by Mercier. For a handsome payment the bed could be reserved for a night of frolic and fun. Music played, seductive perfumes wafted around the chamber and vestal virgins added an element of sensuous mystery to the evening. It was claimed that children of heavenly beauty would be conceived by the couple who made love on the bed.[23]

Paris at that time was engrossed with magic and illusion. There was a fascination with science, with mechanical fireworks and experimental physics; with the wiles of Mesmer and the use of hypnotism and mind-reading. Charlatans thrived on the boulevard, and serious scientists in the *salons*. Marie, who grew up in this tough, uninhibited world of entertainment, became a watcher and a trained observer. All her descriptions of people are minute and she depicts their clothes and appearance in great detail, but she never mentions their feelings. Somehow she was able to remain detached from the emotional turmoil around her.

This detachment was to serve her in good stead when, at the age of nineteen, she was swept from the raucous camaraderie of the boulevard du Temple into the dangerous intrigues of the court at Versailles.

TWO

'The royal family is a spectacle'

When Marie went to Versailles in 1780, as art tutor to Madame Elisabeth, she discovered that life in the streets of Paris and life at the court of Versailles were worlds apart.

Versailles was an unreal world of effete privilege and vast wealth, and there was much corruption at court. Madame de la Tour du Pin wrote: 'Among the Court Nobles could be found instances of every form of vice. Gaming, debauchery, immorality, irreligion, all were flaunted openly. . . . The rot started at the top and spread downwards. Virtue in men and good conduct in women became the object of ridicule and were considered provincial.'[1] There was much jostling for position, and the court was riddled with spiteful intrigues. Places in the royal household could be sold to raise revenue, but more often the positions came from jealously guarded hereditary rights. Many situations were obtained through influence, and much of the extravagance of the court was fed by this long-established system of hangers-on and royal perquisites. Upper-class bourgeoisie sought to become aristocrats. Lower-class bourgeoisie tried to better themselves. All were seeking posts which might lead to ennoblement, since aristocrats and the clergy were exempt from the payment of taxes. The question of precedent became all-important. Madame Campan, lady-in-waiting to Marie Antoinette, observed:

The art of war is constantly exercised at court: ranks, dignities, private audiences, but above all favour, keep up an interrupted strife, which excludes thence all idea of peace. . . . The man of the greatest merit will have some failings, or commit some errors; they [the courtiers] reckon upon them, look out for them, exaggerate them, circulate them in society, and they are reported to the prince, under the mark of zeal and perfect devotion to his interests; in the end they generally succeed in the object. . . . Death and disgrace excite only the same idea at court. By whom will he who is fallen be replaced?[2]

When Louis XV's only son died in 1765, his five grandchildren were left in the indifferent care of a succession of tutors and governesses. The eldest surviving boy, eleven-year-old Louis, became the dauphin, his younger brothers, the Comte de Provence and the Comte d'Artois. There were also two younger sisters, Madame Clotilde and lastly Madame Elisabeth Philippine Marie Hélène, born on 3 May 1764. She was later to become Marie Grosholtz's employer and friend.

On 16 May 1770 sixteen-year-old Louis married Marie Antoinette, who was only fourteen-and-a-half years old. Louis was a short, plump, rather plain young man, with a brusque manner. An excellent horseman, he enjoyed hunting above all else, riding out every day and keeping a meticulous record of all game killed. He was fascinated by mechanics, especially locks, and had his own workshop in the palace under the supervision of a master locksmith. Marie said that many of the locks on the palace doors were made by him. He also became an expert on naval matters, spending much time studying maps and charts. He had a rather juvenile sense of humour, often at the expense of his guests – for example, he would have the fountains turned on unexpectedly when they were promenading, and laugh uproariously at their discomfort.

His brothers were very different. Monsieur, the Comte de Provence, who coveted the throne, enjoyed the society of thinkers and writers, looked after his own interests and did not impart confidences, whereas the Comte d'Artois was a playboy, careless, graceful and fun, who liked women, horse racing, frivolity and excesses of all kinds. The influence of the Comte d'Artois on Marie Antoinette was strong and she developed a passion for gambling and for jewellery. The Austrian ambassador in Paris, Mercy d'Argenteau, wrote about her to her mother, the Empress Queen Maria Theresa: 'Her play has become very dear; she no longer plays games of commerce, in which the losses are necessarily limited: lansquenet has become her ordinary play, and sometimes faro.'[3]

On 10 May 1774 King Louis XV died of smallpox. He lay in his bed in the palace of Versailles while his body, weakened from a life of excess, slowly rotted from the disease. The nineteen-year-old dauphin became King Louis XVI. Marie Antoinette wrote to her mother: 'May God watch over us! The king died this day about noon. . . . My God what is to become of M. le Dauphin and me! We are terrified of reigning so young. Oh my kind mother, do not spare your advice to your unfortunate children.'[4] The instant the death of Louis XV was known in the royal palace, the strange noise of stampeding courtiers could be heard in the corridors of Versailles as they rushed from the royal apartments, down the stairs and into the apartment of Louis XVI, to swear allegiance to their new king.

Marie was just fourteen, and still living in the boulevard du Temple, when the coronation of the new king and queen took place on 11 June 1775 at the cathedral in Rheims, where the kings of France were traditionally crowned. Some muttered that it was a far more expensive place for a coronation than Paris. However, at the beginning of Louis XVI's reign, although France was in the midst of an economic crisis, there was much goodwill towards the young couple. The Comte de Maurepas, a kindly and considerate man, was summoned to become prime minister and adviser to the young king. Madame Elisabeth found the courtiers surrounding each of the princes very different: 'Honest men near Louis XVI. Politicians near the Comte de Provence; the frivolous and volatile, near the Comte d'Artois. Thus the friends of the king were few, those of Monsieur numerous, those of Comte d'Artois innumerable.'[5]

After his coronation Louis XVI gave Marie Antoinette the Petit Trianon in the park at Versailles as a private refuge, away from the stifling etiquette of the court. Originally built by Louis XV as a present for Madame de Pompadour, it was not finished in her lifetime. Marie Antoinette transformed the formal French gardens into a landscaped English garden, with lakes, a hamlet and a farm. The gardens were open to the public, with grottoes, lawns and paths shaded by trees, among which were fountains and statues. There was a white marble temple on a small mound dedicated to the God of Love, and a small but magnificently decorated theatre. Marie, when she became a member of Madame Elisabeth's household, remarked that many Italian operas and French plays were performed there, 'the audience consisting entirely of the royal family, and such of the nobility as happened to be at the court'. If an ambassador or any other important person was invited:

> a play was always acted, expressly for the purpose of paying him a distinguished compliment and the best performers which France could produce were selected. . . . They had nought to employ their minds, but to devise new inventions for varying their enjoyments; but whilst experiencing a succession of these luxurious delights, whilst following a career of extravagant dissipation, and whilst basking in the lap of voluptuous ecstacy [sic], it must not be imagined that the pleasant vices were wholly banished from the palace of Versailles. Gaming, in particular, predominated to an excess, the queen and princess losing deeply, whilst the Duke of Orleans won to an immense amount.[6]

Routine at the royal court was governed by ceremonial rules. A timetable of the order and precedence of every action ruled every moment of the day and followed the royal family even to the marriage bed. The Duchesse de Noailles, mockingly called Madame l'Etiquette behind her back, was the strictest enforcer of tradition.

Madame Campan, Marie Antoinette's lady-in-waiting, described how age-old rules were laid down as an unbreakable code; custom dictated the right to offer a glass of water, to put on a dress or to remove a basin. It was a performance and had to be done in the prescribed form. The *dame d'honneur* dressed the queen in her body linen, the tire-woman in her petticoat. There was a principal lady-in-waiting in attendance and two inferior attendants. Each had their own duties. If a princess of royal blood should happen to enter the chamber, then the *dame d'honneur* handed the garments to the chief lady-in-waiting, who handed them to the princess, who handed

16

them to the queen. Dressing became a slow and laborious business and, in the winter, very cold. Madame Campan observed: 'Queens have neither closets nor boudoirs. Kings have no privacy.' She also said: 'Marie Antoinette found in the Palace of Versailles a multitude of established and revered customs which appeared to her to be insupportable.'[7] The young queen, brought up in the German courts where the routine was simpler, found the French court stifling, and soon did away with some of the more tedious formalities. She wrote to her mother in August 1770: 'My life, although I have nothing to do, is still full of affairs: it is not at all like what it was at Vienna or Schönbrunn: even the life of the royal family is a spectacle.'[8] The king's aunts disapproved of the young queen and her 'flighty' ways, and the conservative courtiers, clinging to their positions, resented any changes to the time-honoured traditions. It was from them that the first attacks on her character sprang.

Madame de la Tour du Pin, a young member of the queen's household, described the daily routine. After the queen was dressed by the ladies in attendance on that day, the door of her bedchamber was opened and everyone admitted. They stood at the edges of the room in rows, sometimes two or three deep, but left a clear space at the centre of the room and by the door. When the king was queen, in full court dress:

> would go to meet him with a charming air of pleasure and deference. [The king] was so shortsighted that he could not recognise anyone at a distance of more than three paces. He was stout, about five foot six or seven inches tall, square shouldered and with the worst possible bearing. He looked like some peasant shambling along behind his plough; there was nothing proud or regal about him. His sword was a continual embarrassment to him and he never knew what to do with his hat, yet in court dress he looked really magnificent. He took no interest in his clothes, putting on whatever was handed to him.[9]

The court of young Louis XVI was very different from that of his grandfather. As Madame Campan reported:

Society presented a new spectacle. Manners were not improved but altered. By a strange abuse, apologies were found for depravity in the philosophical ideas which daily grew more fashionable. . . . Men might be inconstant husbands and women faithless wives as long as they spoke with respect, with enthusiasm, of the sacred duties of marriage. The love of virtue and of mankind was sufficient without practical morality. Enthusiasm gained on every mind; it was at the tables and in the drawing rooms of the first nobles that the distinctions of rank were boldly treated as prejudices. . . . It became almost an acknowledged truth that merit was superior to birth.[10]

This was partly due to the influence of Rousseau and his *Contrat Social* which advocated that man should return to a more natural past. At court, however, the strange confusion of simplistic ideals and licentious behaviour was further compounded by traditional, and often irrational, rules of etiquette.

Among the intimate friends of the young queen was Marie-Thérèse, Princesse de Lamballe, a beautiful woman six years older than Marie Antoinette who had been widowed in 1768 at the age of eighteen after only a year of marriage. When Marie went to Versailles she saw the princess frequently and described her as being 'rather under the middle stature; remarked for the extraordinary whiteness of her skin; had light hair, a good colour, aquiline nose, and blue eyes, the chin rather too long and prominent, and, altogether, more pleasing than handsome; but her amiable qualities and sweetness of manners endeared her to all'.[11] A loyal and affectionate friend, she was appointed Superintendent of the Royal Household by the queen. Another close intimate was the Princesse de Guémenée, a young woman surrounded by a group known for their wit, gaiety and passion for gambling. She had been a governess to Madame Elisabeth, and later became one of the controllers of her household. It was fashionable at court to have a special friend known as the *inseparable* and in 1776 Marie Antoinette became infatuated with Yolande, Comtesse de Polignac, who had been introduced to the court by her much older sister-in-law Dianne de Polignac. Yolande, whom the

Duchess of Devonshire called 'little Po', was attractive and coy. Her devotion was tempered by discretion, but she was surrounded by hangers-on demanding favours and this caused resentment among the other courtiers.

The queen was very fond of riding and was always spectacularly attired. Marie described one elaborate dress, a green riding habit, which was 'splendidly embroidered with silver, and a Spanish hat with feathers, presenting so charming a picture, as she sat her horse with graceful ease, that had she been but a private individual, she must have still riveted the attention of every beholder'.[12] The Duchesse d'Orléans had introduced Rose Bertin to the queen as a dressmaker. For the queen to have her own *modiste* was an innovation and much frowned on by the traditionalists, who favoured the old-fashioned, heavy court dresses. Marie Antoinette, however, under the influence of Rose Bertin, became interested in fashion and clothes, and her enthusiasm inspired others to do the same. Headdresses became more and more ornate, and at one stage became so outrageously tall that carriages were not high enough to accommodate them, and the wearer had to hold her head out of the carriage window to avoid crushing the creation. Marie observed of the courtiers:

Whatever could be added to the fascination of colloquial powers, by adorning the person, was not neglected; the expense and richness displayed in their costumes far exceeded that which is exhibited in the present day, lace frills, powder, a sword, and diamond buckles, also much contributed to give éclat to the male costume of that day, whilst the stomachers of the females were often one blaze of jewels.[13]

The queen, like so many at the court, had a passion for jewellery.

Emperor Joseph II of Austria, Marie Antoinette's brother, came to Versailles on 18 April 1777 to check on the alarming stories of his sister's frivolous behaviour, spread in Vienna by Cardinal de Rohan. While in France, Joseph stayed at the Hôtel de Tréville in the rue de Tournon, where he gave his name as Count Falkenstein. A pompous and self-righteous man, he criticised his young sister the queen for many things, including her manner of dressing, for wearing too much rouge and for paying her bills without checking them. As Marie commented after meeting him, he 'was cheerful, affable, and had always much to say'. Too much, it seems. He lectured the king on the habits of his court, which he considered flagrantly immoral, and suggested that Louis would be a better ruler if he visited his own subjects more frequently and spent more time in Paris. He also came to counsel the king, who suffered from a congenital deformity called phimosis, a tightness of the foreskin which made intercourse so painful that he was unwilling to perform full penetration – or so it was reported by the courtiers. The queen had written to Mercy d'Argenteau, the Austrian ambassador in Paris: 'I never cease to think of the strangeness of my situation, the way the king neglects me. I am afraid of being bored and I am afraid of myself. To escape this obsession I need movement and noise.' It is probable that the king's lack of sexual ardour was one of the reasons why she had become so flighty and frivolous. Joseph was able to persuade the king that he should be circumcised, so that he could consummate the marriage and produce the longed-for heir.[14] The operation was performed, the problem corrected and the marriage was finally consummated. On 19 December 1778, to much national rejoicing, Marie Antoinette gave birth to her first child, Marie Thérèse Charlotte. According to royal custom the birth took place in public, in the queen's bedroom, which, because of the design of the palace, also acted as a corridor connecting it to all the other rooms in that wing. Although a low balustrade divided the bed from the rest of the room, there was a great crush of people, some standing on chairs for a better view, and numerous people pushing and shoving around the bed. It was so hot and airless that the queen passed out. The king himself, with unaccustomed energy, forced open the windows which had been sealed with strips of paper to shut out the winter draughts, and ordered that the room be cleared immediately. The queen was bled in the foot and recovered. After that episode the royal tradition of observers was abolished.[15]

During his stay in Paris Joseph II visited the boulevard du Temple to discuss optics with Comus, who had conducted some experiments for him on the decomposition of light.[16] He also went to see Curtius's *Salon de Cire* and was shown around by Curtius himself who explained 'every interesting circumstance connected with the different figures'. The emperor bought several objects from Curtius, including two figures of Venus modelled in wax, and gave permission for Marie to take a mask of his features. She described him as 'a tall fine looking man, rather a fair complexion, with light hair, powdered, a well-formed aquiline nose, but the under lip rather prominent; he was as plainly dressed as possible having merely a cocked hat, and grey great coat, but wore a very long tail which reached all down his back. He was much older than his sister, Marie Antoinette.' Marie thought he was then about thirty-eight. He asked if he could visit the studio, but as he was being taken downstairs he smelt the German sauerkraut being cooked by Marie's mother and 'he lifted up his hands, and threw back his head, exclaiming with an expression of extreme pleasure, "Oh, mein Gott, there is sour krout!"' In order to reach the studio they had to pass through the dining room, where they discovered the family at dinner, and the emperor asked if he could join them:

His Imperial Majesty seated himself at the table, not suffering any individual to rise from it, but joined the group *en famille*, and ate, drank, talked, laughed, and joked, with all possible affability and familiarity, making himself as much at home as if he had been in his palace of Schönbrusen [sic], and consumed a large dish of sour krout. . . . He spoke German all the time, and appeared pleased to have found those who could talk it with him.

The emperor returned Curtius's hospitality by inviting him to breakfast at his hotel. Marie later commented: 'Many are of the opinion that he also came to an untimely end, supposed to have been poisoned, through the instigation of the monks, whom he deprived of a considerable portion of their wealth.'[17]

Two years earlier, on 4 July 1776, America had declared its independence from Britain, and certainly no one in France could have foreseen how far the ripples would spread. Nineteen-year-old

Gilbert Lafayette, in search of adventure, obtained the post of major-general in the colonial forces in America, but Louis XVI forbade him to leave France. Benjamin Franklin, John Adams and Arthur Lee, all newly arrived in Paris as representatives of the breakaway colony, also warned him against going. Ignoring their advice, Lafayette purchased a ship and setting off with eleven companions, evaded the British cruisers sent in pursuit and arrived in Georgetown in South Carolina in early 1777. Finding on his arrival that his lack of experience was not welcomed, he offered to serve as an unpaid volunteer in the American army and the offer was accepted. He met George Washington with whom he formed a close bond, regarding him as a surrogate father.

The American War of Independence was demanding considerable financial and military aid from France. In the French administration, only Turgot was opposed to French involvement, citing the crippling cost of fighting a war on the other side of the world. In late 1777 a Treaty of Alliance was signed between the American insurgents and France, and in 1778 France declared war on Britain in support of the Americans. Indeed, George III, the English king, was looked upon by the French as the aggressor in the war. General Lafayette returned briefly to France in 1779 bearing a commission from the American Congress to appoint 73-year-old Franklin as sole plenipotentiary of the United States to the court of France. Lafayette often visited Curtius, and Marie remembered him as:

> a tall handsome young man, dressed in the costume then worn by a gentleman who affected not the extreme of fashion, nor the reverse; he was elegant in his manners, full of vivacity, and extremely enthusiastic; an ardent advocate for liberty, to the indulgence and dissemination of which feeling may be imputed much that has since befallen France. He was constantly with Franklin.[18]

When Lafayette returned to America, he took with him Axel Fersen, the handsome Swedish count whose attachment to the queen was causing considerable gossip in court circles.

Benjamin Franklin remained in Paris as the American ambassador, living quietly at Passy, away from court. There was much French support and enthusiasm for the American cause, and Franklin, a Quaker, was seen as the embodiment of the bluff pioneer settler, whose demeanour contrasted markedly with the effete foppery of the court: 'The simplicity of his manners and costume, the mild dignity of his deportment, the frankness of his air, the wisdom of his observations, and the correctness of his conduct, made a most forcible impression upon the reflecting portion of the Parisians, and even many of the gayest of the courtiers conceived the highest respect for him.'[19] With his grey hair undressed, and wearing a plain coat, he was dubbed the 'Electrical Ambassador', and the lightning bolt became his symbol. Paris admired his scientific learning and his image appeared everywhere, on porcelain, snuffboxes and glass. Franklin wrote to his daughter in America in 1779: 'The numbers [of medallions] sold are incredible. These, with pictures, busts and prints (of which copies are spread everywhere) have made your father's face as well known as the moon, so that he durst not do anything that would oblige him to run away, as his phiz would discover him wherever he should venture to show it.'[20]

While Franklin was in Paris, Marie modelled him and found him 'an agreeable companion; his personal appearance was that of most perfect simplicity, and his manners truly amiable'. She remembered dancing with him on one occasion: 'He was a stout man, about five feet ten inches in height; his eyes were grey, his complexion light; he dressed in black; his clothes were in the old style; he was remarked for having particularly fine legs.'[21] Marie thought that Doctor Franklin's visit to Paris was a contributing cause to the French Revolution. 'Lafayette was not alone in becoming the disciple of the transatlantic philosopher; for the minds of numbers of young enthusiasts amongst the French nobility also became impregnated with the seeds of republicanism.'[22]

Lafayette was keenly pro-American, and his house attracted those with Franco-American loyalties. Madame Elisabeth, too, was inspired by all things American, and so, according to Madame Campan, was the king. 'The impolitic desire of diminishing the power of England had induced Louis XVI to embrace the cause of the American insurgents against the mother country. Liberty prevailed; they returned triumphant from France, and brought with them the seeds of independence.'[23] Marie agreed: 'From the period of the Doctor's arrival may be dated the change of sentiments which took place in the minds of the French upon political subjects, and which, improperly guided, overwhelmed France with ruin.'[24]

In the spring of 1780, two years after France had declared war on England, sixteen-year-old Madame Elisabeth was given her own suite at Versailles consisting of eight rooms on the first floor. The rooms faced south-west and overlooked woods, the Grand Canal and the road to Saint-Cyr. It was at about this time that Madame Elisabeth visited Curtius's famous wax museum at 20 boulevard du Temple, where she met nineteen-year-old Marie Grosholtz and became intrigued by her skill. The art of wax modelling was at that time a fashionable pastime, and Marie was appointed to teach the princess. The two girls became friends and Madame Elisabeth asked Curtius if Marie could come and live at Versailles as her art tutor, as she desired 'to have the constant enjoyment of her society'.[25]

Taking up this prestigious position at court, Marie was living in surroundings very different from those at the *Salon de Cire*, but her early life on the boulevard du Temple had trained her well. Not only had she lived among the unruly street people, but she had also met and conversed with many of the notables and intellectuals who gathered around Curtius's dinner table. Alert and keenly observant, she described her new employer:

> In person, Madame Elisabeth was rather handsome than otherwise, somewhat below the middle stature; she had blue eyes and a fair complexion, and light hair, powdered; latterly she became very stout, but ever remained elegant in her deportment, and most amiable in her manners, and was always very affable towards her inferiors; was very regular in her manner of living; dined at four, retired early, and seldom gave parties; like all the French royal family, she was particularly partial to the Swiss.[26]

The princess's predilection for the Swiss may be one reason why she became so fond of Marie, who, though born in Alsace, declared herself to be Swiss.

When she was seventeen, the king gave Madame Elisabeth her own house, Montreuil, on the condition that she must not spend the night there until she was twenty-four. The king had bought the house from the Princesse de Guémenée, whose extravagant lifestyle had led to her bankruptcy and subsequent resignation as controller of Madame Elisabeth's household. The gift was a deliberate surprise. One day the queen took Madame Elisabeth to Montreuil on the pretext of visiting the Princesse de Guémenée, then announced, 'Sister, you are in your own house. This is to be your Trianon. The king, who gives himself the pleasure of giving it to you, gives me the pleasure of telling you.'[27]

The house, near the barrier at the entrance to Versailles and on the road to Paris, gave Madame Elisabeth a refuge from the unwelcome pomp and splendour of the court. Built in 1776, Montreuil was white, semicircular, two storeys high and surrounded by 12 acres of land. Around the house were extensive gardens and, some distance away, a dairy, an orangery and farm buildings. Marie was now a member of Madame Elisabeth's household, which at that time consisted of more than seventy people. She had her own room at Versailles, which at the princess's request was next to hers, 'in order to be always near her',[28] and spent the days at Montreuil with her employer. The princess would frequently rise at six, ride for an hour or two and then after breakfast would occupy herself 'with tambour-working, reading, writing, and sometimes playing upon the harpsichord, which, with other elegant amusements, generally occupied the greater portion of her time. She was very fond of modelling in wax, figures of Christ, the Virgin Mary, and other holy subjects, many of which she gave away to her friends.' It was the custom to make a wax model of an afflicted limb and then place this in a church in the hope that the saint to whom it was dedicated could produce a cure. 'Madame Elisabeth, therefore, with pious zeal, would often model the legs and arms of decrepit persons, who desired it, which were afterwards suspended at the Churches of Saint-

Genevieve, Saint-Sulpice, and des Capucins du Murché des enfans rouge.'[29] Marie, who helped her with these models, did not state whether the results of their efforts were successful. She did notice, however, that Madame Elisabeth did not 'enter much into the gaieties of the court, being rather of a retired character; she never frequented the theatre, not being partial to it, but sometimes went when it was the etiquette that she should do so, with the court; she would occasionally play cards of an evening with the royal family'.[30]

Friendly with all her siblings, and especially the queen, Madame Elisabeth spent much time with her at the Petit Trianon where she had a small suite on the second floor. Marie remembered her employer as being 'strictly religious, and charitable, in the purest sense of the word, in all her thoughts and actions; benevolence, and an excess of generosity, characterized all she did'.

The princess studied botany with M. Le Monnier and M. Dassy, mathematics with M. Mauduit and drawing with M. Van Blarenberghe, and much enjoyed needlework. She also liked overseeing the farm, the kitchen gardens and the poultry yards. Generous with her charity, she would distribute ointments and salves to the sick; and to the needy gave vegetables from her gardens and milk from her dairy. Often it was Marie who took money to her pensioners, and several times, following a visit from 'the female who resided with Rousseau', Marie was sent in a carriage to Paris with money to relieve Rousseau's family from their difficulties. Marie thought this all the more remarkable as Rousseau's principles on theological subjects were known to be completely at variance with the princess's. Madame Elisabeth was so impractical with money and so generous with her charity that she frequently gave away her allowance before she had received it, and had to borrow from Marie, 'rather than reject an appeal of an individual who, she thought, merited relief'.[31]

The king often visited his sister at Montreuil. If Marie was present she always offered to retire but he seldom allowed it. '*Restez, restez, mademoiselle*' he would say and motion her to remain. She frequently had a chance to talk with him, and always 'found him very easy and unreserved in his manner, which was untainted with any assumption of pride or superiority, and his demeanour perfectly free from that appearance of condescension which persons of his rank so often adopt towards their inferiors'.[32] Another visitor was Madame Elisabeth's brother, the Comte de Provence, whom Marie remembered less fondly. Meeting him on the staircase one day he tried to kiss her and she

> judged it high time to give him a slap on the face; which so covered the prince with confusion, that when questioned by Madame Elisabeth, his hesitation in replying at once displayed that he was not so perfect at subterfuge and repartee at that period, as he has since proved himself to be. . . . For the future his Royal Highness restricted his expressions of politeness and regard towards [her] within more moderate bounds.[33]

Madame Elisabeth's ladies-in-waiting were some of the young women with whom she had studied – the Marquise de Bombelles ('Bombe'), the Marquise de Raigecourt ('Rage') and the Marquise des Monstiers-Mérinville ('Démon'). If Madame Elisabeth chose to dine at home, they dined with her. Their simple meal consisted of three courses and was superintended by the chief butler. A gentleman of the chamber attended, as did four footmen dressed in the king's livery which Marie described as 'entirely blue, trimmed with white silk lace on ordinary occasions and silver lace on state occasions, silk stockings, shoes and buckles, hair powdered; also with buckles and a tail. A chaplain said grace. Four ladies' maids attended upon Madame, who were selected from the poor nobility.'[34] Marie could dine with these ladies' maids if she wanted company, or if she preferred she could have her meal in her own private room. Madame de Bombelles, one of the ladies-in-waiting, wrote to her husband about the jealousies among the courtiers surrounding the queen at Versailles, who 'think they are in a position to judge the rest of the world. They are so frightened that someone should insinuate themselves into favour, that they hardly ever praise anyone, but tear them to pieces at their leisure.'[35] Madame de Bombelles much preferred life at Montreuil, which was:

just like that spent by any united family in a château a hundred leagues from Paris. Hours devoted to work, to walks, to reading, either alone or in common. Everything was methodically regulated. The luncheon hour reunited the princess and her ladies around the same table. She had fixed her habits in this way. Towards evening, before the hour for returning to court, we all gathered in the drawing room, and, as is the custom in some families, we had evening prayers all together. Then we set out again towards that palace which was at the same time so far and so near, one's heart refreshed by the impression of a day filled with work and friendship, and sanctified by prayer and charity.[36]

There was universal rejoicing on 22 October 1781 when the dauphin, Louis Joseph, was born. The king now had his longed-for heir. Madame de la Tour du Pin remembered being taken to Versailles just after the event. She was present at the ball given for the queen in the Grande Salle des Spectacles and remembered the queen's dress, which was strewn with sapphires and diamonds. 'She was young, beautiful and adored by all.'

After the birth of the dauphin, the Comtesse de Polignac, the queen's *inseparable*, was appointed as the Governess to the Children of France, thereby ensuring that the queen had her constant companionship. When she threatened to resign the queen wrote her a pleading letter:

You ought not to part from me, nor can you do it – your heart could not suffer it – in the rank I fill it is difficult to meet with a friend; and yet it is so useful – so comfortable – to confide in an estimable person! You do not judge me as the common herd do; you know that splendour which surrounds me adds nothing to happiness; you are not ignorant that my mind, full of bitterness and troubles which I must conceal, feels the necessity for a heart that understands them. Ought I not then to thank Heaven for having given me a friend like you – faithful, feeling, attached to me for my own sake, and not for the sake of my rank? The benefit is inestimable; in the name of God, do not deprive me of it![37]

The comtesse stayed.

* * *

At the court of Versailles, although Louis XVI disapproved of his courtiers' lavish spending, he was unable to control them. Marie Antoinette realised this: 'He is overwhelmed by an awkward shyness, a mistrust of himself which proceeds as much from his education as from his disposition. He is afraid to command, and, above all things, dreads speaking to assembled numbers.'[38] Marie agreed: 'He did not enter into all the extravagance and dissipation of the court, but wanted firmness and resolution to repress those costly banquets, and expensive nights of revelry, in which he would not participate. Instead of joining the gay throng, he would oft rather retire to pursue his studies.'[39] Louis, a good father and a faithful husband, cared deeply for his family, but was unable to curb his wife's need for pleasure, diversion and expensive jewels. Marie said that when Louis entreated in vain

> that the queen would renounce or diminish the gorgeous fêtes and entertainments she was giving, with a despairing air he would exclaim, 'Then let the game go on' – and extravagance, pleasure, and dissipation resumed their reckless fling. One sumptuous banquet was but the precursor of another still more costly; each tried to surpass the other in the magnificence of their costumes, the richness of their embroideries, and the splendid display of the most expensive jewels; not only the queen, but many of her subjects, wearing large fortunes upon their persons, comprised in the value of the diamonds by which they were adorned.[40]

This outrageous extravagance at the court of Versailles during a time of famine and hardship in France enraged both the bourgeoisie and the peasants. The excesses and self-indulgence of the royal family and their sycophants aroused in the French people the stirrings of a dangerous revolt.

THREE

'Seduction had its code'

France was a nation of contrasts, semi-feudal in its social and economic structures but forward-looking in its political and cultural ideals. The country was divided into provinces, each under the rule of an *intendant* who employed subordinates to do most of his work. The governor of each province, whose duties were mainly ceremonial, was usually chosen from the local aristocracy. There were three defined levels in society, the nobility, the clergy and the Third Estate. Those wishing to pursue a trade had to belong to a guild; as the king extracted much money from the guilds, his officials often divided the existing ones to increase the revenues. For example, the Wigmakers Guild was split into 'masters' wigs' and 'servants' wigs'. In order to survive, of course, most wigmakers had to join both guilds – and pay twice as much. (One fee was payable to a guild on apprenticeship, another on becoming a journeyman and a third on becoming a master.)

Tax collectors were elected at random from the ranks of the Third Estate and even with an armed guard theirs was dangerous work. The *taille* tax on land was the heaviest, but there were also the poll tax, income tax and the infamous *gabelle*, or salt, tax. Every person over the age of seven was required to buy exactly 7lb of salt a year. They were not allowed to use seawater, even if they lived by the sea, and the penalty for smuggling salt was death. The *Gabelon* was the hated clerk of the salt tax, and the name was used as a term of insult.

Another feared group were the Farmers-General, who had contracted with the Crown for the right to collect certain taxes, such as those on salt, tobacco, leather, ironware, soap and the movement of wine. They were given the right to erect a customs wall around Paris, with gates manned by their paramilitary force, which was both uniformed and armed. This force was allowed to enter and search property and to seize goods, and because of their power the Farmers-General controlled prices.

As well as state taxes and indirect taxes to the Farmers-General, there was also the tithe or *dîme* payable to clergy. Peasants were not allowed to move their corn from the fields after harvesting until the priest had come in person to choose his sheaves, and if he were tardy the crop would be ruined. The seigneurs had hunting rights over peasants' fields, and between 1 May and 24 June tenants were not even allowed on to their own land to protect their crops from the ravages of partridges and other game birds. There were tolls on roads at the *péages* and tolls on ferries. There was a tax on selling wine and only the seigneur was allowed to sell in the first forty days after the vintage. There were taxes on the use of the mill, the manorial wine press, the village oven and even the services of the bull. The rules were draconian and the peasants much oppressed. The many evils in the constitution of the government and widespread abuses in the administration of the laws enraged the people further. France was ready to erupt.

Into the seething resentment caused by the inequitable laws and taxes stepped the aristocratic liberals, the 'physiocrats' who quoted the works of Rousseau and advocated a return to the laws of nature. They called for class barriers and taxes to be annulled. They demanded a more liberal economy, favoured free trade and believed that agriculture was the key to improved national wealth.

Searching for a solution to the country's mounting debts, the government put the Genevese banker Jacques Necker in charge of French finances in 1776, a post he held until 1781. Although some economies were made at his instigation, they were insufficient, and deeply resented by the courtiers. Necker, like so many others, came to Curtius's *salon* in the boulevard du Temple, and his head was modelled in wax:

Necker was a countryman of M. Curtius, and a true Swiss in appearance; a tall stout man, of rather an ordinary mien, the expression of his countenance very grave and abstracted; but when he began to converse his society became very pleasant: his exterior savoured more of the countryman, than of one who had been accustomed to fill the highest stations and commune with royalty.[1]

Because he was a Protestant and not from the exclusive ranks of the nobility, Necker was given the title of Director General of Finance, instead of the more prestigious Controller General. He resigned in May 1781 when Maurepas and Vergennes refused his request to be admitted to the Royal Council. He was succeeded by Calonne, who stayed in office until 1788, when he was dismissed and Necker reappointed.

Prince Paul of Russia and his wife, travelling incognito as the Comte and Comtesse du Nord, were welcomed as guests at Versailles in May 1782 when Marie was there. They visited Curtius's *salon* during their stay. Marie formed a very poor opinion of the prince, and thought him

> a very ugly little man, rough and abrupt in his manners, and by no means agreeable in his address and general demeanour; he was afflicted with the evil, and wore a very high cravat, coming quite over his jawbone, to conceal the effects of the malady; but still they were visible: in fact, his exterior was as disagreeable as was his character, for which the only apology that could be given was, that he was mad; he was dressed in silk, but perfectly plain. His wife was a German princess, and a remarkably fine woman, possessing more agreeable manners than her imperial husband.[2]

Another visitor from Russia was Prince Radzeiville (sic), an exile who caused much gossip in Paris on account of the remarkable baggage he carried with him. Marie remembered that he was accompanied on his travels by 'the figures of the twelve apostles as large as life, and of massive gold'. Curtius went to see them, 'but probably for the want of money, the prince had one melted, and converted into cash'.[3]

George Rose, the English politician, came to Paris in 1782 and wrote in his diary: 'During my stay at Paris very little occurred worthy of notice; but I was struck with surprise at the freedom of the conversation on general liberty, even within the walls of the King's palace.' He found that M. Chauvelin, then the first *valet de chambre* to the king, 'was talking loudly and freely'.[4] Rose was a loyal Tory, and when Pitt formed a government in 1784 he became Secretary of the Treasury.

In 1783, when Marie was twenty-two, Curtius opened the *Caverne des Grands Voleurs*, a second *salon* at 20 boulevard du Temple. The occasion was reported thus in Bachaumont's *Mémoires Secrets* of 11 May that year:

> This ingenious artist who has the art of natural representation of all the personages known under the name of 'the models of Curtius', has had the idea of assembling in the same place those of notorious villains, foreign or national, which he calls the Cavern of the Great Robbers. He has been established on the boulevards and fairs for several years. As soon as justice does away with someone he models him and puts him in the collection, which thus offers something new all the time. The show is not expensive as it only costs two sous. Recently the barker has been crying to the crowd 'Messieurs, come in. Come and see the great robbers!' The Marquis de Villette was passing and asked loudly, 'Are Monsieur the Prince and Madame the Princess de Guémenée in there?' He was told they were not. 'Too bad: your collection is not complete; I would have given six livres to have seen them.'[5]

Parisians were hungry for new experimental knowledge, and were inspired by such men as Benjamin Franklin and Isaac Newton. Typical of this spirit was the interest in ballooning. In the 1780s Professor Jacques Alexandre César Charles, an eminent professor of physics and chemistry who lectured at the Louvre in Paris, was instrumental in making manned balloon flight possible. He had discovered what was later named 'Charles's Law', which stated: 'At constant pressure every gas expands by the same fraction of itself for a given rise from a given temperature.' He proved this by the use of hydrogen gas in balloons in the place of heated air. His brother

Henri-Louis Charles, a scientist-showman who lived in rue du Faubourg du Temple,[6] became a good friend to Marie, and helped her when she took her Cabinet of Figures to London in 1802. One of Professor Charles's pupils was Etienne-Gaspard Robert, who later changed his name to Robertson, and acquired fame as the inventor of the parachute, as a balloon aeronaut and, according to his memoirs, as the creator of the first and best phantasmagoria show.[7]

Under the guidance of Professor Charles, Robertson first released an unmanned experimental balloon on 27 August 1783 from the Champs de Mars. The balloon rose to 3,000 feet and remained in the air for about three-quarters of an hour. The watching crowds were so fascinated that even a heavy shower of rain did not deter them. However, when the balloon fell to earth in a field about 15 miles away, the field workers, terrified of the sky monster, attacked it and ripped it to pieces.

On 19 September, when Marie was at Versailles, the famous Montgolfier balloon managed an eight-minute flight from the courtyard of the palace, watched by a huge crowd that included the royal family. Montgolfier's principal scientific collaborator on this occasion was Professor Jacques Charles. Suspended below the balloon was a cage containing a duck, a cock and a sheep, which thus became the first aerial travellers. They were quite uninjured apart from the unfortunate cock, whose wing was broken by a kick from the terrified sheep. The first human to ascend in a balloon was M. François Pilâtre de Rozier on 15 October and the excitement in Paris was enormous. Six weeks later, on 1 December, Professor Jacques Charles and Monsieur Robertson went up together in a balloon from the Tuileries. When released, the yellow and red striped balloon rose to 2,000 feet, stayed aloft for two hours and landed 27 miles away at Nesles. Here M. Robertson got out to the cheers of the delighted crowd, but the professor, impatient to study the cloud formation, did not wait for sufficient ballast to replace Robertson's weight. He cast off again on his own and rapidly shot up to a height of about 2 miles, during the course of which he was able to observe the sunset twice. He experienced a violent pain in his jaw and ear on this rapid ascent, but stayed aloft for about half an hour. However, in spite of the excitement, he never went up again. The next day a procession of well-wishers accompanied the now deflated balloon back to Paris.[8] For the eager bystanders who flocked to the launchings, the sight of the beautiful balloons rising freely into the air symbolised a new, more idealistic, way of life.

It was at about this time that Marie was asked to model portraits of the royal family. 'So much did the taste for resemblance in wax prevail during the reign of Louis XVI, that he, the queen, all the members of the royal family, and the most eminent characters of the day' submitted to Marie while she took models of them. The process of taking plaster casts from a living head required complete cooperation from the subject – and some courage. First the face was oiled and the hair pomaded to prevent the wet plaster mould sticking to the skin. Plaster was then applied over the face and quills inserted into the nostrils to allow the subject to breathe. The plaster had to be left in place until it was sufficiently hard for the cast to be removed. It was then allowed to dry completely. In order to make a wax replica, molten wax was poured into the completed plaster mould, and when this had hardened enough, any surplus was poured off, leaving an exact replica of the subject's features. Another method, which was more likely to have been used in the case of the royal family, was to make a sculptured likeness of the subject, and to use that to take a plaster cast, which was made in sections so that it could be removed. These sections of the mould were then bound together and the resulting shell filled with molten wax, which, as before, was poured off when the wax cast was thick enough. Once finished and trimmed, the face was hand coloured and glass eyes inserted, and then it was mounted on a body made of horsehair. The limbs were often carved from wood, though hands could also be moulded in wax. Whenever possible, Curtius and Marie used the sitter's own clothes to dress the model. If real hair was to be used for the head, it had to be painstakingly inserted into the wax of the skull one hair at a time, but at a time when wigs were generally worn it was usual to make a wig in a style appropriate for each sitter.

When Marie was asked to model the royal family, it was because of her growing reputation and her skill. She said of the queen:

35

She was above the middle height, and had a commanding air, but such as did not exact, but won obedience; her complexion was extremely fair . . . her eyes were blue, and the expression peculiarly soft. Her hair was light, and she always wore powder; she was rather inclined to *en bon point*, but not to a degree to alter the naturally graceful form of her figure . . . her feet were small, and her hands remarkably beautiful; her voice, even when speaking, was particularly harmonious, and she sang with much feeling and sweetness.[9]

Marie formed her opinion from a thorough knowledge of Marie Antoinette's character, 'which she had the best opportunity of acquiring, from having so long lived under the same roof as her royal mistress'. She admitted that the queen was fond of pleasure, dress and admiration, 'but that she ever was induced to be guilty of any dereliction from morality' Marie regarded 'as the foulest calumny'.[10]

Marie remembered the dauphin as having a fine head of curling hair, which flowed on to his shoulders, light blue eyes and a countenance that had much sweetness of expression. He wore a little blue jacket and trousers like those of an English sailor, though his were of silk not linen. The dauphiness visited her aunt, Madame Elisabeth, almost every day, and Marie said she had hair like her brother, 'which flowed in rich profusion over her fair neck; she was decidedly a handsome child; was lively and engaging in her manners, ever ready to talk freely; intelligent, and generally in high spirits'.[11]

Marie's wax portraits of the royal family, which can still be seen at Madame Tussaud's in London, were displayed in Curtius's cabinet and the queen gave permission for Rose Bertin to make the dresses for her portrait figure. According to Marie, Rose Bertin 'then enjoyed the first-rate celebrity, and was a person of large property, but lost it in the revolution, and died in poverty in London'.

The king and queen approved of Marie's work and she was allowed to make a tableau of 'The Royal Family at Dinner'. For a long time it had been an established custom that the royal family ate their dinner in front of the curious public. Anyone could come and watch as long as they were 'full-dressed', that is, having a bag wig, sword and silk stockings. Even if their own clothes were threadbare, they were not turned back; but no one, however well dressed, was admitted without the appendages which etiquette required. The king and queen, sitting at a horseshoe-shaped table, were fenced off from the too-curious public by a phalanx of Swiss Guards, whose costume Marie described as magnificent: 'the same as that worn by Henry Fourth, consisting of a hat with three white feathers, short robe, red pantaloons, or long stockings, all in one, slashed at the top with white silk, black shoes with buckles, sash, with a sword and halberd'.[12]

One of the ladies in attendance on the queen, Madame de la Tour du Pin, was often present at the ceremony. She described how a small table with two places was laid in the first salon, with two large green armchairs placed side by side.

> The backs of these chairs were high enough to screen completely the persons seated in them. The tablecloth reached the ground. The queen sat on the king's left. They sat with their backs to the fireplace, and about ten feet in front of them, was arranged a semi-circle of stools for the duchesses, princesses and other ladies whose office entitled them to this privilege. Behind them stood all the other ladies, facing the king and queen. The king ate heartily, but the queen neither removed her gloves nor unfolded her napkin, which was a very big mistake. As soon as the king had drunk his wine, everyone curtsied and left.[13]

The English diarist and farmer Arthur Young, visiting France in 1787, also remarked on the strangeness of the custom. He described how on 27 May he went out to Versailles to attend the investiture of the Duc de Berri, the Comte d'Artois's ten-year-old son, with the *cordon bleu*. Afterwards the king and the nobles walked to a small apartment where the king dined.

> The whole palace, except the chapel, seems to be open to all the world; we pushed through an amazing croud [sic] of all sorts of people to see the procession, many of them not very well dressed,

whence it appears, that no questions are asked. But the officers at the door of the apartment in which the King dined, made a distinction, and would not permit all to enter promiscuously. The ceremony of the King's dining in public is more odd than splendid. The Queen sat by him with a cover before her, but ate nothing; conversing with the Duc d'Orléans, and the Duc de Liancourt, who stood behind her chair. To me it would have been a most uncomfortable meal, and were I a sovereign I would sweep away three-fourths of these stupid forms; if Kings do not dine like other people, they lose much of the pleasure of life.

He thought the palace of Versailles 'not in the least striking. More like an assemblage of buildings, but not a fine edifice.'[14] He was not impressed with Paris either, and found it incredible how dirty, narrow and crowded the streets were, and how dangerous and inconvenient without a pavement. When he went to Nicolet Audinot's *l'Ambigu Comique*, the theatre on the boulevard du Temple near Curtius's *salon*, he found it 'a pretty little theatre with plenty of rubbish on it. [There were] coffee houses in the boulevards, music, noise, and *filles* without end; everything but scavengers and lamps. The mud is a foot deep; and there are parts of the boulevards without a single light.'[15]

In 1783 the building of the queen's model village and farm, the *Hameau*, was begun in the park at Versailles. It took five years to complete. The project was regarded by the ordinary people as another example of the folly and extravagance of the court. According to the unreliable recollections of Doctor Poumiès de la Siboutie, in the finished village the king himself took the part of the lord of the manor, while his brothers were the bailiff and the schoolmaster. Cardinal de Rohan was the vicar and Marechal de Richelieu the village constable. The queen played the part of a dairywoman and supervised a model dairy. Each adopted the country dress of their office, the women wearing simple white muslin and taffeta dresses with straw hats decorated with ribbons and flowers. Away from the restrictions of the court, the queen stopped wearing the uncomfortable and over-ornate, bejewelled court dresses, and replaced them with this simple peasant costume (which was, of course, made of the finest materials). Rose Bertin introduced to court much lighter materials and simpler designs, again aping the rustic idealism inspired by Rousseau. It was fashionable to admire Rousseau and to follow his call to return to the rural life. In truth, these 'simple' dresses were as far removed from real peasant attire as their wearers were from the peasants, but once again the arbiters of protocol disapproved of the new-fangled fashions and blamed the queen for introducing foreign ways. The courtiers were even more annoyed as no ladies of honour or ladies of the bedchamber were allowed at the *Hameau* or at the Petit Trianon, where the queen could dispense with formalities and only admit her friends. When the First Gentleman of the Chamber voiced his complaint, the queen responded: 'You cannot be the first gentleman when we are the actors. Besides I have already intimated to you my determination respecting Trianon. I hold no court there, I live like a private person, and M. Campan shall always be employed to execute orders relative to the private fêtes I choose to give there.'[16]

The displeasure of the courtiers began to show itself in more subversive ways. When Beaumarchais's new play *The Marriage of Figaro* was first read in 1783, the play was considered so treasonable that it was banned by the censors. In one speech Figaro, a servant, declares: 'Nobility, wealth, rank, office – all that makes you very proud! What have you done to deserve these blessings? You have been born and no more.' The play caused much consternation at court, and on 12 June Madame Campan was summoned by the king and queen to read the play to them in private. The king was so furious when he listened to it that he declared the ban must continue. Beaumarchais then promised to remove all the offending material and on 26 September the play was performed by actors from the Comédie-Française before an audience of 300 people in the private theatre at the château of M. de Vaudreuil. However, in defiance of the king, little of the offending material had been removed. The first public performance of the play was to be at the hôtel des Menus Plaisirs in Paris in 1784. The king, when he learned of this on the actual day of the performance, ordered the theatre to be closed. Beaumarchais was sent to prison and the king was roundly condemned for oppression. When eventually the play was presented, the continued opposition of the court was enough to ensure that it became a huge success.[17]

The Paris *salons* wielded enormous power and soon became another focal point for political intrigue. This was the world of *Les Liaisons Dangereuses*, written by Choderlos de Laclos, secretary to Mirabeau and a close friend of the Duc d'Orléans. Here life was portrayed as a contest for sexual power, wherein, through betrayal and cruelty and the playing of Machiavellian games, the contestants pitted their wits against one another, the losers facing death or dishonour. According to Madame Campan:

> there it was considered right to love without pleasure; to yield without resistance; to part without regret; to call duty a weakness, honour a prejudice, delicacy affectation – such were the manners of the times; seduction had its code, and immorality was reduced to principles. Even these rapid successes soon tired those who obtained them; perhaps because the facility with which triumphs were gained diminished their value. Vice became a mere luxury of vanity; and the condition of a courtesan led rapidly to fortune.[18]

Some of the key courtesans in this game of wits were the beautiful Félicité de Genlis, Grace Dalrymple Elliot and Mary Nesbitt. Félicité de Genlis was not only the governess of the Duc d'Orléans's children but also his ex-mistress, an author and the hostess of a leading *salon* which met on Tuesdays in the Palais-Royal. Grace Dalrymple Elliot was another ex-mistress of the Duc d'Orléans and a spy for the British Foreign Office. One of the most beautiful of the London courtesans, she had once been a favourite of the Prince of Wales, by whom she claimed to have had a daughter. Mary Nesbitt was another lady with a scandalous past, and she later befriended Marie Grosholtz when she was working in Paris. Born Mary Davis in 1735, 'her origin may be traced to a wheelbarrow', declared the contemporary scandal sheet *Letters from Junius*. A courtesan who plied her trade in the West End of London, she became a wealthy woman after her marriage to Alexander Nesbitt. By 1771 she had been widowed and was living with Captain Augustus John Hervey, shortly to be the 3rd Earl of Bristol. They divided their time between Park House in Norwood and the earl's house in St James's Square. Mrs Nesbitt's past, like Grace Elliot's, excluded her from the respectable social world in London, though her house became a political meeting place for the men who later helped to form Pitt's government. After the earl's death in 1779 Mrs Nesbitt lived abroad a good deal, and during the French Revolution was believed to be working in Paris as a spy for Pitt.

The Duc d'Orléans, who inherited the title when his father died in 1785, was one of the leading figures in this circle of pleasure-seeking dissipation. Marie, who knew him quite well, thought him

one of the most dashing characters of the day; he kept a great number of horses, many of which were British, as also were most of his grooms. He affected the dress of the English, and followed what the French considered the most prominent vice of that nation – that of drinking to excess. His features were by no means bad, but his face was disfigured by pimples and red pustules; he was well made, rather stout than otherwise.[19]

Madame de Stael, Necker's daughter, 'at that period good looking, but, although very young, inclined to be stout',[20] was the doyenne of the Thursday *salon*, which was patronised by friends of the queen including Axel Ferson, newly returned from America, and Gilbert Lafayette, hero of freedom, and Commander-in-Chief of the King's Dragoons.

Another player frequenting the circle of the Duc d'Orléans, who, like Marie, was in the employment of Madame Elisabeth, was Sebastien Roch Chamfort. In 1784 the Comte de Vaudreuil, Chamfort's patron, arranged for his appointment as Madame Elisabeth's librarian at a salary of 2,000 francs per annum. She was not pleased; she disapproved of his morals, and disliked both the man and his writing. A notorious libertine, constantly ill with venereal disease and depression, his life was typical of many in that uncaring world of dangerous intrigue. Yet, he was a gifted writer and playwright, and a member of the French Academy. He wrote: 'I have seen in society nothing but dinners without digestions, suppers without pleasure, conversations without trust, associations without friendship, and love-making without love.' Chamfort had many friends at court, including the influential Comte de Vaudreuil who was responsible for the first performance of the inflammatory *Marriage of Figaro*. In 1784 the Comte de Vaudreuil took Chamfort with him to live at his apartment in the rue de Bourbon, but Chamfort complained: 'My health is delicate, I am short-sighted, up until now I have acquired nothing out in the world but mud, colds, inflammations and indigestions, to say nothing of the risk of being run over twenty times a winter.'[21] Shortly afterwards Chamfort took an apartment at 18 arcades du Palais-Royal, where he became part of the large group surrounding Mirabeau and the Duc d'Orléans. Marie remembered Madame Elisabeth saying to her one day that she considered the Duc d'Orléans as 'a disgrace to the family'.[22]

Few could have foreseen that what had begun in the Paris *salons* as a dangerous game would evolve into an unstoppable movement for change, irresistibly gathering momentum until it eventually destroyed most of those who had so idly set it in motion, including Mirabeau, Chamfort and the Duc d'Orléans himself.

FOUR

'Nests and hotbeds of sedition and revolt'

The Duc d'Orléans was given the Palais-Royal by his father in 1780.[1] Needing money, he decided to convert the perimeter of the garden into a series of arcades and pavilions which he could then let. Much opposition was voiced by the Parisians and he was booed when he appeared in public, but the plans went ahead. A total of 180 semicircular arcades were created between 1781 and 1784 with premises to be sold or leased to merchants and performers. The new market galleries were ready for their tenants by 1 April 1784 and it was then that Curtius decided to lease two of the boutiques in the galerie de Montpensier, on the western side of the central gardens.

Each arcade consisted of a market gallery at ground level, a mezzanine floor and four storeys above that. The second storey was reserved for private owners, the third for artists and women and the fourth for servants. In the upper storeys were gaming houses, chess clubs, colonial societies, a planter's club, an art society and numerous lodging houses. There were also museums and private clubs in rooms above the arcades, leading one commentator to call the Palais-Royal 'the brain of the capital'. The Musée du Comte d'Artois moved into the Palais-Royal in November 1784. Founded in 1781 by Pilâtre de Rosier, the pioneer aeronaut and colleague of Professor Jacques Charles, the club was a meeting place for scientists, artists and amateurs from many scientific persuasions. It was very popular and within a month of its opening had over 700 subscribers. In the evening there were lectures, exhibitions of inventions, readings and performances.[2] It would seem almost certain that Curtius, with his wide interests, was one of its members.

As the Palais-Royal was the private property of the Duc d'Orléans, it fell outside police jurisdiction. It was administered under a set of sixteen articles governing the behaviour of those leasing the arcades and stalls. Stalls were to be kept clean and quiet, and untidily dressed servants, lackeys and tradesmen were prevented from entering the central garden. The only time this rule was relaxed was on the birthday of the Duc d'Orléans, 25 August. The three main wings were the galerie de Montpensier on the west side, the galerie de Beaujolais on the north and the galerie de Valois on the east side.[3] The arcades are little changed today, although nos 7 and 8 where Curtius set up his *Salon de Cire* now house a shop selling medals and military memorabilia. The space in the arcades was small: each one was only about 12 feet wide and 20 feet deep with glass windows and entrance doors facing into the central promenade and garden. Curtius's exhibition was next door to the Café du Foy, a fashionable coffee shop.

Marie, installed at the court of Versailles, was in a unique position to supply Curtius with figures of the royal family. One of his most popular attractions was Marie's tableau, modelled from life, of 'The Royal Family at Dinner', where for a small fee the curious could see how the royal family dined, without having to travel all the way to Versailles. The exhibition room was hung with mirrors and pictures, and illuminated with special lighting and chandeliers. A balustrade protected the wax models from the too-close attentions of the crowd, as at Versailles. The *salon* was divided into two parts. Patrons paying twelve sous could view from the front, those paying two sous, from the back. A barker outside shouted: 'Come and see the splendid *salon* of M. Curtius! Come and see the Royal Family! Come and see the dinner at Versailles!'[4]

Wax figures were only part of Curtius's attractions; in addition he employed a ventriloquist who performed twice a day for the payment of a further twenty-four sous,[5] and on his mezzanine level he also exhibited two curious children. An advertisement dated 1787 for '*Phénoménes Extraordinaires de la Nature*' is illustrated by a drawing showing two '*enfans vivans*' [sic] who can be seen in his *salon* at the Palais-Royal. Allegedly found in Guadeloupe, the children were described as two freaks of nature: the six-year-old 'Negresse' was black, but with piebald black and white spots on her arms, legs and over the whole of her front; the Mulatto boy, also aged six, had patches of white on his body, with black spots on his forearms, shins and diaphragm. Sieur Curtius stated that he had had the honour of presenting these two interesting children to the royal family, and now displayed them to the curious and the scientists alike at the Palais-Royal. The entrance to his exhibition was advertised by the presence of the gigantic Paul Butterbrodt, aged fifty-six years and weighing 476 pounds. Live freaks were eagerly sought by showmen. They could be dwarves or giants, grossly fat or painfully thin, or, most popular of all, exotic natives such as American Indians or the naked Hottentot Venus from Africa with the outsized posterior, who was put on display in London and subjected to the most humiliating pinching and poking.

Not far from Curtius's *salon* was the bookshop of Robert-André Hardouin, who took a nine-year lease on arcades 13, 14 and 15 with two boutiques as well as an apartment on the first floor and another on the second. In the same galerie was a Flemish Grotto, a distiller named Lafayette, an auction room, a children's museum and the Café Tantes, where, supposedly, ladies of ill-repute were not admitted. The famous Café de Caveau was in the galerie de Beaujolais on the northern side. In the galerie de Valois, to the west, was Sieur Pelletier's *Cabinet de Mechanique, Physique et Hydraulique*, a harness maker, a bookshop, an engraver, a miniaturist, a lottery office and a cutler named Badain, from whom Charlotte Corday bought the knife with which she killed Marat. The famous marionettist Dominique-François Séraphin presented his show in arcade 127. His *Ombres Chinoises et jeux arabesques du Sieur Séraphin, breveté de Sa Majesté* was a sophisticated form of optical magic lantern, using black silhouettes painted on silk, which told a story when passed in front of the lamp and projected on to a screen.

The gallery on the south side, named the galerie d'Orléans, was different from the others. There the duke, who had now run out of money, erected three rows of covered wooden boutiques, called the *galerie de Bois*, divided by two walkways and protected by a canopy. This rapidly acquired notoriety as the haunt of thieves, prostitutes, pickpockets and delinquents. Nicknamed the *Camp des*

Tartares, it was lit by forty hanging lamps and was heated in the winter, which made it a popular place for assignations. Inside were more freak shows featuring such attractions as Mademoiselle Lapierre, a Prussian lady who stood 7 feet tall, and a nude reproduction in wax of *la belle Zulima*, whose waxy bare breasts were partly covered by her long hair.[6] For the prurient, and the payment of a few extra sous, her charms could be further explored by lifting the skimpy cloth that covered her lower body. The notoriety of the *Camp des Tartares* attracted large crowds and the Palais-Royal soon became known as a place of excess.

When Arthur Young visited in 1789 he was surprised that it no longer seemed like a palace but was more like a pleasure garden, such as London's Vauxhall. He noted that much of the garden had been replaced by gambling dens, brothels, cafés, workshops, shops and entertainments of all kinds. It had become one of the main sources for the printing and distribution of subversive tracts. There were numerous cafés around the arcades and central garden, where every afternoon people gathered to discuss matters of philosophy and literature. Later, when the conversation became more radical, the cafés nurtured political groups obsessed by intrigue and subversion, and also served as meeting places for the preaching of impromptu revolutionary speeches. Arthur Young was amazed at the 'eagerness with which they are heard, and the thunder of applause they receive for every sentiment of more than common hardiness or violence against the present government, cannot be easily imagined. I am all in amazement at the ministry permitting such nests and hotbeds of sedition and revolt.'[7] The lessees of the permanent arcades looked down on the raucous showmen who roamed the wooden *Camp des Tartares*, but the noise and bustle of the coffee houses and the spectacles brought business to everyone, and the Palais-Royal prospered as one of the social and political centres of Paris.

An intrigue in 1784 focused unwelcome attention on the royal family. Although it was not of their making – they were merely the victims of a daring confidence trick – the 'Affair of the Queen's Necklace' did much to alienate many who might otherwise have supported them. It started innocently enough. The jewellers Böhmer and Bassenge, knowing the queen's fondness for diamonds, had made up a magnificent and very costly necklace, believing that she would buy it. However, the queen, who was sensible of the criticism of royal extravagance, refused the offer. Enter Madame de la Motte, an adventuress. Born in Champagne and brought up in very humble circumstances, she had risen in the world largely by trading on her charms and her de Valois ancestry. She was also said to be the mistress of Cardinal de Rohan from whom she had borrowed money. The cardinal was looked on unfavourably at the court of Versailles since his spying days in Vienna, when he had passed on scurrilous, and sometimes fanciful, stories of the queen's behaviour. As the Grand Almoner of France he had great power and influence, but he wished to regain favour at court. Madame de la Motte, professing to be a friend of the queen, offered to act as his intermediary. Her ties with the court were questionable. She had once been given help by Madame Elisabeth who had taken pity on her and found her a place to live at Versailles. She also had a remote lineal connection with the Comtesse Dubois de la Motte, a lady-in-waiting to the Comtesse de Provence. In order to prove to the cardinal that she had the ear of the queen, she promised to deliver personally any letter he wrote to her, and to return with the queen's reply. The cardinal duly sent a letter of apology to the queen, with an explanation of his behaviour in Vienna, which Madame de la Motte agreed to deliver. Instead, through her husband, she obtained the services of a skilled forger, Rétaux de Villette, and dictated a letter purporting to be from Marie Antoinette. It read:

I have read your letter: I am rejoiced to find you not guilty. At present I am not able to grant you the audience you desire. When circumstances permit, you shall be informed of it. Remain discreet. Marie Antoinette de France.[8]

The cardinal was convinced, and Madame de la Motte forged several more letters from Marie Antoinette inviting the cardinal to make contributions towards various projects. The cardinal naturally entrusted this money to Madame de la Motte, who by this means fraudulently obtained for herself and her companions 120,000 livres.

She then became more ambitious. Knowing that Böhmer, the jeweller, was still desperate to sell the diamond necklace, she decided to use the cardinal's vanity to obtain the diamonds for herself. She approached Böhmer and assured him that the queen wanted the necklace, but because of the high price it would have to be paid for through an intermediary and over a considerable period of time. She then told Cardinal de Rohan that he was to be this intermediary, and that he was commissioned to purchase the necklace 'in the queen's name'.

The cardinal seized on this as proof of his re-establishment, and while awaiting further instructions took himself off to his residence at Strasbourg, accompanied by the Baron de Planta, a man he had employed as his emissary during his spying days in Vienna. Then another trickster arrived on the scene – the Count de Cagliostro, a flamboyant charlatan who had acquired renown throughout Switzerland and Strasbourg as a skilled physician, capable of performing miraculous cures. His fame had spread far and wide, extolling his alleged concern for the poor and his contempt for the rich. Cardinal de Rohan heard of this man and determined to visit him. With difficulty he obtained an audience, and was impressed by Cagliostro's powers and his knowledge of botany and chemistry. The cardinal confided both his ambitions and his plans to Baron de Planta and Cagliostro. They spent several happy months together enjoying 'frequent orgies of a very expensive nature' while waiting for the summons from Madame de la Motte. It was later reported by Madame Campan that 'the tokay flowed in rivers, to render the repast agreeable'.[9]

When Madame de la Motte was ready, she sent a courier to the cardinal with a gilt-edged letter purporting to be from the queen: 'The wished for moment is not yet arrived, but I wish to hasten your return, on account of a secret negotiation which interests me personally, and which I am unwilling to confide to anyone, except yourself. The Countess de la Motte will tell you from me the meaning of this enigma.' Again it was signed 'Marie Antoinette de France'.[10]

The cardinal sped back to Versailles and arrived in the bitter cold of January 1785.

Cagliostro also arrived in Paris, hot on the heels of the cardinal, and was consulted as to the wisdom of the proposed plan. He 'mounted his tripod, Egyptian invocations were made at night, illuminated by an immense number of wax tapers', and the scheme was approved. Cagliostro pronounced 'that the negotiations were worthy of the Prince; that it would be crowned with success; that it would raise the goodness of the queen to its height, and bring to light that happy day which would unfold the rare talents of the Cardinal for the benefit of France, and the human race'.[11] Mercier described Cagliostro as 'the dictator of Parisian society through his Freemasonry and promises concerning the Philosophical Stone'.[12]

The cardinal began negotiations with Böhmer for the purchase of the necklace, and on 30 January 1785 he showed the jeweller his note of authority, stating that the first of the agreed repayments was to be made on 30 July. On 1 February Böhmer entrusted the necklace to the cardinal, ostensibly so that it could be worn by the queen at a grand fête to be held at Versailles. Madame de la Motte was to be the intermediary who would deliver the necklace to the queen's messenger. At dusk on that same evening the cardinal arrived at the house of Madame de la Motte at Versailles, followed by his *valet de chambre* carrying the casket containing the necklace. The cardinal entered the place of assignation, an alcoved apartment with a glass door, behind which he was asked to wait. The lighting was dim. After a pause he observed a door opening into the room, to reveal someone whom the cardinal believed to be the queen's confidential *valet de chambre* at Trianon. It was in fact the forger Villette, dressed in the queen's livery. The casket was handed over, the swindle was successfully completed – and the casket and the necklace were never seen again.

After the handover the cardinal celebrated his role as the queen's messenger with Cagliostro and his friends, happily anticipating his reward of favour from Her Majesty. As the time approached for the first payment to the jewellers, Madame de la Motte suggested to the cardinal that the queen might need to borrow the sum from a third party. This the cardinal arranged with M. Saint-James, a protégé of Count Cagliostro's who was keen to buy favour for himself at court, and sent a letter, via Madame de la Motte, suggesting this solution. At that moment the forger Villette was away from Paris on some other business, so the letter remained unanswered. The cardinal was surprised to receive neither an answer to his generous offer nor any covert sign of recognition when he encountered the queen in public, and asked for reassurance from Madame de la Motte that all was going to plan.

La Motte quickly invented a new plot. She said that the queen, unable to acknowledge him publicly, had offered to meet him privately late one evening in the groves of the gardens at Versailles, and at that meeting she would give him a sign to assure him that he was restored to her favour. The cardinal agreed. A prostitute, Mademoiselle d'Oliva, who much resembled the queen, was hired by Madame de la Motte to represent Marie Antoinette. The girl was told that the queen wished to play a joke on some courtiers, and that she would be well paid. She would be accosted by a tall man in a blue riding coat and wearing a large flat hat, who would approach and kiss her hand. She was then to give him a small box and a rose, and say: 'I have but a moment to spare; I am satisfied with your conduct, and I shall speedily raise you to the pinnacle of favour.' Immediately there would be a noise of people approaching and she was to say: 'Madame [de Provence] and Madame d'Artois are coming; we must separate', and then leave at once. The plan was not inconceivable as the queen was in the habit of walking with companions in the gardens of Versailles late at night. On the evening of 28 July the meeting took place as arranged. The next day the cardinal received a gilt-edged letter regretting that the meeting had been so abruptly curtailed. The audacious scheme had so far exceeded all expectations, but then good fortune deserted the plotters. Their nemesis arrived in the guise of the jeweller Böhmer. Despairing of obtaining payment, and unaware that both the diamonds and his money had been stolen, he had the temerity to write a note to the queen reminding her of 'the agreement'. The queen, mystified, threw the note away. Desperately in need of settlement the jeweller then approached Louis XVI. Enquiries were made, and the jeweller discovered to his dismay that he had been the victim of a major fraud. It was established that the queen was innocent of the whole affair when one of her supposed letters was produced. It was signed 'Marie Antoinette de France', which was proved not to be her signature as she always used only her name. In spite of this evidence her enemies tried to discredit her by associating her with the whole farcical business. The cardinal was arrested on his way to say Mass on 15 August, and escorted to the Bastille on 17 August 1785 by the prison's ill-fated governor, the Marquis de Launay. There he remained for several months. Monsieur and Madame de la Motte and Monsieur Villette, having burnt the incriminating letters, tried to flee, but were quickly captured and also imprisoned in the Bastille. Under questioning, Madame de la Motte denounced Count Cagliostro as the author of the plot and receiver of the necklace, and swore that he alone had benefited from it. Cagliostro and his wife were then also arrested and taken to the Bastille. Count Cagliostro made a flamboyant witness.

> He made his appearance before the magistrates dressed in green, embroidered with gold; his locks were curled from the top of his head, and fell in little tails down his shoulders, which gave him a most singular appearance, and completed his resemblance to a mountebank . . . the accused entered boldly on his defence. He interlarded his jargon with Greek, Arabic, Latin, and Italian; his looks, his gestures, his vivacity, were as amusing as his speech.[13]

Monsieur and Madame de la Motte and the forger Villette were transferred to the Conciergerie prison at the end of August, and the sensational trial of those involved in the 'Affair of the Queen's Necklace' began. The accused were tried individually before the grand council, with the examinations lasting from six in the morning until half past four in the afternoon. The court pronounced their sentences at nine o'clock on the evening of 31 August 1786.

The letters that formed the base of the lawsuit were declared forgeries, falsely attributed to the queen. Monsieur de la Motte was condemned to the galleys for life.

Madame de la Motte was to be whipped, branded on both shoulders with the letter V (for Voleuse) and imprisoned for life. Rétaux de Villette was banished from the Kingdom. Mademoiselle d'Oliva was discharged and Cagliostro was acquitted. The injurious accusations against the cardinal in the evidence of Madame de la Motte were suppressed, and he was released from prison.

The king and queen were furious that the cardinal had been acquitted, and that the integrity of the royal family had been called into question by someone who held such a high position at the court. Although he was exonerated in the eyes of the law, the king dismissed Cardinal de Rohan from his post as Grand Almoner of France and banished him to Strasbourg. The post of Grand Almoner was given to M. de Laval-Montmorency.

Madame de la Motte, when taken from her cell to be branded, fought her gaolers vigorously. She bit the hand of the man who was to brand her, and fell to the ground shrieking and with violent convulsions. Eventually they had to tear off her clothes. Because of her struggles, the branding iron slipped and she was marked on the breast instead of the shoulder. After ten months as a prisoner in Paris, she managed to escape and made her way to England, where she continued to plot and scheme to get revenge on the queen. Her image found its way into Curtius's *Cave des Grands Voleurs*.

* * *

In 1787 an embassy from Tippoo Sahib, the Sultan of Mysore, came to Versailles seeking French support for the sultan's fight against the English. The ambassadors much enjoyed their visit and stayed several months in Paris as the guests of the king, being taken everywhere in a carriage drawn by six horses. One of the sights they visited was Curtius's *Salon de Cire*, and Marie was commissioned to make life-sized portraits of the ministers and several sepoys. She dressed the figures in exact copies of their 'eastern and picturesque costumes', noting they were all of fine, light Hindu colouring, with white beards to their waists, and very richly dressed. The figures were set up in a tent in the gardens of the Petit Trianon. At one point during their stay at Versailles a joke was played on the sultan's ministers:

After they had seen the public exhibition of M. Curtius, of wax figures, they were shown, as they supposed, such as were at the palace of Versailles; but instead of their being placed under the glass cases prepared to receive them, the courtiers themselves entered them, whilst the king and queen were highly amused with the remarks of the Indians, who were much struck with the wax figures, as they imagined them to be, so exactly imitating life.[14]

As an example of Curtius's skill, there is still in existence a remarkable head and shoulders bust in the Musée Carnavalet in Paris. A 'presumed self-portrait' made of wax, glass, material, metal and wood, it was donated to the museum by a M. Henri Cain in 1908. The bust, which must be over 200 years old, shows an amazingly lifelike portrait of a good-looking, middle-aged man, dressed in the style of the late 1700s. It is the work of a highly talented artist, and an excellent advertisement for Curtius's *Salon de Cire*.

Madame de la Tour du Pin remembered seeing the ambassadors often at the opera and in other public places. 'At the Opera a fine stage box was reserved for them. Seated in large armchairs, they often propped their yellow, babouche-shod feet on the edge of the box, to the delight of the public who, let it be said, had no fault to find with this custom.'[15] Eventually the ambassadors, who had been given little more than fine words, had to return empty-handed to Seringapatum, the capital of Mysore, whose sultan, Tippoo Sahib, is remembered for his fascination with tigers. (There is still an automaton of a life-sized tiger on display in London at the Victoria & Albert Museum, which was captured by the British when the sultan was finally overthrown. Known as Tippoo's Tiger, when it is wound up it growls and roars and eats a model of one of the English invaders.)

While the king played jokes on his visitors, unrest mounted in the streets of Paris, fuelled by a combination of high taxes and hunger.

A severe cash flow crisis in France had been aggravated by the cost of ships and troops sent out to America to support the fight for independence. The ministers called for increased taxes. As the nobility and clergy were largely exempt by privilege from paying taxes, the Third Estate realised that most of this burden would fall upon them. That year the *parlement* of Paris had demanded the summoning of the Estates General, to which Louis XVI reluctantly agreed. Sebastien Mercier was harsh in his criticism.

It may be said in 1788 there were five or six kings in France. The queen was a king, fat Monsieur was a king [Comte de Provence], and all disputed the authority of the king in the matter of nomination to place and office, employment, benefice, and pay; and very little they recked of the king and royalty. It might be seen from their conduct, procedure, and particularly from their talk. I can declare that Louis XVI was the perpetual butt of their mockery and contempt.[16]

Madame Elisabeth wrote to a friend on 9 June 1788:

The king returns upon his steps, as did our grandfather. He is always afraid of being mistaken; his first impulse passed, he is tormented by a fear of doing injustice. It seems to me, that it is in government as it is in education: one should not say *I will*, unless one is sure of being right; then, once said, nothing should be given up of what has been ordained. . . . I see a thousand things he does not even suspect, because his soul is so good that intrigue is foreign to it.[17]

Calonne had been dismissed as Controller General on 25 August and replaced by Archbishop Lomémie de Brienne. Marie well remembered M. Calonne:

He was a short stout man, but had a polished address, and was amost complete courtier; his devotion to the queen surpassed that of any other minister, consequently, he was a great favourite at the court and proportionately disliked by the people. . . . The day of reckoning arrived; he declared the immense deficit in the public accounts, execution followed, and he retired from the storm, and took shelter in England, taking with him several objects of *vertu* which belonged to the nation.

Marie was told later by his housekeeper that these had been sold 'to defray certain expenses which had been incurred'.[18] As events became more chaotic in France, Necker was recalled from Switzerland and was reappointed to his former position of Finance Minister. Supported by the Duc d'Orléans, he was able to make some economies at court and abolish some of the sinecures. In December of that year the Duc d'Orléans sold his art collection from the Palais-Royal to London collectors, and the people believed that much of the 8 million francs he received from the sale had been used to give relief to those who had suffered during the great storm of the previous summer. Marie, who knew the duke quite well from his frequent visits to Curtius, commented: 'by giving away large sums of money he rendered himself very popular with the people, as also by taking the democratic side of the question; his fortune being so immense that it enabled him to purchase popularity'.[19]

To compound the misery, that year the winter in Europe was bitterly cold. Bread and firewood were distributed in Paris by the Duc d'Orléans and the king. In Versailles, which was vast, damp and freezing cold, it was hard to dry out enough wood for the fires, which smoked and gave out little heat. There were shortages of both bread and firewood. Not only did the king donate large sums of money to help his people, but he also went out on foot through the snow seeking out distressed families to give them aid. Marie often saw him dressed in a polonaise coat: 'It was a light grey colour, trimmed with dark brown fur, and was called a jura; with it he wore leathers, and a three cornered hat.' Like her brother, Madame Elisabeth also distributed food, firewood and medicine. Marie said:

It cannot be denied, that the royal family were most generous in the sacrifices they made, and the sums they gave away, and thousands, no doubt, were relieved by their bounty; but all their efforts could not ameliorate the condition of the millions who were suffering from the deeply rooted corruption of the government, and the maladministration of the laws and of justice in general, particularly throughout the country, by the provincial *parlements*.[20]

Marie thought it remarkable how little notice was taken throughout the palace of the disturbances and political storms which were raging and fomenting outside its walls. She felt that such ignorance may have been the result of an understanding among the attendants in the palace 'that politics was a forbidden subject'. She discussed this with 'her most intimate friend, Madame Campan', and said that it was only by accident that she ever learned anything of the transactions occurring between the monarchy and the government.[21]

It was this failure of the courtiers at Versailles to see the dangers in the world beyond the narrow unreality of their life, that was soon to bring the walls tumbling about their ears.

FIVE

'Most curiously moulded in wax'

C urtius's *Salon de Cire* was arguably the most famous of the numerous wax museums in Paris in the 1780s. He was doing well enough to buy some land at rue de Fosses du Temple, where he built a house and then leased it. By the beginning of 1789 his fame had spread overseas, and he was selling heads and figures to fellow artists in England. However, he was by no means the only modeller in wax; there were many artists in Europe and America exploiting the fascination of the famous and infamous. One of the most skilled of the early wax modellers in France was the Frenchman M. Benoit, who died in 1704. He was reputed to have found the secret of making faces come alive, especially those of the most delicate and beautiful women. Thus without risk to their health or beauty, the wax portraits gave them eternal life. He was especially renowned for his skill in making lifelike eyes in enamel, and he always reserved the right to destroy the mould after making only two or three models. The first completed figure he gave to the subject; the second he kept for display; and the third he would sell to anyone who would pay a good price.[1]

In London in the late seventeenth century, Mrs Goldsmith made models of royalty and other figures which she displayed at her premises in Green Court, Old Jewry. One of her most famous funeral effigies, still in Westminster Abbey, is that of the Duchess of Richmond. Another well-known artist, Mrs Mills, exhibited in the Exeter Change in the Strand. Royalty and nobility formed the backbone of her display, with Mark Anthony and Cleopatra supplying dramatic relief. Mrs Salmon was another artist of repute. Following her husband's death in 1718 she took over the waxworks and exhibited in Fleet Street near Chancery Lane. She displayed dramatic scenes such as the execution of King Charles I and Boadicea being defeated in battle. Many of her figures were mechanised, either by the use of simple wind-up clockwork, or by treadles concealed in the floor. Her figure of Old Mother Shipton, the famous English prophetess, was stationed by the door and kicked out at any of Mrs Salmon's departing patrons who inadvertently stepped on her treadle. Another more eccentric wax artist was the American widow Mrs Patience Wright, a Quaker from Philadelphia, who left America in 1772 during the fight for independence and settled in London. She modelled wax portraits, busts and groups of figures, and exhibited these in her house in Cockspur Street. A friend of Benjamin Franklin and John Adams, at that time Washington's representatives in England, and a staunch republican, she was believed to be a spy, concealing information about British troops in the wax models she made for the Americans. She was extrovert and outspoken, insisting on calling the king and queen George and Charlotte. Her house became a meeting place for artists and eminent men. Mrs Adams visited her in 1784 and was not impressed, either by her appearance or by her manner:

'Well I am glad to see you', said Mrs Wright. 'All of you Americans? Well I must kiss you all.' Having passed the ceremony upon me and Abby she runs to the gentlemen. 'I make no distinction' says she, and gave them each a hearty kiss from which we would all rather have been excused for her appearance is quite the slattern.[2]

On 14 April 1785 a collection of wax figures under the patronage of M. Sylvestre arrived in London from Paris. The detailed advertisements give a good idea of many contemporary waxwork exhibitions:

An Inspection for the Curious. At the Lyceum, near Exeter Change in the Strand is an entirely new EXHIBITION just arrived from Paris, containing a cabinet of Royal Figures, most curiously molded [sic] in Wax, as large as Nature, and taken from life by an eminent artist, of the Royal Academy, at Paris. It comprises Twenty Royal Personages now living. The Emperor of Germany, Empress of Russia, their Majesties of France, Spain, and Portugal, with their respective families, dressed in their national habits, in a most august & splendid manner, all sitting, *en famille*, at table. The King of Prussia, and the Prince of Orange, at table, in council of war. A sleeping Venus, of exquisite beauty. Hunting parties of Henry VIth, with the family of Meunier. Dido, Queen of Tyre. Voltaire and other figures, which are too numerous to be particularly specified.

The whole forms an exhibition which gratifies the Artist as much as it pleases the curious Inspector, from the different figures being a most beautiful and correct imitation of animated human nature.

Ladies and Gentlemen may have their portraits taken in wax, or miniature by this artist. Those who would please to honour him with their Commands, are required to apply to the curator of the Cabinet. Should the portraits not be thought the most striking and correct likeness, he will not expect anything for his trouble.[3]

The exhibition created quite a stir in 1785 and was 'daily honoured by the presence of the most distinguished personages in the Kingdom and receives the highest admiration for its amazing resemblance to nature'. The images of 'Their Majesties of France are the greatest likenesses yet seen of their Royal Personages'. On 1 July a new attraction was added, and the reviewer became lyrical:

The artist, to shew that his abilities were not exhausted, has lately produced an additional piece which outdoes his former outdoing; it is a *female figure*, reposing: *toute déshabillée*, on a couch, the perfect symmetry of whose limbs, the soft languor of whose eyes and countenance joined to the bewitching posture in which she is displayed make every beholder regret that he has not the power of Prometheus, and cannot animate a figure that exceeds 'all that painting can express or youthful poets fancy when they love'.

59

The sleeping Venus of April 1785 had, by the end of July, become 'the curious figure of the Sleeping Leda'. This figure was the most admired piece in the collection. 'It is impossible to conceive anything more beautiful; it appears to vie with nature for effect. I would not wonder if the artist should become a second Pygmalion, and adore his own creation. However beautiful and curious his other models undoubtedly are, yet this model must be esteemed the Chef d'Oeuvre of his Cabinet.'[4]

On 22 February 1786 more attractions were added:

An Entire New Exhibition is just arrived from Constantinople, a Cabinet, containing an exact representation of the Seraglio, most curiously moulded in wax, as large as Nature and taken from Life by an eminent artist Mr. Sylvestre, of the Royal Academy, at Paris. They consist of a Grand Signior, and many of the most beautiful Turkish & Armenian Ladies, his own mistresses, all richly dressed after the newest and most splendid taste of their respective countries.

By this time there were 'more than Thirty Royal Personages', and, for those with short memories, 'a sleeping Venus of exquisite beauty, who has never appeared before'.[5]

It is interesting that so many of these figures are identical to the figures displayed by Curtius in his Paris salon, and one can only assume there was a trade in popular figures between different artists. The Sleeping Venus may well have come from the mould of the beautiful Madame du Barry, made by Curtius in 1765. It is still on display at Madame Tussaud's in London today as the Sleeping Beauty. Once the original had been cast, any number of likenesses could be made, provided the mould survived.

Sylvestre's exhibition remained in the 'Grand Salloon' at the Lyceum off and on for the next three-and-a-half years, though for six months in 1786 the Cabinet of Figures went to Holland. By the time it transferred to Spring Gardens in April 1787, it included some English royalty, the 'figures of their Majesties, the Princess Royal and the Prince of Wales'.

As well as these, there was a model of the beautiful Countess du Barre (du Barry), sometimes known as the Sleeping Venus, and two very notorious additions, 'both now under confinement in Paris'. One was the infamous Countess de la Motte, the confidence trickster who had stolen the queen's necklace, thus creating a grand scandal at the court of Versailles, and the other was Le Montroisin, the famous fortune-teller. By 24 November 1788 Sylvestre's exhibition was back at the Lyceum with another new figure:

> The distinguished character of Baron de Trencke is found standing in the 60lb weight of chains with which he was loaded for twelve years in a dungeon. The figure of Baron Trenk [sic], in the prison, is certainly one of the finest imitations of nature ever yet finished by the hand of genius. The manliness of the figure, with the laxed attitude of misfortune are most inimitably blended. Every beholder must revere the dignity; while the compassionate, the situation of this unfortunate character; in a word it is impossible to describe its variety or excellence; so that this accession to the other Figures in this justly popular Cabinet, must tend to increase, if possible, its general estimation.

Other additions were 'an admirable likeness of Mr Fox, also Mr Hastings'. And, of course, 'a figure of exquisite beauty and delicacy, the universally admired figure of Venus sleeping'.[6]

The museum was the tabloid press of the day and the addition of new figures would often reflect the political situation at that time. The figures on show needed to be famous or notorious, but above all topical.

*   *   *

The first signs of King George III's illness became manifest on 12 June 1788. At first the symptoms – consisting mainly of endless, irrational conversation – were so mild that they could be ignored, but by November he was very much worse and it seemed that he was unable to govern. The Prince Regent, aided and abetted by the

Whig leader Charles Fox, was eager to assume power. However, a regent could only be appointed by an act of Parliament, and Parliament couldn't be recalled without the king. The result was a political void, with confusion and bitter in-fighting.

There was much unrest in 1788. The Americans were still trying to come to some agreement on their constitution. Britain, worried by the king's illness, was lacking an effective ruler; and the French, with severe financial problems, were about to become engulfed in revolutionary turmoil.

At the beginning of 1789, when Curtius realised that problems were brewing in Paris, he wanted Marie back at 20 boulevard du Temple. He 'was anxious to have his niece once more residing with him under the same roof; accordingly he repaired to Versailles, and made every arrangement for her departure, and, with reluctance she took leave of Madame Elisabeth'.[7] Madame Elisabeth offered to give her any of the furniture from her room, and Marie took two chairs by the famous cabinet-maker Jacob.

When Marie returned to her home at 20 boulevard du Temple she realised that the calibre of Curtius's visitors had changed during her absence. Formerly they had been philosophers, and devotees of literature, the arts and sciences – but no longer. Voltaire and Rousseau were dead, Franklin had returned to America and Lafayette and Mirabeau were deeply involved in politics. In their place were 'furious politicians, furious demagogues, and wild theorists, for ever thundering forth their anathemas against monarchy, haranguing on the different forms of government, and propounding their extravagant ideas on republicanism'.[8] Curtius had now become involved with the more extreme political figures of his day – 31-year-old Maximilien Robespierre, Georges-Jacques Danton, Camille Desmoulins, Beaumarchais, Marat, Hébert and the Duc d'Orléans. Marie updated Necker's portrait head and added Danton to the collection. She made a cast of the head of the Duc d'Orléans, though she disliked the man:

He would sometimes at M. Curtius's, make himself extremely agreeable; but at last he would become intoxicated, and then

M. Curtius would contrive to get him out of the house, by inducing him to go to a tavern opposite, called the Cadran Bleu, which stood where the Jardin Turc is now situated, where he would remain carousing with his companions for hours, and become so riotous and disorderly as to break the windows, and commit other excesses.[9]

Curtius still had two *salons*, one in the Palais-Royal and the other at 20 boulevard du Temple, with the addition of the *Caverne des Grands Voleurs* for murderers and more sensational exhibits, including the figure of Madame de la Motte.

Museums, or Cabinets of Curiosities, were popular on both sides of the English Channel, often being little more than collections amassed by gentlemen who had been on the Grand Tour. Curtius's museum was a hoarder's paradise of miscellaneous things jumbled in together. There were wax modelling materials in every room, and also pictures, figures, busts and collections of strange objects from around the world. Lighting was of paramount importance with lamps and mirrors placed to show the figures to their best advantage.

Lighting, electricity and optics were some of the interests Curtius shared with Jean-Paul Marat, a fellow Swiss. In 1777 Marat had returned to France from England, where he had practised very successfully as a doctor. The respected author of several books on philosophy, optics and electricity, he was also a follower of the doctrines of Rousseau. His fame as a clever young doctor had preceded him and he obtained an appointment as brevet physician to the bodyguard of the Comte d'Artois, 'owing to the report the Comte had heard of the good and moral life, and of the knowledge and experience in the art of medicine, of J.P. Marat'.[10] For this he was paid 2,000 livres a year and allowances. Marat was a popular doctor and, ironically, in view of his later history, was much favoured by the aristocracy. He spent much of the next few years studying science, especially the properties of heat, light and electricity, but had dared to disagree with the teachings of Newton. As a result he was rejected by the traditional *Académie des Sciences*, of which Professor Charles was a leading member. The professor, who had exceptional qualities, attracted many students. Robertson was one of his pupils and remembered him as 'tall, well proportioned, imposing, simply dressed and elegant. He wore a large hat of black fur and a coat of green silk fastened by a belt. He was a good speaker.'

A strange event took place one day. Marat tried to make a fool of the professor by attempting to prove that his views were contrary to those propounded by Newton, who thought that certain objects produced electrical emissions. To prove this, Marat claimed that resin would conduct electricity. Professor Charles disagreed, but the experiment was duly conducted and was apparently successful – however, when the resin was examined later it was found to contain a needle. Marat, furious that his experiment had been discredited, was convinced that Professor Charles had spoken disparagingly of him in one of his public lectures. When he called on him to demand an explanation, there was a fierce argument. Marat, enraged, drew his sword, but finding the professor unarmed resorted to fisticuffs. In the ensuing fight, Marat was knocked down and his sword removed, and he was escorted home.[11]

In April 1786 Marat resigned from the service of the Comte d'Artois because he wanted to devote more time to his studies and his scientific writing. He made a new translation of Newton's *Opticks* in 1787, and in 1788 published a book on lighting and electricity called *Mémoires Académiques, ou Découvertes sur la Lumière*. He was a frequent visitor at Curtius's table and Marie noted:

He generally dressed in a blue coat, or pepper and salt, *à la mode Anglaise* with large lappelles [sic], buff or white waistcoat, light coloured small clothes, and top boots, frill to his shirt, and the collars worn large above the neckcloth, a round hat with a broad brim, and had usually a dingy neglected appearance, and seldom cleaned himself. He always spoke German to M. Curtius and his family.

Marie's mother, who did the housekeeping, cooked mainly German-style food, which pleased Marat who, Marie says, 'was very fond of good eating. He generally showed some anxiety as to what was for dinner.'[12] With increasingly strident demands for change, Marat became involved in the more extreme politics of the day, and became an ardent reformer and revolutionary. He advocated the calling of the Estates General. Later, when he became famous as the writer of incendiary pamphlets, his early skill as doctor and scientist was largely forgotten.

With much unrest on the streets and a looming sense of danger, the number of visitors to the *Salon de Cire* fell. Needing money, Curtius wrote to his lawyer in Mayence on 10 April 1789 about an inheritance he hoped to claim from his uncle, Raban Maures. Curtius had already been paid his portion of the legacy, but was making enquiries as to the share of his brother, Charles, who had been missing for fifteen years and was presumed dead. He was told there should be no problem in resolving the matter if he would grant power of attorney to the Secretary of the French Legation at Mayence.[13] However, events in Paris were about to change the lives of all her citizens, making Curtius's claim impossible to pursue.

On 13 April 1789 there was a riot at Faubourg Saint-Antoine, during which the house and factory of the wallpaper manufacturer M. Réveillon were attacked and destroyed. Réveillon employed 350 people and had stood for his district, Sainte-Marguerite division, as its representative for the Estates General. The deep-seated cause of the protest was the soaring price of bread in relation to payment of low wages. A rumour was started that Réveillon had advocated the cutting of wages to bring down the price of bread, and that another merchant, M. Hanriot, had supported him. However, Réveillon was a successful and popular employer, and had been paying the standard wage. His men refused to join in the attack. It was believed that the Duc d'Orléans had deliberately stirred up the mob and was behind the unrest. That day there was a race meeting at Vincennes, and the rioters were obstructing the carriages of the nobility. The Duchesse d'Orléans insisted that the barricades in front of Réveillon's house be removed so that she could drive her carriage through, and immediately the crowd followed her carriage through the breach. In the following mêlée, Réveillon's house, Titonville, was burnt and the contents destroyed. Hanriot, the owner of a saltpetre works, lived in la rue Cotte and his house was also attacked and destroyed. When the cavalry arrived to disperse the crowd the rioters climbed on to the roofs and hurled down tiles at the soldiers. In retaliation the Garde Française fired on the rioters and 300 people were killed in the rue Montreuil. There was widespread looting, cellars were ransacked and there was much drunkenness. The affray was thought to have been started by just a few agitators – many of the dead and wounded were found with six-franc pieces on them, indicating they had been bought. There was some speculation as to whether the riot had been incited by the Duc d'Orléans, the English or possibly both. Certainly it was a foretaste of things to come.

On 23 April 1789 the king held a council meeting to discuss the economic crisis and the necessity of recalling the Estates General. Large detachments of soldiers were moved into positions around Paris to quell possible riots. Almost one-third of the troops were foreign, including many Swiss and German regiments. The previous September the Paris *parlement* had urged that the Estates General be summoned in the old 1614 format with one vote per deputy. This would have ensured the defeat of the Third Estate as the nobles and clergy voted together, thus considerably outnumbering the Third Estate. But on this occasion, mainly owing to Necker's influence, the Third Estate was granted double representation, which gave them an equal voice in the votes.

In the spring of 1789 representatives began to gather in Versailles. Chamfort commented: 'Nobility, say the Nobles, is a medium between the King and the People. Yes – as a hound is the medium between the Hunter and the Hare.'[14]

The choosing of the deputies was a slow process, but eventually it was completed. On 1 May the king received members of the three estates separately. The clergy he saw first, in the Hall of Mirrors, followed by the nobles. Last of all came the Third Estate representatives, who were not considered worthy of such an elevated setting and so were received in a lesser hall. A procession wound its way through Versailles to the vast church of Saint-Louis, where a service was held asking for God's blessing on the convocation. The official opening of the entire Estates General took place on 5 May in a hall behind the Hôtel des Menus Plaisirs in the rue des Chantiers at Versailles. The estates, as was the custom, then separated to examine the credentials of their members and discuss procedures. Matters dragged on.

By now Axel Fersen, the queen's favourite, had returned to Versailles, again in the service of King Gustavus Vasa of Sweden, another notable who had visited Curtius's salon. Marie recounted how 'he sat for his own likeness, which certainly made a most extraordinary portrait, his countenance being of a description rarely met with; it somewhat resembled a hare, and one side of his face was considerably smaller than the other. He was about five feet seven or eight inches in height. Altogether, his person was far more remarkable than dignified or majestic.'[15] King Gustavus, who trusted Fersen's opinion far more than that of his official ambassador Baron de Stael, had sent him back to Paris to keep the Swedish court informed of events there. Once again Axel Fersen renewed his close friendship with the queen. That spring she gave him her portrait, and a beautifully bound little pocket book.

On 4 June the court went into mourning when the dauphin died. The child had been ailing for some time so the death was not unexpected, nevertheless it was a severe blow. The queen was heartbroken.

The next day the Estates General met again at Versailles. Honoré-Gabriel Riquetti, Comte de Mirabeau, had been rejected as a candidate by the nobles, and so had been elected as a member of the Third Estate. Marat and Robespierre were deputies, as were Danton, Camille Desmoulins and Alexandre de Beauharnais, now separated from his beautiful wife Josephine. Mirabeau was a man of enormous appetites, an avid collector of gossip, erotica and women. Marie had a poor opinion of him from his visits to Curtius, as he was 'so addicted to inebriety, that, before he quitted the house, he became so disgusting, that her uncle always declared that he never would invite him again; yet, when Mirabeau paid his next visit, such were the effects of his fascination, that he was sure to receive another invitation. . . . Although of noble birth, to display his contempt of rank and title, he took a shop, and sold cloth by the yard. He was a great libertine and a spendthrift.'[16] Marie when she modelled him, noted he was:

> five feet ten, and proportionately stout; wore a profusion of his own hair, powdered, ever in a wild state; he usually dressed in black corded velvet, and adhered to the old fashion in regard to the make of his costume. He was much pitted with the small-pox, and had very dark eyes, and his countenance was particularly animated when speaking; his powers of oratory were considered to exceed those of any other individual who figured in the Revolution; but their merits suffered much detraction from his violence and proneness to revenge. He was supposed, however, to have been a sincere patriot, whether mistaken or otherwise, as to the means he adopted of serving his country.[17]

Mirabeau was believed to be a leading member of the Society of Thirty, an undercover political club. He was also suspected by many of being a pawn of the English and was thought to be a government agent for both England and France, with friends and enemies on both sides of the Channel. Certainly he was a skilled politician and a gifted orator. An opportunist who always looked to his own political and financial advantage, he was a charismatic leader, but the meetings of the Third Estate deputies at Versailles were unruly and the debates tumultuous. Mirabeau's control was hotly debated, mainly because of his reputation. There was much argument and discussion about procedures, and little progress on the financial crisis.

Severe shortages of grain in France meant that by June 1789 Paris was, once again, on the brink of starvation. English newspapers reported that the imported American wheat was infested with insects and unfit to eat. The French appealed to Pitt, who was in favour of sending 20,000 sacks of flour to France on humanitarian grounds. When the House of Commons debated the matter at the beginning of July, the majority felt that the situation of the French was no more than divine justice, and a fitting retribution for their support for the Americans in the War of Independence. Permission for the export of flour to France was refused.[18]

On 17 June the Third Estate deputies found themselves locked out of Versailles while alterations were made to prepare the hall for the official opening. Interpreting this as a ruse to separate them from the nobility and the clergy, they met separately in the tennis court at the rue du Vieux Versailles, and declared themselves to be the new National Assembly. Many of the clergy, especially the poorly paid priests and village *curés*, voted to join them. On 20 June 1789 the members of this new National Assembly took the 'Tennis Court Oath', swearing 'to God and the *Patrie* never to be separated until we have formed a solid and equitable Constitution as our constituents have asked us to'.

Five days later forty-seven of the more liberal aristocrats, including La Rochefoucauld-Liancourt and, of course, Philippe, Duc d'Orléans, joined the deputies of the Third Estate. Marie said that the Duc d'Orléans had frequented the court occasionally when she was living at the palace, 'but was never liked or much respected by the royal family; with the queen, particularly, he was on bad terms'.[19]

One week later, on 27 June, Louis XVI accepted the demands of the new National Assembly and ordered all three estates to vote together. There was general rejoicing at this victory and the streets of Versailles were packed with people singing and dancing. The king and queen and their two surviving children came out on to the balcony of Louis XVI's bedroom and were cheered by the crowd.

Versailles, the home of the French court, was a six-hour walk from Paris through the Bois de Boulogne, or a two-hour drive in a carriage, but it was at the Palais-Royal in Paris that the spirit of true freedom and liberty was growing. There the crowds were avid for change and their growing sense of power created a breeding ground for euphoric and drunken defiance. At the Palais-Royal on 30 June the crowd which had assembled in the Café Foy next door to Curtius's *salon*, was buzzing with rumours that eleven French guards were to be conveyed to the Abbey prison at Bicêtre. The crowd swelled to some 10,000 people who marched to the prison vowing to free the guards, but this time there was no violence. Bread prices were now so high that there was near famine in Paris, and there was a widely believed rumour that this was deliberate. The people thought that the aristocrats were to blame, while the court blamed Necker. On 10 July the king told his brothers, Provence and Artois, of his decision to sack Necker and to appoint Breteuil in his stead. On the evening of 11 July a deputy named Dominic Huber was a dinner guest in Necker's house. He later told William Eden, the British ambassador to Madrid, that Necker had informed his guests he would take an airing, then left the table and never reappeared. According to the historian M. Rabaut, Necker had received a letter of dismissal from the king with strict orders to remain silent and leave the country within twenty-four hours. He and his wife disguised their departure, then drove to Coper and from there changed horses and took the road to Brussels. 'With him went the confidence of the nation.'[20]

Rabaut continued: 'It is impossible to show the immense effect which this blow had on the entire town of Paris. The citizens ran to the Palais-Royal, their usual meeting place. Driven by concern for their interests, they were engulfed by the fury of the mob.' The young lawyer Camille Desmoulins made an impassioned speech at the Café Foy. Climbing on to a chair and brandishing a pistol, he urged the Parisians to take up arms to defend themselves. They must wear cockades to show they were for the people. Did they want the green of hope, he asked them, or the blue of Cincinnatus, the colour of free America and democracy? But green was the colour of the despised Comte d'Artois, so the choice was changed to the Parisian colours of red and blue, with white, the colour of the Bourbons, for the Duc d'Orléans. Thus was born the tricolour.

Curtius reported what happened next:

On 12 July, following a motion proposed at the Palais-Royal. On the occasion of M. Necker's departure, of which one had just received the news, a crowd of citizens repaired to my salon on the boulevard du Temple. They fiercely demanded from me the wax bust of that minister, and that of M. le Duc d'Orléans [now threatened with exile], to carry them in triumph to the Capital. I hastened to hand them over, begging the crowd to make no ill use of them. No one is unaware that this is the age of our liberty.[21]

Marie added that 'they then demanded that of the king, which was refused, M. Curtius observing that it was whole length, and would fall to pieces if carried about'. She said that when they came to her uncle's to demand the busts, they were 'very civil, and their general bearing was so orderly, that she felt no alarm whatever'.[22] From the *salon* in the boulevard du Temple, Curtius's busts of Necker and the Duc d'Orléans were taken by the angry crowd and paraded through the streets. As a mark of respect and support for the disgraced Necker, the procession walked bare-headed, with the busts draped in symbolic black crêpe. M. de Bersaucourt reported that the cortège went via the rue Saint-Martin, la rue Greneta, la rue Saint-Denis, la rue Ferronnerie and the rue Saint-Honoré to the Place Vendôme, gathering people all the way. On the way there was some opposition from the German troops under the Prince of Lambesc, who charged the crowd, wounding several people including a private of the French Guards. The Guards, already in dispute with the Germans, retaliated and fired on them. The Germans then retreated into the garden of the Tuileries and charged at the people who were peacefully walking there. Several bystanders were killed and many more wounded.[23] Curtius in his account says:

I will not retrace here the horror which they committed during this ever memorable day. I will only say that the man carrying the bust of M. le Duc d'Orléans was wounded by a bayonet thrust in the hollow of the stomach, and the man who carried M. Necker was killed by a Dragoon in the Place Vendôme. The bust of M. le Duc d'Orléans was brought back to me undamaged, but that of M. Necker was only returned six days later by a Swiss of the Palais-Royal. Its hair was burnt and its face showed the marks of several sabre cuts. Thus I can glory in the fact that the first act of the Revolution began at my house.[24]

71

Reports again sped through Paris that the people had been attacked. Rabaut claimed that: 'Frightened women and children shouted and screamed, the cannon roared and all Paris was afoot and called to arms.' The Duc d'Orléans was accused by his enemies of masterminding the confrontation in order to further his own ambitions to become regent. However, according to the memoirs of his English mistress, Grace Elliot, he had spent the day with her at his house at Raincy to the east of Paris. He returned to Paris in the evening, but decided that he would be wiser not to return to the Palais-Royal because of the fighting, and went instead to Monceau. There he learned from his servants that they thought he had been beheaded. Many believed that the uprising was an Orléanist plot.

Rabaut continued:

The tocsin was rung and the citizens broke into the shops of the armourers. Anywhere where there were weapons, guns or swords, was ransacked. The uproar continued all that day, but as evening fell, brigands from outside Paris burnt down the barriers and entered the city, where they were received with joy. Paris now had two hundred thousand men to defend her, but she had no leaders to command her.[25]

The people, desperate for bread or flour, ransacked the monastery of Saint-Lazare, a commercial depot, and all the supplies of grain, wine, vinegar, oil and cheese were stolen. The hated city wall containing the customs posts built by the Farmers-General was stormed, and forty of the customs posts were sacked. Marie thought this was the work of the same brigands who had plundered and burnt the house of Réveillon.

The next morning, 13 July, in response to the lawlessness, a National Guard was hastily formed. Eight hundred volunteers were enrolled for each section and Curtius was nominated as captain for his district. He wrote: 'I hastened to provide the State with all the arms I possessed, and I took, at my own expense, four intelligent men whom I set to keep continual watch, and who came every hour to inform me what was going on.' He was warned that brigands planned to burn down the Opéra and the other boulevard spectacles. 'Indeed they arrived between midnight and one o'clock.' There were more than 600 fire raisers, but Curtius was ready for them with his troop of 40 men. 'The torches were ready and without my vigilance they would have burnt down one of the most beautiful quarters of Paris. I put myself at the head of my troop and spoke to them. I was fortunate to reassure them, they abandoned their evil intentions and I had the great satisfaction of seeing them go away.'[26]

From now on Curtius became increasingly involved with the revolutionaries. Often on duty as a captain for the District of the Pères Nazareth, he had to leave most of the running of the wax museum to Marie. As the Revolution consumed the people of Paris, Marie, living at the heart of the unrest, was to witness some terrifying sights.

SIX

'Paris in an uproar'

As the *Salon de Cire* in the boulevard du Temple was only a ten-minute walk from the Bastille, Marie increasingly found herself in the midst of rioting revolutionaries:

> The greater part of the respectable inhabitants dreaded the effects which might be expected from an armed rabble, whilst others were fearing to be attacked by the royal troops; which induced the citizens to assemble, and for their mutual protection, to form themselves into a sort of civic guard . . . this may be considered to be the origin of the National Guard.[1]

Desperately in need of arms, this new National Guard ransacked the *garde-meuble* near the Tuileries, the store for old furniture, stage props and weapons. There they found ancient pikes and halberds, and an antique cannon inlaid with silver. 'They then went on to l'Hôtel des Invalides and took 300 guns and six cannon. Eventually six hundred men were armed.'[2] They needed powder but this had already been taken from the Arsenal to the Bastille for safekeeping. Learning of this, a motley collection of attackers, made up of National Guards and patriotic civilians, stormed the Bastille on 14 July 1789.

The Bastille, a massive fortress with 5-foot thick walls and eight 70-foot high towers, was surrounded by a ditch 120 feet wide. It was the prison for enemies of the State – often incarcerated on the king's *lettres de cachet* – an arbitrary warrant bearing the king's seal. Minor offenders were also imprisoned there, such as religious prisoners, seditious writers and young delinquents whose families wanted them out of the way. Cardinal de Rohan had been housed there in some comfort while awaiting trial in 1786 for his part in the queen's necklace affair. The governor was allotted money for the care of his prisoners, most of whom were housed in octagonal rooms within the eight towers. Each of the rooms was 16 feet in diameter and was furnished with a table, chairs and a bed with green serge curtains, and all had a stove or chimney, and access to the windows. Food was good and included bread, wine and cheese. Prisoners could also order in their own provisions and were allowed their own possessions.

The myth of the Bastille was that it was a place of grim incarceration, but that was no longer true. It had applied to the old unused dungeons, deep under the towers. By 1789 the Bastille was one of the better prisons, although it was almost empty. It was scheduled to be demolished and replaced by an open colonnaded square in honour of Louis XVI, the 'Restorer of Public Freedom'. The Marquis de Sade was a prisoner there until the week before the Bastille fell, and lived in great comfort and luxury. He and the other prisoners were allowed to take exercise in a walled garden courtyard and to walk on the towers. This privilege was only removed from the marquis when he began to shout abusive obscenities at passers-by. When the governor refused to allow him to walk on the tower, the marquis continued to harangue the passers-by, shouting at them through the metal funnel that conveyed his excrement from his cell into the moat.[3] Alarmed by this extra incitement from within his own prison, at the beginning of July the governor, Bernard-René de Launay, had the Marquis de Sade transferred to Charenton, the prison for the insane.

When the crowds gathered outside the Bastille on 14 July, Governor de Launay found himself with a major problem – namely, the 250 barrels of gunpowder held within the prison. Many troops had now been removed from the centre of Paris and the Bastille was severely undermanned. There was a permanent force of only eighty-two *invalides* (pensioner soldiers) who, on 7 July, had been reinforced by thirty-two men from a Swiss regiment. Moreover, the Bastille had no water supply and very little food, so any prolonged defence was out of the question. Outside the walls, in front of the outer courtyard, were about 900 jubilant revolutionary Parisians led by M. Santerre, the owner of the Hortensia Brewery. The crowd wanted gunpowder. Two delegates from the Hôtel de Ville were admitted to the Bastille to speak to the governor, and he invited them to take lunch. The mob outside became restless. Guns were withdrawn from the ramparts, but de Launay refused to hand over the gunpowder until he had received instructions from Versailles. After one o'clock the mob, impatient for action, broke into the outer courtyard by cutting the drawbridge chains. There was confusion and some musket fire from the defending soldiers. The attackers, not knowing that it was one of their own men who had cut the chains, believed that de Launay had deliberately let down the drawbridge so that his soldiers could open fire. In the rage and confusion it was impossible to restore any kind of order. The defenders flew a white handkerchief of surrender from one of the towers, and the guns ceased. The governor asked for an honourable evacuation in return for the powder, threatening to blow it up if this was not granted. But the demand was refused, and the attackers, the *Vainqueurs de la Bastille*, rushed into the courtyard and overcame the guards. When the attackers searched the fortress they found only seven prisoners, whom they set free. They then took possession of the gunpowder and disarmed what troops they could find, though most of the soldiers had prudently removed their uniform coats in order to blend with the crowd. The citizens' army lost eighty-three men killed, with many more wounded, while one of the *invalides* had been killed and three wounded. The crowd vented their rage on de Launay. His sword and baton were taken from him and he was marched towards the Hôtel de Ville through a vindictive and angry crowd. Spat upon, knocked down and beaten, eventually he lashed out at his attackers with his boots, and kicked a pastry cook, M. Desnot, in the groin. De Launey was then beaten to the ground, savagely attacked and killed. Desnot was handed a sword to decapitate him but he preferred to use his own pocket knife to saw off de Launay's head, which was placed on a pike and paraded in triumph. The next victim was de Flesselles, the Provost of the Merchants, who was held responsible for impeding the people's search for arms at les Invalides on the previous day. The English courtesan Grace Elliot remarked: 'The streets, all the evening of the 14th, were in an uproar; the French Guards and all those who were at the taking of the Bastille were mad drunk, dragging dead bodies and heads and limbs about the street by torch-light.'[4]

Curtius, who was on duty when he learned of the attack, engaged his company to rush with him to the Bastille. He arrived 'in time to share the last dangers and the glory of a victory which set a seal on our liberty'. He was also able to save the lives of a few of the *invalides*. He accompanied them to the Hôtel de Ville where he 'pleaded for grace for those unhappy veterans. The abuse, the threats, the blows of those frenzied individuals who only thirsted for blood, did nothing to halt me. I asked the Gardes Françaises to join me and they finally agreed. I led the *invalides* to the Nouvelle France where I saw they were given supper.'[5] Engaged in this act of mercy, Curtius was not at the *Salon de Cire* when the mob rampaged up the hill to 20 boulevard du Temple, bearing on pikes the heads of M. de Launay and M. de Flesselles. Delighted with their bloody trophies they demanded that Marie take casts of the heads to commemorate the actions of the day, which she did reluctantly, insisting on working outside on the pavement, for she refused to let the mob into the *salon*. She was observed by the English showman Philip Astley, who made a note of the event in his diary. Astley, a soldier and skilled equestrian, was the founder of Astley's Westminster Amphitheatre in London, where nightly the audiences were thrilled by his amazing feats on horseback. He had taken his show to Paris in 1782, and opened the *Amphithéâtre Anglois* in the rue du Faubourg du Temple, not far from Curtius's *Salon de Cire*. The show became immensely popular, and Astley was commanded to give a performance at Versailles for the royal family and 600 courtiers. However, Paris had now become a dangerous city, and shortly after he had noted Marie modelling the victims of the storming of the Bastille, he fled to the safety of England, taking with him copies of the models of the severed heads.

Of the seven prisoners released from the Bastille, four were forgers or debtors, one of whom bore the memorable name

Clotworthy Skeffington Lord Masareen; according to Marie, he had passed half his life in confinement for the non-payment of debts. The fifth prisoner, the Comte de Solanges, had been imprisoned for 'libertinism', while the other two were lunatics, who were quickly sent on to Charenton. The prisoner whom Marie described as the Comte de Lorge may have been Major Whyte, a confused old man with a long white beard, who seemed to the mob to epitomise those who had suffered in the Bastille. He was paraded as a hero of the Revolution and taken to Marie so that she could model his head, which she did, but he was disorientated and suffering from dementia. Marie said that all he wanted was to be taken back to the safety of the prison, 'having lost all relish for the world'.[6]

Once the Bastille was liberated, all Paris flocked to visit the dungeons before the building was demolished, Marie among them. She recalled:

The cells were dark and hideous, without windows or apertures, to admit either light or fresh air. They were secured by double doors of three inches thick, the interior covered with iron plates, and fastened by strong bolts and heavy locks. The most horrible receptacles were the dungeons wherein the iron cages were fixed. These cages, the disgrace of human nature, were eight feet high, by six feet wide and formed of strong beams strengthened further by iron plates.[7]

Marie, visiting with her uncle and some friends, met Robespierre, Collot d'Herbois and Dupont as they, too, toured the old prison. While Marie was descending the narrow stairs to the dungeons, her 'foot slipped, and she was saved from falling by Robespierre', who observed 'that it would have been a great pity that so young and pretty a patriot should have broken her neck in such a horrid place'.[8] Robespierre took this opportunity to harangue the crowd on the evils of 'monarchical dominion', and urged 'every patriot to hurl down the banners of arbitrary power'. Marie said that he was able to cajole the mob by 'introducing continually in his speeches such words as "the oppressed people", "the despotism of aristocracy", "the necessity of liberty and equality", and "the common rights of man", &c.; and at last, without possessing any brilliance himself, he saw his more talented rivals sink under his power, and saw them perish on the scaffold'.[9]

On 15 July, in an effort to restore calm to the capital, a one-time astrologist, M. Jean-Sylvain Bailly, was elected Mayor of Paris and, according to Marie, he made a great effort to pacify the people. She found him 'a most amiable man, and possessed of much talent, which he exerted to the utmost to soften the prejudice and errors of both parties. His appearance was not prepossessing; his face was shaped like that of a horse, his figure tall and thin; he used to go to her uncle's very often. He was not only respected as a man of the most unblemished honour, but considered a profound philosopher.'[10]

When the news of the fall of the Bastille reached the king at Versailles, rather belatedly as he had been out hunting, the royal family were urged to flee. It is said that it was the Duc de la Rochefoucauld-Liancourt who brought the news to the king at midnight on 14 July, with the ominous words 'Sire, this is not a riot, it is a revolution.' The queen, fearing especially for the safety of the children, was prepared to leave the country, but after much debate it was decided that they would remain in France. On 15 July the king met the National Assembly at Versailles. He entered the Assembly without his accustomed train of courtiers, but flanked by the Comte de Provence and the Comte d'Artois, and announced the withdrawal of troops from Paris. There was much applause. The next day he went to Paris for a public meeting with the mayor at the Hôtel de Ville. Curtius reports that he was ordered to go and receive the king at the entrance to the Place de Grêve, near the Quai de Gesvres where the crowd was greatest, and saw him step out on to the balcony where he accepted a tricolour cockade and was enthusiastically cheered by the massed crowds. Lafayette was given command of the new Paris militia and the king returned to Versailles. Marie thought this temporary amity was 'the awful calm which precedes the storm; and many, perceiving that it was only pausing to gather strength, took the opportunity of quitting

France'.[11] The Comte de Vaudreuil left for England on the night of 16 July, and the Comte d'Artois and his wife went to Turin where they stayed with their uncle, the King of Sardinia. The Comte de Provence, however, stayed. The Polignacs also left with all speed, taking with them their daughter and their money. When the queen's *inseparable*, the Duchesse de Polignac, fled, Madame de Tourzel was appointed as governess to the royal children. The Prince de Condé and his household escaped, and many of the noble fugitives fled in disguise. Two days after the fall of the Bastille Necker was recalled from Switzerland but, disillusioned by the new government, he resigned in September 1890.

* * *

Pierre-François Palloy, stone mason, friend of Curtius and *Vainqueur de la Bastille*, began the demolition of the hated prison a few days after it had been liberated. Mirabeau, a one-time inmate, swung the first pick to begin the removal of the stones. Many patriots joined him. The prison was ransacked for souvenirs, guided tours were taken around it and keys and papers were burnt or confiscated. By the end of November the work was almost done. The ruins of the Bastille became one of the most popular sights of Paris. Souvenirs were made from the stones, including models of the prison, paperweights and dominoes. Inkwells were made from the fetters, and Palloy ran a souvenir business on the side. He also financed and mounted a travelling display depicting the fall of the Bastille. On 18 January 1790 Curtius bought a Bastille stone with a certificate of authenticity to display in his Cabinet. He later lost it and had to ask for a replacement.

The next victim of the revolutionaries was Joseph-François Foulon, an old man of eighty, who had been a finance minister in the government which replaced that of Necker. He lived in the Hôtel Foulon, near Curtius's *salon* in the boulevard du Temple. It was rumoured that Foulon had told the starving peasants to eat hay if they were hungry. The old man was forced by an enraged mob to return to Paris from the country where he had gone for refuge, and was tied to a cart 'with a collar of nettles round his neck, a bunch of thistles in his hand, and a truss of hay tied to his back'.[12] He was taken to the Hôtel de Ville on 23 July, hung from a street lantern and then decapitated. His head was stuck on a pike, wreathed in white carnations by the market women, and his body dragged roughly along the cobbled street. His son-in-law Berthier de Sauvigny, the *intendant* of Paris, was the mob's next victim when he was forced to return from his country house at Compiègne. Grace Elliot wrote:

When they got near to Paris, a fresh mob, with some of the French Guards, met him, and with sabres cut off the top of the *cabriolet*. They then beat him and pelted him, and cut his legs and face. When they got to the Porte Saint-Martin, they brought his father-in-law's head, and made him kiss it, and then they forced him to get out of the cabriolet, and hung him up on a lantern. The bodies were mutilated and dragged over the cobblestones, through the streets. They carried Berthier's head to the house of his father-in-law, where Madame Berthier, his poor wife, was lying-in. They took the head into her room; and she expired the same evening from fright.[13]

As Foulon's house in the boulevard du Temple was close to the *Salon de Cire*, the mob took the heads in to Marie at no. 20 and insisted that she make casts of them. Grace Elliot herself had a frightening experience: 'I was unfortunate enough to try and go to my jewellers that evening, and met in the rue Saint-Honoré the soldiers of the French Guards carrying Monsieur Foulon's head by the light of flambeaux. They thrust the head into my carriage: at the horrid sight I screamed and fainted away. . . . I did not attempt to go further but returned home almost dead. I was put to bed and bled, and indeed was very ill.'[14]

Lafayette, disgusted at the barbarity of these acts, resigned his command of the National Guard, but, according to Marie, 'for the good of his country was induced to resume it'.

On 4 August the equality of rights was declared throughout France, and on 27 August 1789 the document entitled, *The*

Declaration of the Rights of Man and of the Citizen was finally published, after endless discussion and argument. The National Assembly called for the abolition of many feudal privileges, including provincial, municipal, ecclesiastical and judicial rights, and the privileged entitlement to offices and pensions. This decree spelled financial ruin for many of the aristocrats. One of the deputies, a Breton called Leguen de Kérangel, called for a new start. The deputies went into a frenzy of abolishment and Lally-Tollendal sent a note to the presiding deputy, the Duc de Liancourt, to beg him to adjourn the session. 'They are not in their right mind,' he wrote. This wave of public renunciation and abandonment of privileges swept through the nation, and citizens caught up in the euphoria were offering their money, possessions and plate to the State. Silver buckles were removed from shoes and dispatched, and Curtius donated 48 livres to M. Bancelin, the Commissioner of the District of the Pères Nazareth. Madame Elisabeth wrote to a friend: 'On Tuesday night the Assembly sat 'til two o'clock. The nobles, with an enthusiasm worthy of the French name, renounced all their feudal rights. The clergy also gave up their tithes and perquisites, and the power of holding several benefices. The decree has been sent forth into all the provinces. I hope it may stop the burning of castles.'[15]

The National Assembly, now looking for change, was considering two alternative modes of government. One, favoured by Lafayette, was the American model of an elected government in line with the Declaration of Rights. Another, favoured by Mirabeau, was the British model, with an Upper and a Lower House. In Paris Lafayette tried to keep control over the unruly companies of National Guardsmen, among whom there was heated discussion over precedent. His army comprised 4,800 salaried guardsmen, of whom some were army deserters and others mercenaries, together with a number of unpaid volunteers. There was considerable argument over what uniform should be worn, and Lafayette decreed that blue coats with white lapels, white facings, vests and leggings and a red trim would be issued, to be paid for by the wearer.

Axel Fersen wrote to his father in Sweden:

The Canaille governs now. . . . No one dares to give orders, and no one obeys. This is the liberty of France, and the State to which we have come. Since July 13 there have been 12,750 deserters – not reckoning the Garde Française. All bonds are broken. The authority of the king is gone. Paris is trembling before forty or fifty thousand armed ruffians.[16]

The situation was made worse by Marat, who on 12 September published the inflammatory *Publiciste Parisien*, which four days later was renamed *L'Ami du Peuple*. Through this paper Marat was to wield enormous power over the events of the upcoming Revolution. The press became scurrilous. Marat's paper incited violence and named possible victims. The response of the crowd was gleeful, and the stringing up of suspects and summary beheadings became all too common.

These grim happenings in Paris became a source of entertainment in London, and Curtius was happy to supply grisly exhibits for various shows there. Money was to be made out of revolutions, and Curtius seized on the opportunity. The main part of the show at Astley's Amphitheatre near Westminster Bridge consisted of breathtaking feats of horsemanship by Philip Astley, his son and a troop of daring riders. It also included the ever-popular *ombres chinoises*, fireworks, clowns, magic tricks and *tableaux vivants* – the origin of the modern circus. However, following Astley's return from Paris in the summer of 1789, he advertised a new entertainment: 'Paris in an Uproar, displaying one of the Grandest and most Extraordinary Entertainments that ever appeared, grounded on Authentic Fact.' By the end of September Astley had expanded the original show. He advertised that he had brought to London, from Paris, the heads of M. de Launay, Governor of the Bastille, and M. de Flesselles, Provost of the Merchants of Paris, 'finely executed in wax by a celebrated artist in Paris'. He put the heads on display at the Royal Grove, Westminster Bridge, along with a model of the Bastille, a plan of Paris and a National Guardsman's uniform. He changed the show's name to 'Paris in an Uproar, or the Destruction of the Bastille'.[17]

Astley was not the only showman to use events in France to make money. On 30 August there was a new, and far more sinister, addition to Sylvestre's collection of wax figures in London:

Mr Sylvester [sic], always anxious to gratify the curiosity of the generous public, has added to his grand exhibition, a model of the head of the late Governor of the Bastille: he received the exact likeness from the same gentleman who sent him the likeness of Baron Trencke, who happened to be on the spot when the governor was executed, and got permission of the mob to take it off in plaster, which work he sent to Mr Sylvester.[18]

That 'same gentleman', was M. Curtius, who was supplying models of the decapitated head of Governor de Launay to both Mr Sylvestre at the Lyceum Theatre and Philip Astley at the Circus Amphitheatre at Westminster. It is likely that many of the other figures displayed by M. Sylvestre originated in Curtius's *Salon de Cire* in Paris, including the famed sleeping Venus, the French royal family and the bust of Voltaire. All of these were noted by the writer Mayeur de Saint-Paul as being on display in Curtius's showroom at 20 boulevard du Temple. But what neither M. Sylvestre nor Mr Astley acknowledged was that many of these models from life were, in fact, the work of Curtius's assistant, his 28-year-old niece Anne Marie Grosholtz. It was Marie, not her uncle, who modelled the French royal family and the busts of Benjamin Franklin and Voltaire. It was Marie who took the plaster casts of the bloody heads of Governor de Launay and M. de Flesselles when the mob brought them to Curtius's salon, as Astley very well knew. It was not until much later in her life that Marie's skill was acknowledged.

Other London theatres joined the Revolutionary bandwagon. The Royal Circus in St George's Fields advertised 'The Triumph of Liberty or The destruction of the Bastille', and Sadlers Wells presented two shows, 'Britannia's Relief or The Gift of Hygeia' to celebrate the recovery of George III, and 'Gallic Freedom or *Vive la Liberté*', a tale of the attacking, storming and demolition of the Bastille.

French politics made good theatre.

* * *

While England was enjoying the Revolutionary spectacle, in Paris there was a severe shortage of food, for many of the landowners had fled and the harvests had not been properly gathered. As unemployment increased, unrest spread. Curtius was admitted into the prestigious corps of *Les Vainqueurs de la Bastille*, and in August was ordered to Montmartre with his men to get rid of the brigands who had infiltrated the workshops there and were corrupting the good workers. In two days 'fourteen thousand men were paid, given passports and conducted out of the town'. The inflammatory newspapers became even more scurrilous.

The people wanted a constitutional monarchy and the abolition of the *ancien régime*, but the king refused their demands and insisted that he retain his right of veto. He and the queen were nicknamed 'Monsieur and Madame Veto'. The more tolerant members of the National Assembly sought for a compromise. They suggested the king be allowed to retain his right of veto for four years, but only on the condition that he accepted the Declaration of Rights, and abolished the privileges of the nobility. The king was reluctant to comply. The instability of the situation was exacerbated when the Royal Flanders Regiment was recalled from Douai and stationed at Versailles, arriving on 23 September 1789. A week later, on 1 October, a much-publicised banquet was staged in the theatre at Versailles in honour of the regiment. The boxes were filled with spectators from the court, and officers of the National Guard were among the guests. Much wine was drunk. Later in the evening the king and queen entered the theatre to great applause, although, according to Marie, 'Madame Elisabeth, anticipating some evil consequences, was much depressed, and went to prayers'. The royal family were fêted, and the next day 'the queen expressed herself delighted with the dinner; her words were caught with eagerness, and industriously repeated, and caused an immense irritation in the minds of the people'.[19] Rumour and propaganda were spread by both sides to incite trouble. It was reported that the tricolour was trampled underfoot, and replaced by the white cockade of the Bourbons. Marat and Camille Desmoulins further inflamed the situation by declaring in their papers and pamphlets that the banquet had actually been an orgy.

Parisians reading this on 4 October were outraged and crowds gathered in the gardens of the Palais-Royal, demanding revenge against the slur to the tricolour and the instant removal of the Royal Flanders Regiment. They also wanted the king to sanction the Declaration of Rights and the abolition of noble privileges. The next day, 5 October, a Parisian mob made up mainly of *poissardes*, the market women from Paris, marched on Versailles intending to force the king to return to Paris. Marie commented that it was rather curious that the *poissardes*, who were the most rancorous and violent anti-royalists of the Revolution, were, at the time she was with Madame Elisabeth, the most forward in demonstrating their loyalty, coming to the palace for every birthday of the royal family with a basket of flowers.[20] The marching women had first broken into the Hôtel de Ville and stolen money and arms. There they had been met by one of the *vainqueurs* of the Bastille, Stanislas Maillard, whom Marie knew – he was the son of a bailiff, 'a worthy old man', who lived in her neighbourhood. She thought less of Maillard himself: 'a rough, ferocious, ugly looking fellow; [who] had formerly served as a common soldier in the queen's regiment; [and] had been branded for having robbed his comrades'.[21] Maillard managed to dissuade the women from their first intention, that of burning down the Hôtel de Ville, by promising to lead their march to Versailles. He was accompanied by the commander of the *vainqueurs*, M. Hulin, who left Curtius in command of the Bastille in his absence. He left him with only eight soldiers, and Curtius reported that he 'had a lively altercation with certain individuals, whom I brought to order'.[22]

From her terrace at Montreuil Madame Elisabeth saw the first of the crowd of women coming up the road from Paris, and immediately rode to Versailles where she encountered the Comte de Provence, who had heard the rumours but dismissed them. Madame Elisabeth convinced him that the danger was real, and together they found the queen walking alone in the gardens at Trianon. Madame Elisabeth later wrote to her lady-in-waiting, Madame de Bombelles, now in Ratisbonne: 'You can imagine that I was as quickly at Versailles as I take time to tell you so. I learnt, however, before going, that there were 2,000 women armed with cords, with hunting knives etc. arriving at Versailles. They got there at 5 o'clock.'[23] When they reached Versailles, the women's army, bearing their strange collection of weapons, and wet and muddy from the rain, invaded the Assembly, sat indiscriminately among the deputies and caused much disruption. The king agreed to meet a delegation and accepted their demands for bread. Lafayette, who arrived at Versailles late in the evening, declared that the king and his family must return with him to Paris. The king prevaricated and said he would give his answer the next day. Madame Elisabeth pleaded with him to stand firm and not to go, and the king's friends urged him to leave and take refuge in Rambouillet, but he still hesitated.

Eventually the people, rejoicing in their 'victory', settled down for the night. Many of the women lay down on the benches in the National Assembly and the royal family retired to their rooms. It was after midnight when Lafayette, too, went to bed. Early the next morning, at about half past five, agitators, some said led by the Duc d'Orléans, forced the iron gates and broke into the palace courtyard with the intention of killing the queen. Fierce fighting broke out and spread to the crowds outside. They rushed into the palace heading for the queen's apartments. The two guards outside her door, M. Durepaire and Miomandre de Sainte Marie, shouted out to warn her before they were cut down. The terrified royal family gathered in the Salon de l'Oeil de Boeuf and waited anxiously until Lafayette was able to come to their rescue. With the help of the royal bodyguard he cleared the staircase, but was unable to clear the courtyard. Outside a crowd of half-dressed women shouted for the queen, and drunken, jeering men armed with pikes paraded the heads of the two slain bodyguards.

Lafayette went out on to the balcony overlooking the courtyard with the king, who addressed the people, promising to return to Paris with them later that day. He was cheered. Lafayette then persuaded the terrified queen to go on to the balcony with him, and gallantly kissed her hand. It was pure theatre but the people loved it and roared 'Vive la Reine'. The royal family were then allowed to return to their rooms to get dressed for the journey. At about one o'clock that afternoon the crowd left for Paris with the royal family in their midst. The coach, designed to seat six, was crowded. On the back seat sat the king, the queen and the dauphin. On the front seat sat the Comtesse de Provence, the Princesse Royale and Madame Elisabeth. The Comte de Provence and Madame de Tourzel, now governess to the children of France, sat in the middle. The cortège was huge, with about 60,000 people all crowding and pushing, and progress was painfully slow. Axel Fersen disguised himself as a labourer and by jostling with the crowd managed to keep close to the carriage carrying the royal family. The heads of the two slain bodyguards were triumphantly paraded on pikes in full view of the royal party. Other marchers carried loaves stuck on their pikes, and a train of carts followed carrying flour from the palace. The procession finally arrived in Paris at about six in the evening. At the *barrière* Mayor Bailly presented the king with the keys of the city on a gold plate and made a long speech of welcome. He then insisted that the king and his family go to receive an official welcome at the Hôtel de Ville. They were exhausted, the journey to Paris had been long and terrifying and they had had little sleep the night before. It took a further two hours to force their carriage through the crowd to reach the Hôtel de Ville where they listened to another speech of welcome. Curtius was on duty with his men:

The crowd was even more numerous and the huge procession which accompanied the royal family was preceded by a great convoy of flour, a train of artillery and a multitude of coaches. Immediately I made an opening for the carriage of wheat and cannons. I made another opposite the Hôtel de Ville for the cavalry. My orders were given so clearly and were so well executed that despite the difficulty which was increased by nightfall there was no disorder.[24]

The royal family finally arrived at the Tuileries at about ten in the evening. Madame Elisabeth wrote to the Marquise de Bombelles on 8 October: 'We have left the cradle of our childhood – what am I saying? Left! We were torn from it. What journey! What sights! Never, never will they be effaced from my memory. . . . What is certain is that we are prisoners here; my brother does not believe it, but time will prove it to him. Our friends are here; they think as I do that we are lost!'[25]

Versailles was left locked up and deserted.

SEVEN

'Be my brother or I will kill you'

The palace at the Tuileries, where the royal family were now housed, was divided into three parts: the pavilion de l'Horloge, the pavilion de Marsan and the pavilion de Flore, where Madame Elisabeth was to be lodged. The Tuileries buildings had not been lived in by the royal family for many years, but were inhabited by pensioners who had been allowed to put up partitions and make their own small apartments. When the news of the imminent arrival of the royal family reached M. Mique, the Inspector of the Tuileries, all was chaos. The pensioners were evicted and the dirty, cold, damp rooms were prepared for the royal family with all possible speed, but everything was in disrepair and needed to be refurbished and cleaned. Nothing was ready when the exhausted family arrived late that same day.

In London, one paper, the *St James Chronicle*, suggested that the intention had been to force the king to flee, so that Orléans would be proclaimed Lieutenant-General. However, on 14 October the Duc d'Orléans travelled to England, and although he was granted an audience with George III he was told the English king's sympathies were with Louis XVI. Orléans, a friend of the Prince of Wales, was hissed at in the streets. The English public, who had no sympathy for upstarts, despised both the Prince of Wales and the Duc d'Orléans alike.

In Paris, many of the British who still remained now, decided to leave, including the Duchess of Devonshire. The Duke of Dorset, increasingly uneasy about the situation, left for England on 8 August, leaving his secretary, Lord Robert Fitzgerald, in charge. Paris was awash with rumours of British agents, of brigands and banditti ravaging the countryside, of Orléanist plots and the danger of civil war.

The royal family slowly settled into their new life at the Tuileries Palace. Arthur Young, who was in Paris again in January 1790, was astonished to observe the king walking in the gardens of the Tuileries under guard:

> with six grenadiers of the *milice bourgeosie*, with an officer or two of his household, and a page. The doors of the gardens are kept shut in respect to him, in order to exclude everyone but deputies, or those who have admission tickets. When he entered the palace, the doors of the gardens were thrown open for all without distinction, though the Queen was still walking with a lady of her court. She also was attended so closely by the *gardes bourgeoises*, that she could not speak, but in a low voice, without being heard by them.[1]

The queen and Madame Elisabeth seldom ventured out. They had been deeply shocked by the ordeal at Versailles. Too anxious to read, they worked at large pieces of tapestry to busy themselves, and in the morning they supervised the lessons of the two children. There was constant friction between the old courtiers from Versailles, who insisted on behaving as though nothing had altered, and the revolutionaries. The deputies of the National Assembly, who had all left Versailles with the royal family, took up seats in the manège, the royal riding school in the Tuileries gardens, now the seat of the new Convention. One of the first decrees of the National Assembly was to abolish the existing *parlement* and to create a new court of law known as the *Chambre de Vacations*, presided over by President de Rosanbo. Cardinal de Saloman, one of the lawyers, reported in his memoirs that because of their allegiance to the king, their lives were continually threatened by the revolutionaries. In this idealist phase of the Revolution there was felt a need to rationalise the government of France. The old hereditary districts were to be abolished and replaced by a country divided into eighty or so equal areas. Eventually eighty-three departments were created. Liberty trees sprang up in town squares all over France – sometimes real trees, but often only striped poles, they were festooned with ribbons and became a symbol of the Revolution. In contrast, 1789 was also the year when Doctor Guillotin, a deputy in the Revolutionary National Assembly, suggested a more humane way of execution. He designed the killing mechanism later known as the guillotine, but it was not used until 1792.

By the end of 1789 Curtius had become even more involved with the Revolution and joined the radical Jacobin club, then under the leadership of his friends Mirabeau and Robespierre. The club met in the rue Saint-Honoré, in the former Dominican convent of St-Jacques, from which the Jacobins took their name. When Arthur Young returned to Paris on Christmas Day 1789, he was elected as a member of the club. Chamfort too, who had lost his post at Versailles, joined the Jacobins, becoming their secretary after the massacre at the Champs de Mars in 1791.

As the National Assembly's early unity of purpose began to fragment, delegates divided into opposing factions. As well as the Jacobins, there was a rival confraternity in the Cordeliers section, with the lawyers Georges Danton and Camille Desmoulins, Marat, Loustalot, Fréron and the playwright Fabre d'Eglantine. Another member, René Hébert, was a former box office clerk at a theatre in the rue du Temple, and now the author of the incendiary publication *Le Père Duchesne*. They were all frequent guests for meals at 20 boulevard du Temple and Robespierre was generally seated next to Marie. She found him 'always extremely polite and attentive, never omitting those little acts of courtesy which are expected from a gentleman when sitting at table next a lady, anticipating her wishes, and taking care that she should never have to ask for anything'. Marat, on the other hand, was so busy eating that he took no notice of anyone else at table. Marie found Robespierre's conversation 'animated, sensible, and agreeable; but his enunciation was not good'. She also found him rather dull. He was:

middle-sized man, marked with the small pox, and wore green spectacles, for the purpose of hiding, perhaps, his eyes, which were particularly ugly, the white being of a yellow cast; it has also been stated, that his sight was weak; his features were small, inclining to sharpness; they were not particularly expressive of ferocity, nor had they anything sufficiently remarkable to have attracted notice, had he not rendered himself conspicuous by his enormities.

He was very particular about the way he dressed, and 'usually wore silk clothes and stockings, with buckles on his shoes; his hair powdered with a short tail; was remarkably clean in his person, very fond of looking in the glass, and arranging his neckcloth and frill'.[2]

At the beginning of November the Assembly deemed it time to reform the Church. Tithes were abolished and Church lands confiscated by the Assembly, then sold off in lots to help with France's financial crisis. Payment for this was issued in the new paper money, the *assignats*, and the land was mainly bought by peasants and the bourgeoisie. The confiscation of Catholic Church property received little sympathy in much of France, in Anglican England or in America, where established religion was expressly forbidden. On 13 February laws were passed to further suppress religious orders, and the remaining priests were allowed only to teach and to administer charity. Clergy were now to be paid by the State, not by tithes, and for many lowly paid clerics, including the village curé, this change resulted in a higher income.

Curtius was away for much of the time on revolutionary matters, and Marie took over the running of the *salon*. It was a difficult time for her, as it was for all entertainers. The situation in the boulevards deteriorated; many of the *émigrés* had fled and there was an army of former servants now wandering the streets of Paris without employment or income, and whose lawless behaviour created much fear. As Madame Campan observed: 'All property had changed hands; all ranks found themselves confusedly jumbled by the shocks of the Revolution. Society resembled a library in which the books have been replaced at random, after tearing off the titles.'[3] The heady idealism of the early glorious days of the Revolution turned to uncertainty and terror. Marie's life became focused on death and death-masks. As well as the wax models of figures in the *Salon de Cire*, it displayed a variety of curiosities and relics, anything which might attract the citizens of Paris. When Benjamin Franklin died in Philadelphia on 17 April 1790, aged eighty-five, he was universally mourned, and in Paris a memorial ceremony was held in his honour. Marie placed her figure of Franklin in the *salon* near the entrance where it could be easily seen, and many came to pay their respects.

At the beginning of 1790 an attempt was made to arrest Marat for his intemperate attacks on the *corps municipal*, but he managed to evade the police and escaped to England, only to return in May and continue with his inflammatory diatribes. Embittered by what he perceived as persecution, he was forced to hide in the sewers and cellars. His notorious skin affliction was contracted from the sewers of Paris, and later caused him such severe pain that he was forced to spend much of his time in a medicinal bath. It was during this time on the run that he stayed with Curtius, his friend and compatriot. Marie had mixed feelings about him: 'He came on a Saturday night and requested an asylum, having in his hand his carpet bag, containing what few clothes and linen he required.' He stayed for a week and 'used to write almost the whole day, in a corner, with a little lamp. Whenever he heard a strange voice, he would run away and hide himself, which happened sometimes during dinner, when he never forgot to take his plate with him. He was very poor; but appeared to have a thorough contempt for money; although he appeared, on all occasions to enjoy a good dinner.' She remembered him as '*very* short, with very small arms, one of which was feeble from some natural defect, and appeared lame; his complexion was sallow, of a greenish hue; his eyes dark and piercing; his hair was wild and raven black; his countenance had a fierce aspect; he was slovenly in his dress, and even dirty in his person; his manner was abrupt, coarse and rude'. After he had stayed with them for a week, 'he took his leave, saying they were a very kind family, and telling Marie that she was a very good child; thanked them all for the asylum they had afforded him, and taking his carpet bag, departed'.[4]

Mirabeau, another of Curtius's visitors, was playing a dangerous double-game, as an elected deputy sitting in the Assembly and also as a friend and adviser to the king. He wrote to La Marck:

Louis XVI is incapable of reigning, owing to the apathy of his character, owing to that rare quality of resignation which he takes for courage and which renders him almost insensible to the danger of his position; and, finally, owing to that invincible dislike of brain-work which makes him turn aside all talk, all reflection, on the dangers in which his kindliness has plunged himself and his kingdom. The queen, endowed with intellect and a tried courage, nevertheless lets slip every occasion for taking the reins of government and surrounding the king with faithful persons, devoted to serve her and to save the State with her and by her.[5]

In return for the payment of his outstanding debts, Mirabeau sent the king a declaration of loyalty, and promised stronger royal support. He did this with the encouragement of the British government, which was still hoping for a new French parliament after the English model, with an Upper and a Lower House. English politicians felt that this would be more controllable than a government run entirely by the people. Marat, who had spent some time in England, disagreed strongly and presented a tract to the Assembly, *Tableau des Vices de la Constitution d'Angleterre*, to support his argument.

Axel Fersen was now living at 17 rue de Matignon and visited the queen when he could. He wrote to his father in February 1790: 'What a frightful state this beautiful country is in! It is in the most complete anarchy. . . . The people have been taught to feel their power, and they use it ferociously. . . . The National Assembly continues to do ridiculous things. . . . The king remains a prisoner in Paris. His position – and that of the queen, who feels much more acutely than he does – is terrible.'[6] The royal family had now been living at the Tuileries for eight months, under constant observation, but in May Madame Elisabeth wrote to the Marquise de Bombelles: 'At last we are let out of our den. The king is to ride out on horseback today for the third time; and I have been out once. During that time the Assembly will probably be busy in taking from the king his right to wear his crown, which is about all that is left to him.'[7]

The National Assembly was certainly busy. In a new flurry of activity the deputies abolished all the old district boundaries in Paris, and created forty-eight *sections*. Curtius's Pères de Nazareth became the *section* du Temple. Each *section* was allocated a company, the *Compagnie des Chasseurs Nationaux Parisiens*, who helped the already established National Guard to collect taxes and revenues at the *barrières*. The commune, who appointed the officers, selected Curtius as captain for his *section*, the *battalion de Nazareth*, and to commemorate this he had a portrait made of himself in his uniform.

In July 1790 the National Assembly decided on a celebration to honour the first anniversary of the fall of the Bastille, and announced that the 'Solemn Festival of Federation' would be held at the Champs de Mars. The Assembly hoped that the festival would reaffirm the purpose of the Revolution, and divert the people of Paris from their hunger and misery. The Champs de Mars was a vast area on which students from the Ecole Militaire carried out their exercises. The deputies declared that for the festival a semicircle on the perimeter of this huge field would be raised by 4 feet to create an amphitheatre, and to do this earth must be dug from the centre and piled up around the edge. With only two weeks to get the job done and not enough paid workmen, the citizens were asked to help. Thousands of volunteers from every walk of life worked together in the greatest amity. 'Everyone who owned a carriage horse sent it for a few hours every day to pull earth. All other work was suspended, all the workshops were empty. People toiled until midnight and at daybreak were back again. Many of the workers camped in the nearby streets.'[8] Marie was one of the volunteers who trundled a wheelbarrow across the Champs de Mars. She noted that the Parisians voluntarily gave their time, and

the spectacle became one of the most interesting and extraordinary kind; ecclesiastics, military, and persons of all classes, from the highest to the lowest, wielded the spade and the pickaxe, whilst even elegant females lent their aid . . . every *section* of the city sent forth its contingent, with colours and banners, proceeding to the sound of drums, to the grand national work; and when they arrived, all united in their labours, cheering each other through their toil. Foreigners from all parts flocked to see so extraordinary a spectacle.[9]

The Solemn Festival of Federation, celebrated on 14 July 1790, was preceded by a procession. Fifty thousand National Guardsmen assembled on the boulevard du Temple, Curtius among them. Bearded veterans, a children's battalion, soldiers, sailors and the delegates from the departments all started marching at about eight o'clock in the morning. Drenching rain fell. A massive crowd cheered the marchers on and they arrived at the Champs de Mars at one o'clock. In the first of the three triumphal cars was the Goddess of Liberty, 'personated by a lady of great respectability', said Marie, 'and not, as often erroneously stated, a prostitute. The car was ornamented with symbolic devices.' The next car carried the figure of Voltaire and the last car the figure of Rousseau.

A magnificent pavilion was constructed at the furthest end of the field for the national authorities including the king and the President of the National Assembly, while the queen, the dauphin and other members of the royal family were in an elevated balcony. Talleyrand, the Bishop of Autun, a libertine and friend of Chamfort, conducted the Mass which opened the proceedings at half past three in front of the drenched but patriotic crowd. Lafayette rode to the pavilion where the king was seated and received a parchment inscribed with the words of the Constitutional Oath, and laid it on the altar. Louis rose and solemnly pronounced the words of the oath, and when he had finished all the deputies of the National Assembly shouted 'We swear' in unison. In the emotion of the moment the queen stood and lifted up the dauphin to the people and there was a cry of 'Vive la Reine'. Madame Elisabeth wrote to her friend the Marquise de Raigecourt: 'The people flocked to see Dame Liberty tottering on her triumphal car, but they shrugged their shoulders. . . . It was all very noisy, but flat.'[10]

However, the ceremony predicted a happy and peaceful future, and that night there were parties in the streets, and dancing on the site of the Bastille. The rain continued to pour down, but 'instead of appearing to *damp* the general hilarity, it seemed to *whet* their gaiety, and thousands at once formed themselves into dancing groups, their buoyant spirits opposing a lively contrast to the gloomy atmosphere'.[11] The celebrations lasted for a week, and were expected to symbolise the beginning of a new era. Marie Grosholtz joined in the party on the ruins of the Bastille and danced with Baron Trenck [sic], whom she described as 'a tall, fine, soldier-like looking man, of agreeable manners; his hair very white'. He had achieved fame by selling his memoirs, detailing his adventurous exploits and his amazing escape from an Austrian prison. Curtius had made a life-sized wax model of him in chains, which he sold to Sylvestre in London. The baron, according to Marie, borrowed money from Curtius on several occasions which he 'either from forgetfulness or want of means, never repaid'. He had returned to Paris as an ardent supporter of the Revolution, but aroused the suspicions of the French authorities and was later guillotined as a Prussian spy.

That summer, when the Tuileries became unbearably hot, the king and his family were allowed to go to St Cloud to escape the heat. Marie was asked by some of the deputies in the National Assembly to set up her tableau of royal figures at Versailles. The models were arranged in lonely splendour inside the Petit Trianon surrounded by a few gilded pieces of furniture, for Versailles was now largely deserted, stripped of its ornate furnishings and only visited occasionally at weekends by the curious.

Once again Marie modelled Mirabeau for Curtius's *salon*, but he was already a very sick man and after a short and violent illness he collapsed and died on 2 April 1791, aged just forty-two. There was talk of poison, for he had made many enemies, but the given cause of death was lymphatic pericarditis. He was given a hero's burial at the Panthéon, with 300,000 people following his cortège. To most people Mirabeau had been a heroic figure, but Madame Elisabeth was more cynical. She wrote to the Marquise de Raigecourt: 'Mirabeau has taken the course of going to see in another world if the Revolution is approved of there. Good God! What an awakening his will be.'[12]

All seemed in peaceful harmony – but not for long. At Nancy, a general, the Marquis de Bouillé had remained loyal to the king, unlike some of his soldiers, whom he crushed ruthlessly, executing a number of the 'patriots'. Many of the French regiments were in a state of revolt, and the majority of the senior officers resigned and left France rather than collaborate with the revolutionaries. This became a point of honour, and those officers who stayed with their regiments were accused of cowardice and a lack of loyalty to the royal family. Even children were conscripted to become members of young armies called 'Battalions of Hope'.

The Assembly was becoming more fragmented and partisan. Censorship was lifted and nothing was taboo. This freedom of the press gave the most rabid revolutionaries a powerful tool to incite violence, and the number of new newspapers increased tenfold. Political harangue became the order of the day. The slogan *Fraternité ou la morte* (fraternity or death) was scrawled on walls all around Paris, which Sebastien Chamfort mockingly translated as 'Be my brother or I will kill you'.

By the beginning of November 1790 the *Chambres de Vacations*, the replacement for the old *parlement*, had worked without respite for sixteen months, as Salamon said, 'without honour or profit'. Eventually, unable to continue and exhausted by the constant threats from the more extreme revolutionaries, its members begged the king for a dissolution. 'The king has placed us at the post of danger, it rests with him to relieve us of it. A judge must maintain his courage like a soldier.'[13] The king agreed to their request, and dissolution was granted. Before they parted the lawyers drew up a formal protest against the subversion of the laws of the country, the annihilation of the royal authority and decrees overthrowing the orders of the clergy and nobles. This protest was signed by all members of the *Chambres de Vacations* who were present on that day, and it was agreed that it was to be taken immediately to the king. However, for safe-keeping, the president, M. de Rosanbo, placed the document in his own cabinet.[14] It was to be the death warrant of all but one of those who signed it.

At the end of November 1790 a decree was passed requiring all clergy to take the Civic Oath of loyalty and obedience to 'the King, the Law and the Nation', thereby placing the nation's authority above that of the pope. The king reluctantly signed the decree on 26 December, for he was anxious to keep the peace. Madame Elisabeth wrote to the Marquise de Raigecourt: 'I see persecution coming, being in mortal anguish at the acceptance that the king has just given. I have no taste for martyrdom; but I feel that I should be very glad to have the certainty of suffering it rather than abandon one iota of my faith.'[15] The situation was daily becoming more dangerous, and at the end of February 1791 the king's elderly aunts, Mesdames Adelaide and Louise, unable to accept the State decrees on religion, departed for Rome. They wanted to take Madame Elisabeth with them, but she refused to leave her brother.

Clergy who refused to take the oath were called the Dissidents, while those who swore it were Constitutionalists. In March Pope Pius VI denounced the Civil Constitution of the clergy, and condemned those who had taken the oath. Appalled at the growing heresy in France, in April he issued a Papal Bull. The king, now deeply regretting that he had signed the decree, refused to take communion on Palm Sunday from the Constitutional Cardinal, Père Hébert. The next day, when Louis and the royal family set off to visit St Cloud, the people would not let him pass, as they suspected he might be going to hear Mass from an unsworn priest, or possibly, like his aunts, to escape. Lafayette and Mayor Bailly ordered the National Guardsmen to clear a passage for his coach, but it was obvious that the crowd's mood was ugly and there was likely to be bloodshed. The king and his family sat in their carriage for two hours in the hope of a reprieve, but when it was evident that none would come they climbed out and walked back to the Tuileries.

The royal family, at last beginning to appreciate the real danger of their situation, were considering ways to escape from France. Vague plans were afoot to use a large green berlin, a travelling coach, which had been ordered before Christmas 1790 and was to be fitted out with the utmost luxury and loaded with all necessary comforts. In July 1791 plans for a royal escape became more definite, masterminded by Axel Fersen, the queen's loyal and loving servant. Colonel Craufurd and his friend Mrs Sullivan helped with the preparations. Fifty years later, in England, Marie was to model Mrs Sullivan's son, the Count d'Orsay.

The flight to Varennes on 20 June 1791 was a series of mishaps and blunders. The king planned that the royal party would leave the

Tuileries one at a time during the night, in disguise, and meet at the Petit Carousel, a small square between the Tuileries and the rue Saint-Honoré, where Fersen would be waiting with a hackney coach. Madame de Tourzel, the governess, whose own daughter was one of the party, became 'Baronne de Korff'. On the night, once the three children were ready, she left with them by a side door and met Fersen in the courtyard. Fersen, dressed as a coachman, had a *citadine*, a small shabby omnibus, which he drove around for a while to divert suspicion. Returning to the Petit Carousel, he waited, as planned, outside the Hôtel du Gaillarbois. Madame Elisabeth was the first to arrive. Wrapped in a large hooded cloak, with a hat and veil, she had slipped out through the false back of a cupboard in her bedroom, left the palace through a side door and found her way to the coach. She was to be Rosalie, the baronne's companion. She did not see the dauphin hiding on the floor of the coach and stepped on him when she got in, but fortunately he stayed silent. The king could not leave until his *coucher* had taken place at half past eleven, attended by his servants. Only after this, when the servants had all departed, was the king able to leave the palace and make his way to the Petit Carousel where he found the *citadine*. The queen, too, had to wait for the ceremony of the *coucher* to end before she could make her escape. She was to be Madame Bonnet, the children's governess, and wore a plain dress of grey silk, a black cloak and a dark hat with a veil. She was late arriving, and there was a long anxious wait at the Petit Carousel. On her way out of the palace she encountered Lafayette on his rounds. She had managed to hide herself from him under the gates of the Louvre, but in her panic had got lost in the dark rat's nest of streets around the Tuileries. By this time Fersen was becoming very anxious about the timing of the escape plan. But finally the whole party was assembled and they set off for the *barrière* at the Porte Saint-Martin. The streets seemed endless and it was two o'clock in the morning before they reached the customs post, but the official noticed nothing amiss and let them pass.

The night was dark with little moon, and the sky was overcast. Already late because of the queen, it was some time before Fersen was able to find the berlin. The fugitives then climbed into the comfortable coach. Fersen overturned the *citadine* to make it look like a vehicle abandoned after an accident, and they set off for freedom. At Bondy Fersen left them and went on ahead to Brussels to await their arrival. The slow and cumbersome coach rolled off to disaster. The berlin was high and large, a typical travelling vehicle for a wealthy family. Painted green with yellow wheels and trim, the upholstery was white velvet and there were green taffeta blinds to hide the occupants. Inside was storage for provisions, money and toilet necessities. A heavy vehicle, it was drawn by four horses, which had to be changed between stages.

The journey was slow. A wheel fell off and there was a delay while it was mended, then, at about half past eleven in the morning, the king stopped the carriage and decided he would walk with the children while the carriage climbed a hill, which delayed them still further. The king kept putting his head out of the window as they rolled along, and the postmaster at Petit Chaintry recognised him. As the time was now half past two, the man a royalist, and they were some distance from Paris, the king felt it was safe to acknowledge who he was. He then decided they would stop there for lunch, and the children were given a short rest. Because of all these delays the berlin was over two hours late arriving at Pont de Somme-Vesle, where they found that the expected escort had departed. The Duc de Choiseul, the inexperienced young commander of the sixty soldiers waiting there, fearing something had gone wrong, had sent a note to the other relays to tell them that the plan had failed, and then set off to join General Bouillé. Because of the delays, the rumours of the king's journey had flashed ahead and at Sainte-Ménehould a girl at the inn repeated the story. She was heard by M. Drouet, the republican postmaster, who rode after the coach, overtook it, and then denounced the royal family when they reached Varennes. When the berlin arrived in the town the horses needed changing, but the fresh horses had been left on the far side of the river and no one in the king's party knew where to find them. It was eleven o'clock at night as the villagers surrounded the coach and demanded to know who the travellers were. The royal bodyguard waiting on the far side of the river returned to the town wanting to make a fight of it, but the king, not wishing to cause any bloodshed, refused. The royal party was ordered to leave the coach and they were confined in an upstairs room at the house of M. Sauce, a candle maker, who was also the Mayor of Varennes. There they stayed until the next morning, while the villagers, convinced that this was indeed the king, sent a messenger with all speed to Paris.[16]

When the news of the royal escape reached the ears of Marie in Paris, she was much agitated, 'hoping that the monarch, and all who accompanied him, might succeed in reaching the frontier without molestation, fearing that a bitter fate awaited him if he should once more be delivered into the hands of the French populace'.[17] But it was too late. Early the next morning an escort of National Guardsmen arrived in Varennes. At six o'clock the royal party was forced to return to their carriage, and the slow journey back to Paris began. The next day they shed their disguises. They attended Mass in Châlons in the morning and stayed there to dine, but when word of General Bouillé's approach came, they were hustled back into the coach and taken on to Epernay where they were given a miserable meal and threatened by the villagers. They set out again at six in the evening and were joined by Antoine Barnave, one of the three deputies sent out to escort them back to Paris. The other two were Jérôme Pétion and M. Maubourg. They had orders not to let the king out of their sight, and Barnave and Pétion proposed they should take the places of Madame Elisabeth and the Madame Royale, who were to join Maubourg in the deputies' carriage. However, the party refused to be separated, and so Pétion pushed himself in-between the king and queen, and Barnave sat between Madame Elisabeth and Madame de Tourzel. They slept that night at Dormans in a small inn, and the next day they went on in extreme discomfort. The weather was hot and the carriage uncomfortably crowded. The last ten leagues of the journey home proved to be even slower, the carriage hindered by the marching of the escorting National Guardsmen and a crowd of 6,000 citizens. Curtius was called out with his Chasseurs. Hungry and exhausted, the royal family did not reach the Tuileries until half past seven that night. Madame Royale remembered: 'The crowd we met along the road was innumerable, so that we could scarcely advance. The insults with which the people loaded us were our only food throughout the day. In the faubourgs of Paris the crowd was even greater, and among the persons we saw but one woman fairly well dressed who showed by her tears the interest she took in us.'[18] This woman may have been Grace Elliot, who wrote:

> They were stopped at Varennes, used most cruelly, and brought back to Paris, in a most barbarous manner. I saw them in the Champs-Elysées as they came back, and witnessed such a scene as it is impossible to describe. The insolence of the mob and the wretches that surrounded the travelling coaches they were in was very terrible. The faithful Garde de Corps, who had followed the King, were tied hands and feet with ropes on the coach-box of Their Majesties carriage, which went at a foot pace, that the monsters might follow. They were leaning on the coach, smoking, swearing, and talking the most indecent language. They prevented any air getting into the carriage, though the poor Queen was dying with heat and fatigue, for they had not been in bed since they left Paris, and it was one of the hottest days I ever felt.[19]

The Comte de Provence and his comtesse, who had set off in separate lightweight carriages on the same night as the king, had not stopped on the way, and had reached Brussels in safety. Marie thought the king was largely to blame for the failure of his own escape. 'Had not the king insisted upon stopping to dine, he would not have been recognised, and must certainly have escaped; the queen and the rest of the party were for proceeding without delay, but the Bourbons ever had good appetites.'[20] Their captors now had good reason to confine the royal family more strictly, and from now onwards the royal family lost all semblance of liberty and the king was suspended from his functions as head of the country.

EIGHT

'How bitter was the contrast!'

When she learned of the king's forced return, Marie 'was plunged in the deepest sorrow'. She considered the journey 'ill-advised in the first instance, and worse managed in the second'. From then on, following the humiliating failure of their escape, the royal family were continuously under observation, both day and night; even the doors of the bedrooms were kept open, and there was always a guard in attendance. According to Madame Campan, it was then that the queen's hair turned white. She also reported that, while the deputy Pétion had been deliberately rude on the return from Varennes, Barnave had behaved considerately and politely. The son of a rich attorney of Grenoble, Barnave was often at Curtius's house, and Marie thought him 'a handsome young man, of the middle height, but extremely well made; most gentlemanly and fascinating in his manners'. She added: 'He had the reputation of being a man of two faces, as it was observed by many, that, although he behaved with the utmost courtesy towards the royal family when in their presence, he was yet a staunch revolutionist at heart.'[1] His zeal did him no good. He was condemned and executed on 29 November 1793.

Meanwhile, the deputies decided to bring Voltaire's remains back to Paris. There would be a ceremonial procession followed by interment in the Panthéon, now designated as the burial place for the heroes of France. The lavish celebration was arranged, as always, to divert the people from the miseries of their daily existence, and Voltaire's body was greeted along the route by crowds of people and dignitaries. On reaching Paris the remains were kept in the ruins of the Bastille, under the protection of National Guards and white-clad girls. Once again it was pouring with rain, when on

11 July 1791 the procession for the *fête de Voltaire* set out from the Bastille. The body was in a huge ornamented sarcophagus, on the top of which lay a waxen model of the philosopher at rest on a couch. The coloured model, almost certainly made by Curtius, slowly became more death-like as the rain poured down and the paint washed off. The cortège was very long and eclectic. Editions of all Voltaire's works were carried in procession by toga-clad men, and memorable scenes from his life were represented by small groups of actors. Vestal virgins shared the route with Jacobins, deputies and the *Vainqueurs de la Bastille*, carrying a model of the prison. It was reported that 100,000 people stood in the rain to watch the theatrical procession pass by. The organisers hoped that the celebration would generate enough enthusiasm to silence some of the more extreme agitators.

In a France convulsed by change, many tried to continue with their normal lives. That summer Curtius successfully entered a coloured wax bust for the annual Academy exhibition. Many of his friends were artists, including the painter Jacques-Louis David, whose major works, painted on a grand scale and very popular, were influenced by the classics and had titles such as *The Rape of the Sabine Women* and *The Death of Socrates*. David was also a sensitive portrait painter and at one time had been painter to Louis XVI, who admired his work, and bought many of his paintings. David, now one of the leading revolutionaries, had been born with an ugly wen, which made his mouth crooked and distorted one side of his face. Marie thought his face was most repulsive and his manners were 'quite of the rough republican description, certainly rather disagreeable than otherwise', and yet he was always very good-natured towards her, pressing her to come and look at his paintings. 'David was rather under the middle size, and appeared to have some consciousness of the revolting nature of his countenance, manifesting the utmost unwillingness to having his likeness taken.' Marie was pleased with the likeness she made of him, describing it as 'a most accurate resemblance of that eminent artist'.[2]

It was important to keep the *Salon de Cire* up to date to attract customers, but it was not easy to keep pace with the numerous changes in government, especially as many of the new sitters did not pay. One raconteur described Curtius's *salon* as it was a few years later:

> The entrance is very modest, two lamps adorn the façade, a barker is at the door to attract the crowd. Inside M. Curtius explains the subjects to the audience. The figures are always the same, but change their costumes and their names all the time. Once the functionary guarding the door was a garde francais [sic], and then he became a hussar chamboran, a grenadier of the Convention, trumpeter of the Directoire, lancer Polonaise and now a chasseur of the Imperial guard. Inside, Genevieve de Brabant has been changed into a shepherdess from Ivry or Charlotte Corday. Louis XV and his august family, became the three consuls and their august families, and now the Emperor and his august family.[3]

Curtius, aware of the political situation, could see a trial of strength was imminent. He told Marie that, although he was a royalist at heart, he could not declare it openly, as it would endanger them all. She thought this might explain the 'number of visitors who frequented his house, whose politics were of the most fanatical description, and whose theories respecting the different forms of government, all tended to the subversion of monarchy'. One of the most frequent callers was the Duc d'Orléans, whom Marie regarded 'almost with detestation, as were many of his satellites, by whom he was constantly surrounded'.[4] Marie looked with foreboding at the future, which she often heard discussed among Curtius's friends during meals at 20 boulevard du Temple. Not only did she have a personal attachment to the royal family, but also she had three brothers and two uncles in the *Cent Suisse*, 'which regiment was constantly about the person of the king, and responsible for his safety. . . . Their devotion to the royal family was such, that all who knew the temper of the corps, felt certain they would sacrifice themselves to a man, rather than any personal outrage should be inflicted upon their monarch, or his relations.'[5]

On 17 July some of the more extreme anti-royalists organised a demonstration on the Champs de Mars, and signed a petition denouncing the king. They accused him of deserting his post by trying to leave the country, declaring that by so doing he had virtually abdicated. When the demonstration became violent, Bailly declared martial law, and Lafayette called out the National Guard to disperse the stone-throwing demonstrators. In the subsequent skirmish, which became known as the Massacre of the Champs de Mars, a guard opened fire, and in the resulting mêlée fifteen anti-royalists were killed. The clash split the deputies further and Bailly was dismissed as Mayor of Paris. Lafayette was invited to take his place but, because the queen disliked him, all those with royalist sympathies voted against him. As a result, in November 1791 Jerome Pétion became mayor. Marie thought him: 'A fine looking man, of about five feet ten, with a handsome countenance, and endowed with the most agreeable address, which contributed much towards his attaining that popularity he subsequently enjoyed.' He was, however, 'the decided persecutor of the royal family, and was actively instrumental in precipitating their fate, availing himself of every opportunity to urge the execution of the king'.[6]

On 14 September Louis eventually gave in to the demands of the deputies and agreed to a revised constitution. Parisians celebrated, and a hot air balloon soared above the Champs-Elysées. Among many other changes, all 'honours', and the prerogatives belonging to them, were abolished. Many courtiers resigned. The revised constitution meant a new Constituent Assembly had to be convened, but this contained so many different factions that the uproar and chaos made governing almost impossible. There was fear of an invasion by the *émigrés* who waited on the borders of France for a chance to return, and fear of an invasion by other countries in sympathy with the royal family.

Partly to reassure the people more new decrees were proposed. Those priests who had not taken the oath were to be banished; Louis XVI's personal household guard was to be dissolved; and all *émigrés* suspected of plotting against the nation, including the Comte de Provence and the Comte d'Artois, were ordered to return to France and their properties were to be confiscated. The king agreed to the disbanding of his household guard but to the fury of the Assembly he vetoed the decrees against the *émigrés* and the banishment of non-juring priests.

The citizens of Paris were now becoming more demanding and insistent. They wanted better wages, more food and the abolition of restrictive trading practices. The scarcity of coffee and sugar at the beginning of 1792, said Marie, 'gave rise to many violent scenes, the people insisting it was a monopoly'. Shops were broken into and ransacked, but little food was found, for there was none to find. 'The rabble of Paris, however, having once been aroused and victorious, it was with the utmost difficulty they were kept in order by the authorities.'[7]

Curtius, too, was finding his business less profitable, and visitors to the *salon* were few. At the beginning of January 1792 he tried once again to obtain the inheritance from his uncle, Raban Maures, who had died in Mayence. Curtius was having problems with communication as the mail service was erratic and letters were often opened and read. He explained to his lawyer: 'I have not been able to write to you as I have sent other letters to which no reply has been received, so I suppose they have been intercepted.' He managed to get a private courier, M. le Comte O'Kelly, to deliver a parcel of documents. 'I place my complete trust in you. The parcel which will be sent to you contains my power of attorney passed before a solicitor so that you can collect both interest and principal, which cannot be refused without injustice. You will also find my baptismal papers, Certificate of Life and a letter from the family lawyer, M. Altenbourg who states what is due to me.' He signed himself Curtius, Captain of Infantry.

O'Kelly returned with the welcome news that the secretary of the French legation at Mayence was willing to help Curtius to press his claim. He also explained why Curtius had received no reply previously – his lawyer, M. Altenbourg, had died. In another letter, sent on 29 April, Curtius expressed his hopes that the business could be settled as soon as possible: 'I have told you of nothing but my rights in the estate which I claim. My title is good and my possessions in Paris are more than sufficient to serve as security.' On 6 January 1792 Curtius signed papers which placed three houses, which belonged to him, as security for proceeding with the case. The value of these houses was stated as more than 15,000 livres.[8]

* * *

The persistent Madame de la Motte, who had escaped from prison in Paris and was now in London, wrote a libellous accusation against the queen, calling it 'Memoirs of Marie Antoinette'. She offered to sell her the 'Memoirs' for 1,000 louis, but the queen refused to be blackmailed. The king, rather imprudently, bought the document and gave it to one of his advisers to burn, which was done in the furnace at the Sèvres factory in front of 200 workmen. The action aroused much suspicion and was denounced at the Assembly. It was put about that the memoirs were really letters between the Austrian Committee and the queen. This rumour was not entirely without substance. Axel Fersen had been in constant communication with the queen, and in February 1792 had travelled to Paris in disguise, with his employer M. Reutersvaard. They travelled under false passports, posing as couriers to Portugal. It was a dangerous journey, for had Fersen been discovered he would have been imprisoned or executed. He saw the queen on 13 February and the king the next day, and gave him details of a proposed escape plan. However, the king refused to leave Paris as he had given the Assembly his word that he would stay. All through her imprisonment the queen continued to correspond with foreign powers, using a code and writing with invisible ink. In order to be read, the letter had to be heated and washed with special water. The book chosen for the key to the code was *Paul et Virginie*, and the code itself was based on the use of a specific page and line.

It seems that during this time the courtesan Mrs Nesbitt was acting as a royalist agent for the British government, and newspaper reports indicate that she had often travelled to Paris in disguise:

The accusation of Mrs Nisbett [sic], whether true or false, is calculated to make an impression. Her well known talents, her connections here, her residence in The Hague, will be used as arguments of her agency, and though that clever woman may have merely retired to the Continent from motives that it would not be difficult to explain, her journies [sic] to Pyrmont and to Blankenberg, and finally, her route to Switzerland, will subject the British Court to suspicion, that they were not unconcerned spectators to the Royalist Conspiracy. . . . The connections she formed in the Empire and in Switzerland, her knowledge of the languages, the symmetry of her person which made it easy for her to assume the male habit, and the confidence reposed in her by Ministers pointed her out as a proper agent.'[9]

On 20 April 1792 the National Assembly, urged on by the Girondins, declared war on Austria. It was a rash move. The French army was badly equipped, most of the officers had fled and the troops were disorganised. The citizens felt betrayed, both by the state of the army and by the deputies who had voted for war. When Prussia joined Austria and declared war on France, there was a feeling of panic. The threat of invasion united the citizens who responded enthusiastically to the impassioned call to arms to defend their country. There was a rush to enlist, and Marie thought that 'as many as fifteen thousand persons enlisted, in one day, at amphitheatres, which were erected in the various public places'. Five days after war had been declared, a guillotine was erected at the Place de Grève, in front of the Hôtel du Ville, and claimed its first victim, Nicolas Pelletier, a purse-snatcher.

This rush to enlist caused problems for Marie when two stalwarts from the *Salon de Cire* left to join up, leaving a shortage of able-bodied men in the museum to do the work of moving and lifting the figures. Marie said that 'the quarter in which she lived appeared almost cleared of men'. The people called themselves the *sans-culottes*. They wore striped trousers instead of the courtly knee breeches, shoes which were laced, not buckled, and a scarf around the neck. Their other trademark was the red bonnet, the *bonnet rouge*. Marie believed she once saw the Duc d'Orléans dressed in that 'singular costume'.

The Assembly proposed that during the second anniversary of the fall of the Bastille 20,000 *fédérés*, patriot extremists from outside Paris, should be invited to camp outside the walls. On 19 June the king, to the fury of the revolutionaries, vetoed the invitation. The next day crowds gathered at the faubourg Saint-Antoine under the leadership of the brewer Claude Santerre, whom Marie described as:

> completely the general of the populace, and mostly at their head, whenever they were disposed for either cruelty or outrage. He was a man much above the middle height and stoutly formed; his features were coarse, and harsh in their general expression; his appearance, altogether, being rude and vulgar. He was a man of good property, but low bred, and much addicted to swearing.[10]

The mob, which numbered about 15,000 people armed with a variety of weapons, demanded that the king be stripped of his right to veto. Their rallying cry was 'Down with the Veto'. They drew up a petition and began to march to the Tuileries. There were a few National Guards and some *invalides* among them, but it was mainly *sans-culottes* and women. Early that morning Marie saw this 'most ferocious looking mob of people pouring down from the faubourg Saint-Antoine, armed in various ways, and presenting a very formidable appearance'. Because she had three brothers in the Swiss Guard at the Tuileries, she believed that the royal family would be safe, 'as she judged they were sufficiently guarded to dispel any apprehension of danger on their account'.[11] While she went back to the *salon*, Curtius followed the marchers.

First they invaded the Assembly, but there were so many of them that only a few were admitted. The others forced their way into the Tuileries gardens and then into the palace forecourt. Santerre led the mob up to the great doors and demanded entrance. They stormed into the palace. The king, watching from a large ante-room was pushed back by the crowd into a window embrasure. Others went up the great staircase in search of the queen, who was warned by her guards to flee. Her attendants ran with her from room to room to join her children. Madame Elisabeth stayed with the king. When the door was flung open by the crowd shouting 'Down with the Veto!' she clambered on to a chest in the window embrasure and stood beside her brother. She was in great danger because some people in the crowd thought she was the queen and threatened and jostled her. Legendre, a butcher, stepped forward and demanded on behalf of the people that the king uphold their rights. The king replied that it was neither the place nor the moment for such an agreement, but that he would do all that the constitution demanded. The mob harangued and insulted him and shouted for the dismissal of the royal ministers. The king and his sister were trapped in the window embrasure for four hours, while the few grenadiers placed themselves in a protective ring around the pair. Marie, in her memoirs, said, 'the heat was extreme, and the king appeared very much oppressed by the suffocating effluvia produced by the numbers of people, who were literally crammed together in the apartment'. One of the mob, who 'carried a bottle and a glass, offered Louis some wine; and although he had a presentiment that he should be one day poisoned, he, without the slightest hesitation, drank it off'.[12] The king had a *bonnet rouge* pushed at him on the end of a pike, and he took it and put it on his head.

After some time M. Pétion, the new Mayor of Paris, appeared. Hoisted up on sympathisers' shoulders, he appealed to the mob to disperse, but they took no notice. The situation was tense. The king, in an effort to get the crowd to leave, suggested they visit the State Apartments. The crowd fell silent and then passed through the rooms in reasonable order. When they reached the Council Chamber they discovered the queen, her two children and some of her ladies, with two Hussars, standing silent and rigid behind a table. Santerre, the mob's leader, stopped to harangue the queen. It was reported by Marie that the terrified woman, 'With breathless anxiety watched the mob, whilst she endeavoured to suppress her tears, and to console her daughter, who stood weeping beside her.' One man put a *bonnet rouge* on the queen's head, but she took it off and put it on the head of the dauphin. Eventually the mob dispersed and by ten o'clock, when the last of the crowd had left, calm was restored and the palace was empty. The shaken and exhausted family then went to bed. Madame Elisabeth wrote to the Abbé de Lubersac on 25 June 1792, 'The future seems an abyss, from which we can only issue by a miracle of Providence.'[13]

Following the people's invasion of the Tuileries, Marat's paper, *L'Ami du Peuple*, and René Hébert's *Le Père Duchesne* stirred up strong anti-royalist sentiments. The committees of the *sections* resolved in future to ignore the king's veto, and the Assembly was forced to sanction their decision. Santerre was put in charge of the Paris National Guard, and a tribunal was established under his command with unrestricted power to condemn or pardon. A Revolutionary police state took over power. Curtius, now fully occupied as a National Guard officer, decided that in future his doorman had better replace his National Guard uniform with that of the *sans-culottes*.

In this mood of panic and patriotism, and ignoring the king's veto, the *fédérés* were invited to Paris for the 14 July 'Fall of the Bastille' anniversary celebrations. They began to arrive on 8 July 1792. The *sans-culottes* from Marseilles were particularly vociferous, calling for the abolition of the monarchy and universal suffrage. The rousing song they brought with them, the *Marseillaise*, became the patriotic anthem, and they danced and sang in the streets. The *fédérés*' riotous behaviour, and their reputation for violence, generated considerable fear among the Parisians. Curtius patriotically agreed to have six billeted on him. Marie remembered the arrival of this ferocious band, and was pleasantly surprised. 'They behaved well, and were not of the lower orders, but persons in easy circumstances; they were very polite, and when invited to dine out used always to state they should be absent from dinner, to avoid useless preparations on their account.'[14] After the loss of the assistants who had been conscripted into the army, the presence of six sturdy men would doubtless have been welcomed by Marie. After the Bastille celebrations most of the *fédérés* remained in Paris.

There were other changes at the *Salon de Cire*. Santerre's head, modelled from life, joined those of other patriots, Marat, Danton,

Robespierre and Pétion. It cannot have been easy for Marie and Curtius to keep up with the changing roles of those in power. M. de Bersaucourt wrote cynically:

> Curtius always takes advantage of the situation. He is wily, this German! He changes all the time according to the wind, the situation, the government, the people in power. He removes 'the King at Dinner', and replaces it with figures of the deputies of the Gironde. He is successively *feuillant, girondin, jacobin, maratiste, hébertiste, robespierriste, thermidorien.* He goes with the flow, Curtius. He is a follower of the on-going government, both supporting and applauding their success. One does not have a strong opinion if one is Curtius, 'Volontaire de la Bastille'. Why a volunteer – because of his busts? He complains to the municipality about the loafers who lower the tone of the boulevard du Temple and who misbehave in his Cabinet de Cire. Now what do you think of that![15]

On 14 July 1792 the fall of the Bastille celebrations were held on the Champs de Mars and the king and queen were forced to be present. The Tree of Freedom, erected on a funeral pyre, was hung with objects symbolising the *ancien régime* which were to be ceremonially burnt. The queen wept throughout the ceremony, and screamed when she saw Louis ascend the steps of the altar, for she feared he was going to be killed. Louis remained calm, though he refused to torch the funeral pyre, saying that as feudalism no longer existed there was no need to burn it. After the ceremony the royal family were allowed to return to the Tuileries. It was the last time the king appeared in public.

It was at about this time that the king had a secret iron safe built into the wall of one of the remote corridors at the Tuileries, where he concealed state papers. The safe was installed by Gamin, who for many years had been the king's loyal servant and locksmith, but who was later to betray him. The king, queen and Madame Elisabeth were now in fear for their lives and took elaborate precautions against being poisoned. Madame Campan bought most of their food herself, including their bread, pastry, sugar and wine, and said that during July that year she never went to bed, as she feared an attack on the queen during the night. She was proved right when a servant made an attempt on the queen's life. The locks were changed and the queen moved from the ground floor to a first floor room between the king's and the dauphin's.

France was still being threatened by her enemies. The Duke of Brunswick, in command of the Prussian and Austrian armies, had now been joined by the Comte de Provence and the Comte d'Artois in command of the *émigrés*. On 25 July they issued a joint manifesto. France, and particularly Paris, was threatened with retribution unless the royal family was treated with respect. The document, 'breathing vengeance and thunder against the Parisians, [was] dictated in a haughty tone, befitting that of an imperious master to his abject vassals'. The ultimatum, said Marie, was 'in every respect such a document as was best calculated to ignite the very combustible spirit of the French'.[16] It fuelled the anti-royalist camp; wild rumours of advancing armies circulated and spread panic throughout the country. In fear for the lives of the royal family, Lafayette made a plan to rescue them. Seventy royalists were to meet at the royal stables where horses would be ready for them. The loyal members of the Guard at the Tuileries would then accompany the royal family to a carriage waiting at the Champs-Elysées and from there four companies of the Swiss Guard would escort them on the road to freedom. The queen, however, did not trust Lafayette. According to Madame Campan, she said: 'No, we have once owed our lives to Lafayette; but I should not wish it to be the case a second time.' In spite of the pleas of his advisers, the king refused to sanction the plan, saying that 'he preferred to expose himself to all dangers than begin a civil war'. On 8 August a motion was tabled in the Assembly to have Lafayette arrested and tried as an enemy of France. The motion was defeated, but Lafayette, realising that he was now powerless to help either the constitution or the royal family, fled to Liège. There he was captured and spent the next five years in a Prussian prison.

Distrust and anarchy ruled in Paris. During the night of 9/10 August 1792 the tocsin was rung at midnight at the instigation of one particular *section* which was determined to dethrone the king. Mayor Pétion counselled delay, but an attack on the Tuileries had already been planned by the Insurrectionary Committee, although some among them still had misgivings. Danton remained at the Cordeliers with Camille Desmoulins, from where he addressed the mob and urged them to take up arms to save themselves. Santerre, with Westerman, occupied the faubourg Saint-Antoine; Marat hid in the cellar at Danton's house; Curtius was on duty; and Marie stayed in the *salon* with her mother. The rabble advanced on the Tuileries. The royal family, warned of the danger, did not go to bed but sat and waited nervously for events to unfold. Outside the Swiss Guard and some of the National Guard prepared to mount a defence.

When the mob eventually invaded the Tuileries the danger was so extreme that the king was persuaded to leave the palace and take refuge in the Assembly, although the queen and Madame Elisabeth were strongly against going. Marie said that 'the queen disapproved of throwing themselves on the mercy of those who had shown them so little consideration, but at length, she reluctantly consented'.[17] With the Princesse de Lamballe, Madame de Tourzel and the frightened children they passed between protective lines formed around them by the Swiss Guard. The crowd pressed so close that the queen was robbed of her watch and her purse. However, they managed to escape to the building where the Assembly was in session. The king and his family were given shelter in a small box-like room, the '*loge du logographe*', which was no more than a high booth, a whitewashed space where a newspaper reporter could listen to, and report on, the debates. The next day was very hot, and the royal family, shut into this small confined space for sixteen hours, must have suffered considerably.

Before escaping with his family from the Tuileries, the king had dismissed the Swiss Guard, but in the confusion and fighting the order did not reach them and so they fought on. The invaders were unaware that their victims had escaped, and attacked the loyal Swiss who remained at the Tuileries, along with many nobles and servants. Most of the defenders were killed. The commander of the National Guard, the Marquis de Mandat, was summoned to the Hôtel de

Ville to explain why he had refused to withdraw his men, but was hacked to death as he was being dragged off to prison. The women who were not killed were taken off to prison. Madame Campan was one of them. As she was led away, she saw a mob of *poissardes* parading the decapitated head of Mandat. There was a terrible massacre. Mercier wrote:

> The rash Swiss lost countenance at the sight of a hundred thousand men, but still held out. What cries of grief and rage! What terrible uproar! One heard them fall with their heavy arms, and the dreadful rattle of death in their throats. And now this same people, forgetting its magnanimity, must needs stain its triumph with dishonour. Thirsting for blood and wine, they burst into the cellars and, cruelty turning into ferocity, the most hideous vices were unchained.[18]

He reported that more than 600 men died, most of whom were the king's guards, as well as nearly all of the 800 Swiss, who were deliberately hunted down and killed. Bodies were stripped and mutilated. Mercier continued:

> They are struck down without pity, stabbed and massacred and bayoneted, their very limbs dispersed and scattered, receive fresh mutilation. My pen trembles to set down what I write, for women, veritable furies, roasted them on the fiery braziers of the ruins and watched, unmoved, the smoking entrails. . . . Monsters in human form appeared in hundreds on the vestibule of the south front and danced mid seas of blood and wine.[19]

Marie would later write: 'The terror of that night was beyond all description, or even imagination.'

Once the defenders were killed, the invaders rampaged through the palace, looting and destroying in a frenzy of triumph: 'Broken mirrors fell tinkling under bayonet strokes.' The queen's bedchamber became 'a scene of the most infamous and disgusting outrages'. The mob 'broke open the desks of the king and queen and

Madame Elisabeth and of the ladies of the Court'. Anything they found was stolen including, 'Gold and silver coin, money bills, watches, jewels and jewelled caskets, precious stones.' They went through the wardrobes and 'pillaged stuffs and linen, table silver, liqueurs, candles, and books from the library – anything that could be carried off. And even while this violence was doing, the leaders ostentatiously sent the great silver candlesticks from the chapel, and its silver service, and a purse of a hundred *louis* to the Assembly to lay at rest any suspicion of spoliation.'[20]

It was only when the mob had achieved victory at the Tuileries that the perpetrators showed themselves on the streets. 'Marat, their arch instigator, crept out of his hole, put himself at the head of a band of ruffians, and, brandishing a sword, endeavoured to look as fierce as his diminutive person would permit; whilst Robespierre made his appearance at the Assembly, and emitted his venom against the royal victims of the brutal conspiracy in which he had borne his part as a principal promoter.'[21]

Marie, meanwhile, was in the greatest distress. 'What words can describe the pangs of anxiety of one who had five relatives exposed to the fury of that sanguine combat of 10 August.' She was 'long kept in breathless anxiety, ignorant of the fate of her three brothers and two uncles, who were among the combatants at the palace'.[22] All that night reports of the horrors were brought to her, but it was too dangerous to venture out. The next morning she determined to go to the Tuileries to see if she could discover their fate. Another woman, on a similar quest, accompanied her. They went via the boulevards to avoid any assassins who might still be roaming the streets, and arrived at the Tuileries garden:

All was still; few persons were seen, and of those, perchance some were on the same fearful commission as themselves. The weather was intensely hot; an awful silence pervaded the scene; not a breath was stirring, not a leaf was ruffled. . . . At length they entered the gates of those gardens which had so often been the scene of innocent joy and revelry . . . but now, alas! How bitter was the contrast! Wherever the eye turned, it fell upon many a mangled corpse, and in some places heaps of the slain were thrown indiscriminately together; the beautiful gravel walks were stained with gore; the statues, although somewhat spotted with blood, were uninjured; for such was the extraordinary respect manifested for works of art, even by the murderous mob, that when their victims sought refuge by climbing up the statues, the people would not fire at them lest they should damage the beautiful specimens of sculpture; they therefore kept pricking those who clung to them with their pikes, till the unfortunate wretches were forced to descend, and were dispatched by such means as best suited the caprice of their assassins.[23]

Marie looked with horror and revulsion at the mutilated bodies which strewed the ground but, driven by her need to know the fate of her brothers and uncles, she continued with the search even though it would have cost her her life if she had been seen searching for a Swiss. Finding no one she knew, she went home, buoyed by the hope that they might have escaped. But all too soon the news arrived that they had all been massacred. 'How few individuals are there who have experienced so dreadful a blow as that of losing in one day, by the hands of assassins, three brothers and two uncles!'[24]

A memorial in Lucerne, Switzerland, 'To the Fidelity and Bravery of the Swiss', is dedicated to the 26 officers and 760 soldiers of the Swiss Guard killed on 10 August and 2 and 3 September 1792, 'who, so as not to break their oath, were killed after brave defence'. Among the officers' names listed are, Waltner, Marie's mother's name, and Allemann, the name of Marie's aunt. Both lived at 20 boulevard du Temple.[25]

As soon as it was believed safe, the king and his family were moved from the Assembly to the ancient Feuillants, where they were miserably accommodated. They were in considerable discomfort as they had been able to take nothing with them when they fled the Tuileries, and all their possessions had been looted and lost. On 13 August, at a quarter past seven in the evening, the family were transferred to the Temple prison and placed under the care of Pétion and Santerre. Hoping to be lodged in the Prince de Conti's palace, they found to their dismay that they were to be incarcerated in three floors of the small prison tower in the sequestered apartment of M. Berthélémy, the archivist of the Order of Saint Jean de Jerusalem and Malta. Nothing was ready when they arrived, and for the first night they slept wherever they could. Madame Elisabeth and young Pauline de Tourzel had to sleep on camp beds in the kitchen. After the vast spaces of Versailles and the Tuileries, the Temple was claustrophobic.

The next day the Princess de Lamballe, Madame de Tourzel, her daughter, the ladies-in-waiting and the attendants were taken away to La Force prison, and the royal family were left in the care of their guards. If they wanted to walk in the gardens, they had to pass the many sentinels who lined up to insult them, and during the walk they were taunted by the soldiers. They had to run the same gauntlet on their return to the tower. On 19 August a public proclamation was made that the monarchy had been abolished, and replaced by an Executive Council.

Royalist supporters took up positions in the windows of buildings overlooking the gardens of the Temple, in the hope of seeing members of the royal family. 'An intense interest existed in the minds of the people respecting them,' said Marie, 'and in all the houses round the prison, the proprietors were able to let their lodgings at an extremely high rate, numbers of people paying for admission to those rooms from the windows of which they could obtain a view of the king and his family walking in the Temple gardens.'[26] The *Salon de Cire* was only a few minutes' walk from the prison and Marie did go once to try to catch a glimpse of the royal family, but she was so upset at the sight of them, and the way they were being treated, that she never went again.

The royal family were now helpless prisoners of the Revolution.

NINE

'The blood of the innocent'

By the end of August 1792 Paris seemed to Marie 'like one immense prison: the barriers were closed; boats were stationed on the river to prevent the escape of any individual whatever; nor could the most pressing urgency be received as an excuse to obtain permission from the authorities for quitting the city, whilst the search for aristocrats continued'.[1] It was a time of great unrest; the French army was suffering defeat from the Allied forces, and the men of the Revolutionary Municipal Commune were patrolling the streets and picking up anyone thought to have royalist sympathies. Over 1,000 people were thrown into prison, along with common criminals and the priests who had refused to take the oath. There were rumours of plots and insurrection in Paris, and when reports came of the fall of Verdun it was whispered that royalist sympathisers in the overcrowded prisons would break out and lead a counter-revolution. It was thought the Prussians had obtained entry to Verdun through the treachery of the townspeople, and it was feared that this might happen in Paris.

On 27 August Cardinal Salamon, now the pope's Internuncio at Paris, was seized from his house at the Cour des Fontaines at the Palais Marchand by a group of soldier commissaires of his *section*. He was examined before a committee of five, including Marat, whom Salamon had once consulted as a doctor. 'Even then he bore in his soul – frightful as his face – the germ of his future atrocities, for he prescribed me some medicine, which would have killed me, if the celebrated chemist of the rue Jacob had been willing to give it to me. "I see well enough,"' he said, '"this is no medicine for you, it is medicine for a horse; I recognise the doctor's signature, he is mad."' Following his interrogation Salamon was imprisoned in a small loft at the Palais du Justice with eighty other prisoners, mainly clergy. The roof was so low they could not stand up and there was filthy straw on the floor but no beds: in the full summer heat, the ventilation from the few narrow windows was hopelessly inadequate. One man suffocated. 'It was truly a vestibule of death.'[2]

On Saturday 1 September sixty-three of the prisoners, including Salamon, were herded into hackney coaches and taken to the Abbaye prison, once the home of the Benedictine monks at Saint-Germain-des-Prés. That night, when they heard the tocsin rung: 'A breathless terror paralysed the power of all the peaceable citizens.'

The next day, Sunday 2 September, six more hackney coaches full of dissident priests being taken to the Abbaye prison were attacked and the prisoners massacred. Only one priest survived. The hired assassins, reported to be no more than 300 in number, were recruited from the Parisian butchers. The murderers then moved on to the Carmelite convent where 150 priests were being held; all but one were killed. From there they went from prison to prison, killing indiscriminately. One of the leaders, M. Maillard, who was known to Marie, had led the march of women to Versailles.

The priests at the Abbaye prison, learning of the slaughter, prayed and made their confessions as they awaited their fate. Hearing the yells of the advancing assassins, Salamon and fourteen others managed to scramble through a high window, but then found themselves trapped in a small courtyard with no exit. There the mob cornered them. They were dragged into a large room already full of prisoners. All was disorganisation and confusion. The only question asked was 'Have you taken the Oath?' If the answer was 'No' they were hacked to death, sometimes in the room and sometimes dragged outside. The bodies were stripped and plundered, and there was confusion and shouting and arguments about the distribution of the clothes taken from the bodies. At five o'clock in the morning Salamon was questioned, but escaped death by lying about his identity. Billaud de Varenne had promised that each of the assassins should be paid 24 livres. On the day he was set free Salamon saw a member of the commune paying the men, and those who had killed the greatest numbers were paid the most.

Further carnage followed. At Bicêtre there was a mass slaughter of adolescent boys and at La Salpêtrière first the rape and then the slaughter of thirteen prostitutes. The mob then moved on to La Force prison where they remained for five days, and where Marie's friend, the Princesse de Lamballe, was being held. As Mercier said: 'her sincere attachment to the wife of Louis XVI [was] her only crime. She had played no part even in our most agitated moments. Nothing could have rendered her suspect in the people's eyes, to whom she was only known by her multiple acts of charity.' The princess had earlier escaped from France, but had loyally returned when she heard of the queen's plight. On 3 September she appeared before the Revolutionary Tribunal and her trial was presided over by the scheming René Hébert. She showed much courage when questioned and several voices in the crowd of onlookers supported her. She was released, but outside a vengeful crowd awaited her. She was savagely and degradingly murdered. Mercier wrote: 'Her head and breasts were cut off, her body torn open, her heart snatched out, her head borne on a pike, and paraded through Paris; her body dragged behind.' After the mob had mutilated her body, her head was brought to Marie, who was deeply shocked. She later recalled how:

The savage murderers stood over her, whilst she [Marie], shrinking with horror, was compelled to take a cast from the features of the unfortunate princess. Having known her virtues, and having been accustomed to see her beaming with all that cheerfulness and sweetness – to hear her accents teeming but of kindness, always affording pleasure to her auditors, and then, alas! to have the severed head of one so lovely between her trembling hands, was indeed hard to bear.

Marie 'proceeded to perform her melancholy task, whilst surrounded by the brutal monsters, whose hands were bathed in the blood of the innocent'.[3] The assassins then paraded the severed head of the princess, her hair dressed by a terrified hairdresser, and her hands, genitals and heart stuck on pikes, up the boulevard to the

124

Temple prison to show the queen. What was left of her body was dragged along the road. The queen fainted at the news, and was taken by Madame Elisabeth into another room, but for a long time the Temple walls rang to the yells of the bloodthirsty mob. During the two days of 2 and 3 September almost half of the prison population of Paris was killed. Between 12,000 and 14,000 prisoners were massacred with the blessing of the Assembly. The General Council even paid 850 livres to a wine merchant so that free wine could be distributed. On 16 September 1792 Curtius, sickened by the slaughter, wrote to the Assembly proposing that the remaining recalcitrant priests could be exchanged for sailors and soldiers who had been captured by the Deys of Algiers. His letter was ignored.

On the war front events began to change. On 20 September 1792 the combined Austrian, Prussian and *émigré* forces were forced to withdraw from Valmy after a skirmish with the French army led by Dumouriez and Kellerman. General Adam Philippe Custine, who had served with the French in the American War of Independence, now advanced into Germany and reached Mayence. Custine was a difficult man and had the reputation of being severe and unyielding to the point of brutality. Curtius wrote to him to ask if he would use his influence at the Town Hall at Mayence on his behalf, so that the inheritance due to him could be released. Not surprisingly, there was no reply.

General Dumouriez reported that: 'All the departments (but more especially the wretched city of Paris) were given to pillage, to denunciations, proscriptions, and massacres. No Frenchman, the assassins and their accomplices excepted, had either his life or his property in security.'[4] Danton authorised indiscriminate house searches, which were carried out with brutal efficiency, and the soldiers and municipals were savage with their arrests. Mercier wrote: 'They who defend the massacres will scarcely maintain that the jewellery and diamonds of those arrested were objects of suspicion. Nevertheless, both persons and belongings were seized. This alone gives one a clue to the massacres, one thinks.'[5] Marie agreed. 'Those valuables, which once contributed to give splendour

125

to royalty, were deposited at the *garde-meuble*, and, it appeared, whether from neglect or design, were but indifferently guarded, and the greater part of them were stolen during one night. . . . The greater part of the objects stolen consisted of diamonds and jewellery of different descriptions.'[6] In spite of his lack of money, in October Curtius made a donation of 220 livres towards the costs of the war, and the Jacobin club appointed him to be the protector of the Austrian and Prussian deserters who had applied to them for refuge and assistance. The *fédérés* had now left 20 boulevard du Temple, and so the deserters were accommodated in their place. Some were able to help Marie with the heavy work.

With the purging of the prisons, the Assembly sought a total change to the old regime. Births, marriages and deaths were no longer the province of the Church but became civil matters and, as such, had to be registered at the Hôtel de Ville. The break between Church and State was almost complete. As part of this change, the reformers declared that the new regime must have a new calendar and new divisions of time. Decimalisation was the key to this ambitious, albeit somewhat confusing, plan. There were to be twelve months of equal length in the year, with thirty days in each month. These in turn were divided into three 'weeks' of ten days each, to be known as *décades*, with nine days for work and one for leisure. The five extra days at the end of the year, the *sans-culottes*, were to be used for public holidays of a patriotic nature. The use of 'old calendar' names – such as saints' days, pagan gods or historical allusions – was strictly forbidden after 1793. The months were named after the season, the temperature or the flora of that time of year. Year I of the first year of the Republic of France began at midnight on 22 September 1792. In addition, many of the old districts and roads in Paris had their names changed to others that were deemed more patriotic or secular.

To add to the confusion, one year later, on 5 October 1793, new divisions of time were introduced. The twenty-four-hour day was now to be divided into ten hours of a hundred 'minutes'. Each minute contained a hundred 'seconds'. This may not have been a problem for those who rose with the sun and went to bed at dusk, but it must have been chaotic for people with timepieces. Ornate mantel clocks and fob watches now had to be made with two clock faces, one for the old time and one for Revolutionary time. With this introduction of new names for streets and districts, days and weeks, and the decimalisation of time, the idealists hoped to create a new, centralised world controlled by the State. The confusion was overwhelming. The new calendar remained in force until 1805 but the new decimal time lasted barely eighteen months and disappeared on 18 Germinal Année III (7 April 1795).

All this time the king and his family had been locked in the Temple prison, guarded day and night and treated with little courtesy. On 26 September 1792 a public proclamation was made in front of the Temple tower. Royalty was abolished. A republic had been established. From that day the king was to be known only by the name Louis Capet. Seeking to incriminate the king, a strict search was made of all the rooms and closets used by the royal family, and all paper, pens, ink, pencils and written papers were confiscated. That night the king was transferred to a room in the great tower at the Temple. The queen, dauphin, Madame Royale and Madame Elisabeth were also moved into a different floor of the great tower, where the rooms were damp and cold and they became ill. The high windows were barred and shuttered and they could not see out. In November, on the information given by Gamin, the locksmith who had once worked for the king, incriminating papers were found concealed in a wall safe at the Tuileries, which implicated the king in a counter-revolutionary plot. The papers also linked the once-lauded Mirabeau to financial dealings with the *émigré* royalists, and he was branded a traitor. His remains were removed from the Panthéon.

Following the evidence of the king's so-called treachery, Louis Antoine Saint-Just, Robespierre's 25-year-old acolyte, entered the fray with a powerful maiden speech in the Assembly, calling for the death of the king. Marie knew Saint-Just well and found him:

severe in all his decisions, and inaccessible to pity, yet he always acted from principle. . . . His features were very regular, his

127

complexion was dark, his hair black; there was ever a reflecting expression in his countenance, and his whole appearance suggested the idea of a fanatic. . . . To effect an object which he thought would prove for the public good, he regarded not the sacrifice of human life any more than he would so many livres, and he had a perfect contempt for money.[7]

His speech was persuasive, and the king was committed for trial as a traitor.

From 11 December, when the proceedings began, the king was separated from all contact with his family. The trial, which continued over Christmas, was long and bitterly fought. Voting began on 4 January to decide his fate. After four inconclusive results, the king was finally convicted and condemned, and three days later was sentenced to death by a majority of some seventy votes. One of those who voted for his death was his cousin the Duc d'Orléans, now known as Philippe Egalité.

Marie described the morning of the king's execution:

Every shop, and every window, was closed, and people mostly retired to the backs of the houses, along the line by which the dreadful cavalcade had to pass. Incalculable were the floods of tears which were on that day shed . . . yet a solemn silence reigned, as the carriage, containing the royal victim, passed between the lines of troops, which were under arms, in case any attempt at rescue should occur.[8]

The closed coach drove through the silent streets and arrived at la place de la République, once la place Louis XV. When the king mounted the steep steps to the guillotine he tried to make a speech to the vast sea of spectators, but Santerre, the Captain of the Guard, ordered a roll of drums which drowned out his words. Santerre later said he had been commanded to open fire on the crowd with cannon if the king spoke, and it was to prevent this that he had ordered the drum-roll. The king was strapped to the plank, pushed forward into the enclosing lunette and at twenty minutes past ten on the morning of 21 January 1793 the blade flashed down. The king was dead. There were shouts as the head was brandished in front of the crowd and many rushed forward to dip their handkerchiefs or scraps of material in the king's blood. Pieces of his clothing and snips of hair were sold as souvenirs by Henri Sanson, the executioner, as was his right.

Marie was informed that she must go to the church of the Madeleine, where the king's body was taken, and there, in haste and secrecy, she took a cast of the king's severed head. The king's remains were then buried under a thick layer of quicklime to ensure that all traces would be erased. An old man called Janiquer, who was employed at the Madeleine cemetery, remembered that there were no coffins. 'We received the bodies and heads separately just as they were brought in. Part of the clothing was generally stolen on the way; sometimes even, if the police who accompanied the corpses did not remain until they were put underground, we buried them naked.'[9]

In England, the *Town and Country Magazine* reported: 'The French King murdered by a banditti of Regicides calling themselves a National Convention.'[10] There was much concern in England that the insurrection in France would spread across the Channel. George Rose wrote in his diary: 'Certain it is, that they [the French] neglected no means in their power to stir up rebellion in this country. Chauvelin, an impudent republican who had been Ambassador from Louis XVI, was now the agent of the Executive Council to foment disturbances, by sowing disloyalty throughout the land with the aid of English Jacobins and revolutionists.' In January Chauvelin demanded to be accredited as Minister of the French Republic in England, 'which is refused'. Chauvelin was a friend of Fox and the Whigs, many of whom were sympathetic towards the cause of the revolutionaries. But he proved himself so dangerous an incendiary that he was dismissed from office and on 22 January was ordered to quit England. 'This step his friend Mr Fox chose to consider an act of aggression upon France.'[11]

In France, the Committee of Public Safety came under the ruthless control of Robespierre, who purged all whom he believed to have opposed him. All it needed was a denunciation, and the suspect was shot or guillotined within twenty-four hours. Grace Elliot was one of the suspects:

> From that period everything bespoke terror. Robespierre became all powerful. People did not dare to speak above their breath . . . even in our own rooms you felt frightened. If you laughed you were accused of joy at some bad news the republic had had; if you cried they said you regretted their success. In short, they were sending soldiers every hour to search houses for papers of conspiracies. These soldiers generally robbed people or made them give them money, threatening, in case of refusal, to denounce them. . . . Paris was a scene of filth and riot, and the honest, sober part of the inhabitants were afraid of being seen.[12]

There were many reasons to fear, and Marie, at the centre of events, was very aware of the danger. Many petty grudges resulted in death. She recounted how Robespierre was walking on the boulevard one day with a lady, who admired a house as they passed it.

'Would you like to have it?' demanded Robespierre.

'Indeed I should,' replied the lady.

'Then, Madam, it shall be yours,' said Robespierre.

He carried his courtesy so far, said Marie, as to have the owner denounced as an enemy to the public and immediately executed. The property was confiscated, and Robespierre then donated it to the lady. Marie commented wryly, 'There is no politeness equal to the French, after all.'[13] She told another story about how Robespierre had sought as his mistress a young and very beautiful widow, Madame Sainte Amaranthe, who scathingly rejected him. In revenge, Robespierre brought her before the Revolutionary Tribunal and she was tried, condemned and beheaded. Marie knew her well, because she had sat for her portrait as a present for her brother only a few months before she was guillotined.[14]

Even to be a showman in those inflammatory times was a risky business. Paul de Philipsthal, a German, was working in Paris under the name Paul Philidor, and was showing a phantasmagoria show at the Hôtel des Chartres in the rue de Richelieu.[15] His show, held in a darkened room, promised that terrifying ghosts would arise from their graves amid rolls of thunder and flashes of lightning, and then vanish mysteriously. It was immensely popular and had been running twice a night since December 1792. During a show in 1793 one of Philipsthal's assistants had accidentally allowed an image of the king to appear on the screen, and although the slide was immediately pulled out of the lantern, the king appeared to some zealots to be rising upwards, perhaps to heaven. The Revolutionary Tribunal set up by Robespierre needed no more than a whiff of royalist leanings, and Philipsthal was immediately arrested and thrown into prison. His wife went to Curtius to ask for his help, but he warned her that a considerable bribe might be needed. However, Philipsthal was a rich man, and his wife gave Curtius 300 *louis d'or* with which to buy her husband's freedom from Robespierre. Curtius later told Marie that when he went to visit his friend Robespierre, he was able to obtain an order for Philipsthal's release. He had placed the purse of money casually on a table in the room when he left. As the money was never returned, he could only assume that the 'incorruptible' Robespierre had taken it. When he was released from prison Philipsthal left the country. He was not heard of again until he appeared in London at the Lyceum Theatre in 1801. Later, when Marie needed to borrow money for a journey to England, Philipsthal was instrumental in arranging the loan.

* * *

People were confused and uncertain of the future. By February 1793 there were grocery riots in Paris as the paper *assignat* had lost 50 per cent of its value and the government had to subsidise the cost of bread. Extra taxes were imposed. *Emigrés* were formally banished and their property confiscated; to return to France was death. Talleyrand, now in London, was one of the group of exiled French *émigrés* at Juniper Hall near Boxhill; another, General d'Arblay, would marry Fanny Burney.

The two leading factions, the Jacobins and the more placatory Girondins, continued their struggle for power in the National

Convention. On 13 March a powerful speech was given by the Girondin Pierre Vergniaud, who called on the Jacobins to cease their militant fight and call off the rioting and slaughter. Marat was the Jacobins' most virulent speaker and had just succeeded to the rotating presidency of the Assembly. The Girondins indicted Marat, using his own scabrous writing as proof, and Marat went on the run for three days, but then returned to face trial, to enthusiastic applause from his supporters. Although Marat was admired by his fellow Jacobins, there were many, more moderate, deputies who feared and hated him. However, the judges at his trial were sympathetic and their interrogation less than searching, so Marat was acquitted.

This was a severe defeat for the Girondins, and in June, M. Hanriot, the new commander of the Gardes Françaises, demanded the trial and surrender of their leaders. Realising their danger, most of the Girondins fled to Caen, where many of them were later captured and returned to Paris for trial. Marie, always trying to keep abreast of the changing hierarchy, took a mask of Hanriot's head.

Following the banishment of the Girondins, Charlotte Corday, a fervent supporter of their cause, had taken a diligence to Paris from her home in Caen, determined to eliminate either Robespierre or Marat. Once there, she bought a knife from the cutler M. Badouin in the Palais-Royal. She wrote to Marat asking for an interview and offering to disclose details of the Girondin plots. The next day, 13 July 1793, she called at his rooms at 30 rue de l'Ecole de Médecine, near the rue des Cordeliers. At first she was sent away, but she came back at seven o'clock that night. Simonne Evrard, Marat's woman, stopped her on the stairs, but Charlotte deliberately spoke loudly so that Marat could overhear. He told her to come up and, on entering the room, she found him, as usual, immersed in his bath, where he wrote on a board fitted across it at chest level to support his paper and writing materials. Marat had found that the only way to obtain relief from the pain of his eczema was by immersing his body in a sulphur bath, and wrapping his head in a cloth soaked in vinegar. Charlotte gave him some false information about the Girondins at Caen, and then, as he took up a pencil to write the names of the offenders, she plunged a knife into his heart. Marat called out as he died and

> his housekeeper obeyed the call, and a man, who was near, rushed in and knocked down the avenger of her country with a chair, while the female trampled on her. A crowd was instantly attracted to the spot by the uproar . . . some members of the *section* arriving, they prevented her from being torn to pieces by the mob. They conducted her to prison, protecting her from insult.[16]

Marie, who was quickly summoned to the house by the gendarmes to take a death mask of Marat, had arrived in time to see Charlotte Corday being dragged away. Marie also made sketches of the murder scene at the request of artist Jacques-Louis David, and these, together with the death-mask, became the inspiration for David's small painting of Marat's head. She also visited Charlotte Corday in the Conciergerie, where she sketched her, finding her:

> a most interesting personage; she was tall and finely formed; her countenance had quite a noble expression; she had a beautiful colour, and her complexion was remarkably clear; her manners were extremely pleasing, and her deportment particularly graceful. Her mind was rather of a masculine order. . . . She conversed freely, and even cheerfully, and ever with a countenance of the purest serenity.[17]

Three days after Marat's murder, his funeral was held in the old church of the Cordeliers, very near his lodgings. Masterminded by David, and again inspired by the classics, the funeral was a solemn reverence for a fallen hero. Marat's body was, rather belatedly, embalmed and put on public display, carefully posed to resemble the monumental painting that David was planning to produce. Decomposing rapidly in the heat of July, his remains were placed on a high altar while members of the Convention, numbers of magistrates and his fellow deputies filed past and paid their last respects. There was a vast crowd at his funeral and he was buried in the garden of the Cordeliers, 'whence', says Marie, 'he [had] poured out his iniquity by reading his inflammatory paper to the people'.[18]

On 17 July 1793, four days after Marat's assassination, Charlotte Corday, dressed in scarlet, was taken in a tumbrel to the place of execution and guillotined. Marie made a death-mask from Charlotte's decapitated head, which she used when she created a tableau of the assassination for Curtius's museum. The tableau attracted crowds of people, 'who, in general, were loud in their lamentations'. Robespierre himself visited the exhibit, and as he left he began to harangue the passers-by. A crowd soon gathered, and he encouraged them to enter the museum and see 'the image of their departed friend, snatched from us by an assassin's hand, guided by the demon of aristocracy; but although the form of Marat is torn from our embrace, long may his spirit dwell in our minds, and influence our actions'. He urged them to weep and seek revenge. 'His discourse was received by the populace with the most unbounded applause, whilst people poured into the exhibition to see the likeness of their idolized Marat.' Marie said that for many weeks as much as twenty-five pounds a day was taken, 'so anxious was the public to behold the representation of a man, whose deeds had obtained him so dreadful a notoriety'. It is very likely that David's famous picture of the death of Marat may have been partly based on Marie's tableau at the *Salon de Cire*, as well as on the sketches she had made at his special request.

* * *

In the summer of 1793 Curtius decided to buy a small house at Ivry-sur-Seine in the south-west of Paris. It had a garden where he could grow vegetables and keep chickens, both very important in those times of such severe food shortages. The house had a dining room and a kitchen, plus three other rooms, and extended over two floors. Curtius paid for the house in instalments, the first payment of 5,010 livres being handed over to Citizen Junot at the Agence National.

Food was still very scarce and the price of bread rose alarmingly. Marie said that 'the most imperative measures were taken to compel the farmers to bring their corn to market', and citizens were only allowed to keep one month's supply or be subject to a large fine. In July the death penalty was extended to cover hoarders. House searches were once again instituted, usually at midnight, and, as Marie noted, these were the terror of everyone.

On 8 June the eight-year-old dauphin was removed from the care of his mother and aunt and separated from his fourteen-year-old sister. The little boy was dragged away from his frantic mother in tears, and put under the charge of a *sans-culottes*, the cobbler Antoine Simon. He was still housed in the Temple, but was allowed no contact with his family, in spite of Marie Antoinette's incessant requests. For two days after he had been taken they could hear him weeping, until Simon frightened him into silence. The child, who had never been shown how to fend for himself, was left alone in his cell with only a bell to call for aid, which he was too terrified to ring.

The queen, Madame Elisabeth and the Madame Royale were locked into their room. The guards came in three times a day with meals, and always checked the bars on the boarded-up windows. There was a narrow slit in one of the walls of a little closet, through which they could see the dauphin when he was taken up to the battlements. Marie Antoinette stayed by the opening for hours in the hope of catching a glimpse of her son. Her daughter wrote in her memoirs: 'It was her sole hope, her sole occupation.'

The queen's case was handed over to the Committee for Public Safety. When she was taken away to the Conciergerie for trial, Madame Elisabeth and the Madame Royale were left alone in one small room in the great tower at the Temple prison. They were searched three times a day by drunken, abusive soldiers. The Conciergerie, where the queen was now held, was one of the most feared prisons in Paris. Citoyen Michel, in his *almanach des prisons* written in 1794, paints a chilling picture:

What a contrast. Above are attractive shops selling perfumes and the most elegant fashions. . . . Down below, only the thickness of a vaulted ceiling away, are the bolts, the bars, the groans, the rags, the insupportable stench, and the fetid air. There drunken gaolers, jangling enormous keys and speaking an unintelligible language, are accompanied by large terrifying dogs. . . . O you, who have not been in these buildings, if you want to know what it is to be in prison, ask to be put in the Conciergerie.[19]

Conditions were harsh. There were two gendarmes in Marie Antoinette's room to guard her day and night and she was never alone. For the first ten days she was kept without linen, and when she asked for some to be sent from her belongings at the Temple prison, the bundle packed by Madame Elisabeth was never delivered. Her health was poor and she suffered from frequent haemorrhages, but her gaolers were indifferent to her plight. The prison, infested with rats and lice, was dark, unhealthy and noisome.

In marked contrast to this horror, on 10 August a public ceremony known as the Festival of Unity was held to celebrate the formal acceptance of the new constitution. Devised by David, who excelled at flamboyant public ceremonies, it involved symbolic scenes and figures which, like his paintings, owed their inspiration to ancient Greece and Rome. The emblems of royalty were burned on la place de la Revolution in front of the statue of Liberty, which had replaced the equestrian statue of Louis XV. Marie, who was present at the ceremony, commented: 'An unbiased spectator, reflecting on the scenes of carnage and slaughter with which Paris had been deluged, and which those demonstrations of joy were intended to celebrate, could scarcely avoid the natural conclusion, that he was witnessing the fiend-like revelries of a race of cannibals.'[20]

At the beginning of February 1793 France declared war on England and Holland, and a month later on Spain. Fighting on all fronts resulted in an urgent need for more troops. The costs of war were mounting, and citizens were ordered to surrender all plate and jewellery to the National Convention: 'everyone having been ordered to transmit to the Hôtel de Ville every ounce of silver and gold which they possessed'. It was wise to comply, as random house searches were still frequent and there were attacks on anyone believed to be wealthy. Curtius sent an immense hamper to the town hall containing all his valuables: 'And as he had, by the greatest policy, contrived ever to keep on good terms with the men in power, he never was troubled with a domiciliary visit.'[21]

On 23 August, six months after war had been declared, conscription became enforced and 300,000 men were called up. Forges were set up in the streets to equip this vast army, large houses were sequestered, cannon were cast on the banks of the Seine and watchmakers were used to make the more intricate portions of the matchlocks. Efforts to provision the army included growing potatoes in part of the Tuileries. Curtius, a German speaker, was sent on a mission to the Rhine to gather information, and was appointed to General Custine's headquarters as the 'Envoy Extraordinary of the Republic, and War Commissioner at Mayence'. According to Marie, he was away for about eighteen months, during which time she was in sole charge of the *Salon de Cire*.

The Terror started on 17 September 1793, when the New Law of Suspects came into force. This draconian law covered the whole nation; anyone could be arrested and guillotined on suspicion, and there was usually no formal accusation and no trial. In the country the militant revolutionaries victimised anyone who had associations with the old regime. There was mass slaughter in Lyon after an uprising there was overthrown by the Republican army. In command was the cripple Georges Couthon, whom Marie remembered as 'a smiling monster'. He had 'rather a placid expression, which might have deceived many. He was totally decrepit, and was always obliged to have a servant carry him, and even place him in his chair.' Over 1,900 citizens were slaughtered. In Nantes the victims were stripped, roped together, with their hands and feet tied, and pushed out into the river on barges with holes drilled below the waterline. The populace on the shore stood and watched while the struggling prisoners drowned.

The queen, ill, wasted and shrunken, was brought to trial on 12 October 1793. Her hair was now sparse and white. It was a mockery of a trial, as there was no real crime of which she could be accused. The tribunal president, M. Hermann, interrogated her at great length about the accusations of impurity in body, thought, word and deed. René Hébert, the author of the scurrilous *Père Duchesne* and the queen's bitter enemy, screamed for her head. He accused her of immorality and brought charges of incest against her, saying she had corrupted the dauphin. After long hours of fruitless interrogation, Antoine Fouquier-Tinville, the Public Prosecutor, declared her guilty. She was sentenced to be guillotined the following day.

Unlike Louis XVI, who was allowed the privacy of a closed carriage to take him to the scaffold, Marie Antoinette, her hands bound and her hair cut short for the knife blade, was paraded through the streets seated on a plank in an open tumbrel. Only thirty-eight, she went to her death with dignity. On the day of her execution, 16 October 1793, Marie went to a friend's house to see the queen pass by on the way to the guillotine. But the horror was too much for her and as the cavalcade came into sight she passed out, overcome with emotion, and so did not see the queen's last journey. Once again she was summoned to the Madeleine to take a death-mask. There she found the queen's body dumped unceremoniously beside her severed head.

Marie had known and admired Marie Antoinette during her eight years at Versailles, and was deeply saddened by her murder. However, realising that life for the queen had become unbearable, Marie believed 'that death was hailed by her as a deliverance'.[22]

TEN

'This cavalcade of mockery'

The execution of Marie Antoinette ushered in an orgy of killing. Marie, like thousands of other citizens, could only watch as the beheadings continued. Brissot and Vergniaud were guillotined with twenty-one fellow Girondins on 31 October 1793. When the sentence of death was passed, Vergniaud looked with contempt at his judges and said: '*I* die on the day when people have lost their reason; *you* will die on the day when they shall have recovered it.'[1] Jean-Marie Roland, one of the leading Girondins, escaped to Rouen, but his much younger wife, Manon, was arrested in June and imprisoned at the Abbaye prison. When her husband heard that she had been guillotined in November, he committed suicide. Philippe Egalité, formerly the Duc d'Orléans, was accused of having plotted with General Dumouriez, and went through a mockery of a trial. He heard his condemnation with the utmost indifference, dined well the night before his execution and went to his death bravely.

The killings were accompanied by a wave of anti-religious fervour, which included the smashing of statues and the burning of Bibles and prayer books. The objective was to de-Christianise the Revolution. On 10 November 1793 the cathedral of Notre-Dame, now renamed the Temple of Reason, played host to another of David's pageants. Marie was not impressed by 'this cavalcade of mockery'. The Goddess of Reason, impersonated by the wife of a printer named Momoro, 'was enthroned upon an antique seat, with ivy entwined, and borne by four citizens. She had much of personal beauty, even though modesty might be wanting . . . and the bust of Marat heightened the disgrace of the whole.'[2]

On 11 November 1793 Bailly was arrested. A friend of Marie and Curtius, and erstwhile Mayor of Paris, he was accused of causing the deaths of some anti-royalist rioters at the Champs de Mars in July 1791. He was subjected to much humiliating physical abuse before being guillotined. 'And thus terminated the sufferings of one of the most amiable men, both as regarded his public and his private life; he was besides a first-rate scholar and a profound philosopher.'[3] Barnave, who had escorted the royal family on their return from Varenne, and was another of Marie's friends, was executed in November: 'All his learning, his eloquence, and even his riches, could not save him from the persecution of his enemies.'[4]

The list of those killed seemed endless. Madame du Barry was the next victim. Frightened by the Revolution she went to live in safety in England, but unwisely returned to France to collect some of her jewels. She was arrested at her château and several absurd accusations were made against her. Sent to the guillotine in December, she uttered piercing shrieks and fought frantically with the executioner who was trying to strap her to the board. However, there was no escape and her name joined the list of the slaughtered. She had sat for Curtius when she was twenty-two and her bust was one of his most admired figures. Marie often saw her when she was older and said, 'she was still a handsome woman, tall, and inclining to be stout; her manners were graceful, and highly pleasing'.[5] After her execution Marie went to the Madeleine cemetery, found her head and modelled it.

The Terror became all-invasive and spread throughout the country. There was danger everywhere and many showmen were arrested for imaginary crimes. In December 1793 the London *Morning Post* reported that: 'The Actors of the ci-devant Theatre Français, who have been in custody for these four months, petitioned the Convention to be released, since, after the seals had been taken off their papers, nothing could be found which could affect their innocence. Their request was refused.'[6] Many of Curtius's friends had already left the boulevard du Temple, including Comus, who had once benefited from royal patronage. He was now appearing to great acclaim in London.

In April 1794 a growing difference between Danton and Robespierre resulted in the arrest of the former. Again accusing

Robespierre of being too indiscriminate in his choice of victims, and of punishing the innocent along with the guilty, Danton called for the end of the Terror. Robespierre could tolerate no such criticism. Danton was arrested during the night and taken to the Luxembourg prison. With him went Camille Desmoulins, Hérault de Séchelles, Fabre d'Eglantine, Lacroix, Phillipeaux, and Westerman. All were found guilty, and on 5 April all were guillotined. Shortly afterwards Camille's young wife Lucille was also executed, her only crime being her marriage to Camille.

Lepeletier de Rosanbo, one-time president of the *parlement* of Paris, with his fellow lawyers, including Cardinal Salamon, had written the formal protest to the king in November 1790, when the *parlements* were abolished by decree. When this document was found during a routine search of his house, a warrant was issued for the arrest of Rosanbo and all the members of the *parlement* who had been signatories to the protest. Salamon's name was on the list, but he was warned in time and managed to escape to a friend's house where he hid. Malesherbes, father-in-law of Rosanbo and Louis XVI's defending counsel at his trial, was also accused of plotting against the State and was arrested. In early April he was tried and condemned as a counter-revolutionary, and was guillotined along with Rosanbo, his wife and most of his family. The other forty-nine members of the Paris *parlement* were guillotined on Easter Day, 20 April. The authorities were desperate to find, and kill, the only surviving member, Cardinal Salamon, who had been condemned in his absence, but he managed to evade them by taking refuge in the Bois-de-Boulogne. He slept out in the open and under bridges for three months, and managed to survive by living almost entirely on cooked potatoes which a sympathetic beggar woman prepared for him. Without a card of citizenship he was unable to buy bread or meat.

A decree was passed condemning all the *émigrés* and all aristocracy. Their land and possessions were confiscated by the State, and many were driven out of Paris and went, like Salamon, into hiding. In Paris alone 7,000 people were imprisoned in the different gaols, and altogether in France the numbers reached 200,000.

On 27 May 1794 Madame Elisabeth, Marie's employer and her friend, was taken from the Temple prison to the Conciergerie. Her removal left the young Madame Royale in total isolation, and still unaware of the death of her mother. Madame Elisabeth was taken by hackney coach to the prison, where she was made to wait. At ten o'clock she was taken to the council chamber and arraigned as Marie Elisabeth Capet, sister of Louis Capet, the last tyrant of the French. She was thirty years old. She was tried, condemned and taken back to the Conciergerie. When she asked the Governor, M. Richard, how the queen was, she was told, 'the queen was well, and not in want of anything'. Poor Madame Elisabeth had a restless night, and at eleven the next morning went with the other victims to the entrance of the prison. She charged Richard to give kind messages to her sister, but 'one of the other ladies, a Duchess interposed, saying: "Madame, your sister has already suffered the fate which we ourselves are to suffer."'[7] Only five years earlier Marie had been living at Versailles as the trusted friend of the princess. Now, to her deep distress, her friend had been executed. She did not make a death-mask.

In an effort to turn Parisians' eyes away from the horror surrounding them, the 20 Prairial, Year II (8 June 1794), was proclaimed by David as the First Republican Festival of the Supreme Being and Nature, in which the allegorical figures of Hope, Reason, Nature, Justice and Liberty were prominent. In a symbolic attempt to lessen the influence of those who wished to dechristianise France, Robespierre, his head adorned with feathers and holding in his hand a bunch of flowers, fruit and ears of corn, set fire to the effigies of Atheism, Discord and Selfishness which were displayed in a specially built amphitheatre in the Tuileries. The statue of Wisdom then arose from the ashes, 'but, unluckily for this stage effect of this extraordinary drama', it was 'much blackened by the smoke, occasioned by the burning of its predecessors; which drew upon Robespierre many sneers'.[8] Later the procession went from the Tuileries to the Champs de Mars where the crowd discovered that a monumental cardboard and plaster mountain had been erected by David in the centre of the field. Triumphantly raised on the top of a

50-foot column was a vast statue of Hercules leaning on his club, representing the French people. The procession ended with hymns and sermons in the shadow of the cardboard mountain. The whole outrageous festival was pronounced a great success. David, who had now become the creator of all things spectacular, had organised 'the arrangement, forms and ceremonies that were to be observed throughout the festival'.[9]

The attempted assassinations of Robespierre and Collot d'Herbois triggered the most repressive of all the laws of the Republic. On 22 Prairial (10 June) the Law of Prairial was created, replacing the already savage Law of Suspects. Members of the Convention surrendered their immunity. Citizens could be arrested for spreading false news, for discouragement, or for corrupting or depraving morals. In Prairial, the first month of the new law, the number of executions rose from the previous month's total of 354 to 509. The next month, Messidor, the number of deaths rose again to 796. The Great Terror had begun, which was to last until 27 July 1794.

Marie realised that in this new climate of oppression it was essential to get any politically sensitive wax figures out of the country as quickly as possible. She prepared a shipment of twenty portrait figures for an Italian showman called Dominic Laurency. He would take Curtius's *The Cabinet of Curcius* and another show, the *Optic of Zaler*, to Calcutta and Madras in the spring of 1794. She packed up the figures of Louis XVI and the dauphin, the exiled Comte de Provence and Comte d'Artois and their wives. The Duchess of Polignac, Joseph II, the Emperor of Russia and the King of Prussia, Lafayette, Mirabeau and Pétion were all now disgraced or dead, and it would have been foolhardy to display their figures in the Paris museum. For good measure she sent a model of the Bastille and the decapitated head of Foulon, 'which resembled a head which had just been cut off, the blood seems to be streaming from it and running on the ground'. The exhibition opened in India on 18 August 1794 in Old Mackay's Garden in the Nabob's palace at Madras, and went on to Calcutta in December. It is not known when the exhibition left India, but it seems likely that it was there for about eight months, and was then sent to London as part of the exhibition shown in New Bond Street in late 1795. The sea voyage to England would take at least six months.[10]

In the Paris Convention presidents served in rotation, being elected for a period of only fifteen days. Robespierre's term of office lasted, from 6 Prairial to 1 Messidor (4 to 20 June 1794), and it was during this time that Marie was arrested, along with her mother and aunt, and thrown into the prison de la Garde Force in the Marais district. They were 'carried off in the middle of the night by the *gens d'armes* and placed in a *fiacre*. In the same room where they were confined, she found about twenty females.'[11] Marie, her mother and aunt were accused of being royalists. Marie thought they had been denounced by a neighbour, Jacques Dutruy, who worked as a *grimacier* and a dancer in a little theatre near 20 boulevard du Temple. Maybe he had seen the shipment of royalist figures being packed for India. Maybe he had a grudge to settle. The reason for arrest was of little importance and it was an easy way to get rid of a rival. They were almost immediately transferred to Les Carmes prison, in the rue de Vaugirard, where Marie found that one of the other inmates of the cell was Josephine de Beauharnais, later to be the wife of Napoleon. She had been imprisoned in Les Carmes since late April. Marie became friendly with Josephine, who 'did all in her power to infuse life and spirit into her suffering companions, exhorting them to patience, and endeavouring to cheer them'.[12] Josephine's children, Hortense and Eugène, visited her with the family pug dog Fortuné, which brought in messages concealed under its collar. Some years later Hortense de Beauharnais would marry Louis Bonaparte and become Queen of Holland. In the prison there was no furniture in the crowded cell and nothing to sleep on but straw. Their food consisted of inedible bread, hard peas and beans, 'so old and hard they could scarcely be masticated', and occasionally watery soup, which made them all ill. They were allowed only one bottle of dirty water a day to drink. They could order additional food from friends outside if they so wished, but even if they had enough money to pay, were loath to do so, 'knowing that they ran the risk of compromising anyone who displayed any amicable disposition towards them'.[13] Every week their hair was cropped short in preparation for the guillotine. Grace Elliot was imprisoned in the same cell as Marie at Les Carmes, and was admitted on the same day as General Hoche, with whom she later became intimate friends. She wrote a gossipy and revealing report of life there. Alexandre de Beauharnais, Josephine's estranged husband, was also at Les Carmes. Grace noted: 'His wife and he were both much embarrassed at the circumstance, but in a few hours they were perfectly reconciled.' Grace said of Josephine: 'She is one of the most accomplished, good-humoured women I have ever met with. The only little disputes we had when together were politics, she being what was called at the beginning of the Revolution, constitutional, but she was not in the least a Jacobin, for nobody suffered more by the Reign of Terror and by Robespierre than she did.'[14]

It was not only the aristocrats who were in danger; even the smallest misdemeanour was savagely punished:

> A poor man and his wife, who used to keep a stall for puppets in the Champs-Elysées, were brought to our prison for having shown a figure of Charlotte Corday, which was handsome. . . . We were in hopes, as they were poor, that they would have escaped; but, alas! They were dragged also to the terrible scaffold, and we all wept at their loss sincerely. In short the scenes became so dreadful that it was impossible to exist much longer in such a state of constant woe, to see husbands forced from their wives' arms, children torn from their mothers, their screams and fits, people when they could get a knife even cutting their own throats! Such were the horrors going on in the Carmes.[15]

With no way of contacting Curtius, who was still in the Rhineland, or of finding out what was happening outside the prison, Marie had given up hope. However, in mid-July, soon after Collot d'Herbois began his fifteen-day Presidency of the Assembly, Marie and her family were released without explanation. Collot d'Herbois was a friend of both Curtius and Marie, and she also knew his Dutch wife, whom she thought 'an amiable woman'. It was almost certain that d'Herbois had something to do with her release. She thought his manners 'rather pleasing than otherwise; nor was there anything in his exterior which proclaimed the cruel monster which he afterwards proved'. Collot d'Herbois had earlier advised both Curtius and Marie to style themselves as Alsacians, not Swiss, in their passports, 'even procuring them a false register to that effect, as the popular antipathy was so much excited against anyone from Switzerland, that they would have run the greatest risk of meeting personal violence, in the event of any popular commotion'.[16] Marie thought that his advice on that occasion had been instrumental in saving all their lives. It was almost certainly his influence now which secured their release.

Bitter fighting among those in power was beginning to split the Jacobins. Towards the end of July a conspiracy against Robespierre and Saint-Just began to take shape among the most zealous of the Terrorists. They wanted no Supreme Being but instead a totalitarian state with no religion. There were calls in the Assembly for the arrest of Robespierre and Saint-Just and also for the arrest of Lebas, Couthon and Hanriot, the commandant of the National Guard. Collot d'Herbois, still serving as President of the Assembly, prevented Robespierre from speaking to the deputies and drowned out his protest by loudly ringing a bell. When Robespierre's voice failed with the effort, another deputy, M. Garnier, shouted out: 'It is the blood of Danton which chokes thee.' An indictment was proposed and sanctioned against Robespierre, his young brother Augustin, Lebas, Antoine Saint-Just and the crippled Couthon.

Hanriot was out in the streets, 'galloping about in all directions', says Marie, shouting out the names of the accused in a vain effort to find support for their cause. Meanwhile, Barras was appointed in Hanriot's place as commander of the National Guard. When Robespierre and his associates were being taken to prison, they broke away from their escort and took refuge at the Hôtel de Ville. At about two in the morning Barras arrived with some of the National Guard. When it became obvious to those sheltering inside that they would be taken, they tried to kill themselves. When the soldiers entered the building they found Couthon lying halfway down the staircase; Augustin had tried to commit suicide and his

1 Marie Grosholtz in 1778, aged 17. Artist unknown. (*Madame Tussaud's Archives*)

2 Curtius in his Guardsman's uniform. (*Madame Tussaud's Archives*)

3 Marie Grosholtz as a young woman at the Court of Versailles, from Madame Tussaud's waxworks. (*Author's Collection*)

4 Voltaire, as modelled by Marie Grosholtz in 1778, now in Madame Tussaud's waxworks. (*Author's Collection*)

5 Louis XVI while in prison, by Joseph Ducreux. (*Phototèque des Musées de la Ville de Paris*)

6 Marie Antoinette, by Bernard. (*Phototèque des Musées de la Ville de Paris*)

7 Madame Elisabeth, by Delpech. (*Phototèque des Musées de la Ville de Paris*)

8 The painter Jacques-Louis David by Magneret/Gros. (*Phototèque des Musées de la Ville de Paris*)

9 The Petit Trianon at Versailles. (*Author's Collection*)

10 The Queen's model village, the *hameau*, at Versailles. (*Author's Collection*)

11 Curtius: a waxwork bust in the Musée Carnavalet, believed to be an original self-portrait. (*Author's Collection*)

12 The *Salon des Figures de Cire* in the boulevard du Temple where Marie learnt her trade, by Potemont. (*Phototèque des Musées de la Ville de Paris*)

13 An etching of Marie's tableau of the French royal family at dinner displayed in Curtius's *Salon* at the Palais-Royal. (*Madame Tussaud's Archives*)

14 *Le Cabinet des Patriotes*, by Dargez. (*Phototèque des Musées de la Ville de Paris*)

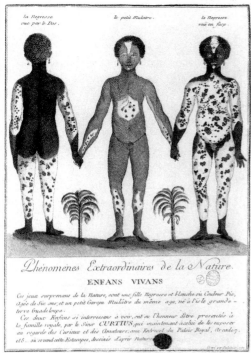

15 Extraordinary Phenomenon of Nature. Picture of two living children displayed in Curtius's *Salon* at the Palais-Royal, by Coutubrier. (*Phototèque des Musées de la Ville de Paris*)

16 Paul Butterbrodt, 56 years old, weighing 476 pounds. Picture of the doorkeeper at Curtius's *Salon* at the Palais-Royal. (*Phototeque des Musees de la Ville de Paris*)

17 'Real life in the Galleries of the Palais-Royal', by George Cruikshank. (*Phototèque des Musées de la Ville de Paris*)

18 The taking of the heads of Necker and the Duc d'Orléans from Curtius's *Salon*, by Janinet. (*Phototèque des Musées de la Ville de Paris*)

19 Curtius's *Salon* at 20 boulevard du Temple. The head on the right is that of Necker, by Feillet. (*Phototèque des Musées de la Ville de Paris*)

friend Lebas had shot himself. Saint-Just, alone, waited defiantly for his captors. Robespierre was wounded, his jaw broken by a shot; though it was not clear whether he had been shot by a soldier or had tried to commit suicide. He was laid on a table and a surgeon arrived to bandage the wound. Marie reported: 'The prisoners and wounded were carried off in hand-barrows to the Assembly. This victory was achieved at three o'clock in the morning, and the most deafening cries of, "Down with the tyrants!" [and] "Liberty for ever!" resounded through the hall.'

They were not given another trial. That same day, 27 July 1794, Robespierre and his followers were denounced as outlaws and conspirators, and guillotined. There was rejoicing in the streets of Paris as Robespierre was taken to his execution, and the carts 'were surrounded by multitudes of relations of persons whom he had caused to be executed'.[17] He lay slumped in the tumbrel, which also carried Couthon and Hanriot, with his head wrapped in a dirty bandage to hold his mutilated jaw in place. When he reached the guillotine, the executioner Henri Sanson roughly tore the bandages from his wound, and Robespierre shrieked in agony as his jaw spouted blood. It was a hideous sight. Mercier reported that when the blade fell, the applause lasted for a quarter of an hour. Seventeen of his followers were also executed. 'A delirium of joy appeared among the people. . . . The prisons resounded with the huzzas of their inmates, considering their liberation as ensured by the death of Robespierre; and newspapers, containing the account of his fall, and that of his adherents, sold as high as thirty francs each.'[18]

Once freed from prison, Marie returned to her work at the museum, but with considerably more caution than before. Business, however, improved with the death of Robespierre and his fellow Jacobins, and the resulting relaxation of some of the more draconian rules. Marie made a cast of Robespierre's mutilated head and immediately displayed it in the museum, where it attracted a large audience. The crowds released many prisoners from the gaols: 'In a short time the number amounted to ten thousand, and diffused such joy, that it became so universal, as to pervade all classes throughout Paris, in which there was scarcely a family whose hearts were not gladdened by having some relative restored to them whom they had given up for lost.'[19]

The power of the Jacobins was broken and many of them were guillotined. Carrier, 'the sanguinary tyrant of Nantes', who had been responsible for mass drownings in the Loire at Nantes in 1793, was arrested in November and guillotined. 'Of five hundred members, four hundred and ninety-eight, voted for the death of Carrier.' Marie said that he met his death 'with calmness and resolution', and she took a cast from the severed head, 'which certainly represents him with rather finer features than otherwise'.[20] When she placed the heads of Carrier and Saint-Just in the *Salon de Cire*, people flocked in to take a look at the oppressors.

Not long afterwards, at the end of July, Curtius returned from his extended mission in the Rhineland. Marie hadn't seen him for eighteen months, and she was shocked at his appearance. He was obviously a sick man. In spite of his close Revolutionary ties, Curtius had always insisted to Marie that at heart he was a royalist, and that he hid his loyalties in order to preserve his family and his museum. He had been her teacher and mentor for the last thirty-three years and was the only father-figure she had ever known. On his return, in the hope that country air would help him recover, he left Paris and went to live in his small house, 3 rue de Suice, at Ivry-sur-Seine. He must have realised, however, that he had not long to live, and on 31 August 1794 made his will with his lawyer Sieur Hubert Gibe. There were two witnesses, Citizen Antoine Boucheron of 14 place de Vendôme and Citizen Jean Dournel, Justice of the Peace, both of the *section* du Temple.

Just under four weeks later, on 26 September, Curtius died, with only his housekeeper Madame Guerin and her husband at his side. As soon as he heard the news, Curtius's friend and neighbour, the theatre owner M. Sallé, went out to Ivry-sur-Seine with Antoine Villon, a grocer, to complete the legal requirements. Marie, who arrived early on the following day was certain that his death, which she had not expected, was unnatural, and arranged for an autopsy to be performed. 'A surgical examination took place, when it was fully ascertained that his death had been occasioned by poison.'[21] Such events were commonplace where allegiances changed as fast as the weather. In this case there was no one to accuse, though Marie suspected the followers of General Custine. When Custine evacuated Mayence, leaving it to the Prussians, his act was considered by the rabid revolutionaries in Paris to be treasonous and cowardly. He was recalled to Paris, where he was accused of conspiring with the enemy. Convicted, he was guillotined. Because Curtius had served under Custine at Mayence and had close associations with the leading revolutionaries, Custine's friends believed him to be implicated in his downfall.

When the will was read Marie found that Curtius had left everything to her, apart from his silver and jewellery, which he wanted to be sold for the benefit of the poor. Most of the other valuables had already been given to the Revolutionary Council. An inventory was taken, then the house was sealed while the will was proven. Seals were also put on the *Salon* at 20 boulevard du Temple.

The inventories for both these houses give some idea of the clutter in which Marie lived and worked. The house in Ivry-sur-Seine had three floors, and every room on every floor was filled with mirrors, pictures, pieces of material, pier glasses, beds and bedding. In the dining room there was:

a round table, eight stuffed cane chairs, a cage, a picture, three mirrors, two marble-topped console tables, a marble-topped buffet, two leather glass stands (silvered), a small model frigate, six serviettes, a cruet stand, six linen table cloths, a table cloth, a folding bed, two mattresses, two sheets, a pillow, a bolster, a wool overlay, a silk overlay, a lamp, two other wool overlays, two pairs of curtains, six cloths, fourteen serviettes, a piece of linen, a mattress, two bedspreads, a bolster, a table cloth, trestles, a cask of wine, a cask containing damsons.[22]

There is no mention of wax modelling materials or figures. The kitchen contained, among other items, four tables, three torches, various plates, soup dishes, glasses, two dozen cups and 120 empty bottles, a red leather casserole, a red leather cauldron, 'and other objects of little value not worth detailing'.[23]

At 20 boulevard du Temple there was the same sort of clutter in all the rooms, but in addition there were wax figures, busts and portraits. In the *Cabinet de Figures* on the ground floor were many mirrors of all shapes and sizes, as well as 'two branched wall chandeliers and three copper candle holders with crystal pendants; three lamps, each with three lights'. There was a clock in its case, three console tables, a barometer and a number of assorted curtains. There were 'thirty-six pictures representing various subjects, painted in oils in their gold frames; 114 others, glazed in their gold frames, and two more looking glasses'. As part of the *Cabinet*, there were sixteen busts in their cases, each with three glass sides; nineteen other cases with glass panels, containing animals; twenty-nine other similar ones containing various objects . . . twenty-eight figures of large size, each clothed in its costume; ten other figures to the waist, also clothed; three other figures recumbent on beds; sixteen heads; an infant, clothed, in its little chair with seat stuffed with straw; and another little child naked. There were also a wide assortment of tables and chairs, and a variety of lights and lamps including some special Argand lamps.[24] In these eight pages of closely written inventory, there are listed a large number of camp beds with bedding, no doubt first used by the *fédérés* who were billeted on Curtius, and later by the Prussian deserters.

In November 1794 Curtius's will was officially registered, and Marie found that along with the two houses and their contents, and a third rented house in rue Fosses du Temple, she had inherited a considerable debt of 55,000 livres. It was then that she realised she would need to borrow money in order to keep the *Salon*. And so, eight months after Curtius's death, on 26 Floréal, Year III (16 May 1795), a mortgage document was drawn up between Anne Marie Grosholtz and Citizen Marie Anne Henriette Horry and her brother, Didiès François Horry, for a loan of 55,000 livres. Marie desperately needed the loan to pay the next instalment on the mortgage on the Ivry-sur-Seine house left to her in Curtius's will, and she also needed money to keep the exhibition going. Security for this loan was the third house, the rent from which was to go towards the payment of the interest. There was a clause in the contract stating that if Marie should get married her husband would be equally responsible for her debts. Another insisted that she must not leave Paris until eight years had passed from the date of the signing of the document.[25]

To attract customers, it was essential that Marie should keep her exhibition up to date with the latest victims, especially the most notorious. She noted with wry amusement that when Fouquier-Tinville, the former public prosecutor, was guillotined on 7 May: 'as he ascended the scaffold, he did not appear to derive the same pleasure from viewing the preparations for his own death, that he had on so many occasions evinced, when contemplating the requisite arrangements for the execution of others'. Marie had met Fouquier-Tinville, and had thought how repulsive his face was. 'He was rather tall, his complexion sallow; he was pitted with the smallpox, had dark hair, and a narrow forehead; like most of the functionaries he dressed in black. . . . He inspired much terror in his office of public accuser, and showed, on all occasions, his utter disregard of the value of human life.' Marie said the only time he seemed to enjoy himself was when he was watching the victims suffer whom he had sent to the guillotine, 'when his iron features softened into a smile'.[26]

By the spring of 1795 France's wars with her neighbours were reaching an end, and between May and the end of July peace treaties were signed with Prussia, Holland and Spain.

With this peace, and the downfall of the Jacobins, royalist groups were again on the ascendant in the provinces, and deputies once again began to jostle for supremacy in the National Convention. New groups were formed, one of which, the *Jeunesse dorée*, was so named 'on account of their costume being as studied and elegant as that of their adversaries was the reverse, and many contests occurred between the two parties'.[27] The members were young, mainly artists or writers, well dressed and determined to repudiate the excesses of the now disgraced Jacobin Club.

While the government of France sought to stabilise the regime, the death was announced in the Temple prison of the former dauphin, now Louis XVII. Forgotten by most of the world and abandoned by his royal relations, he met a pathetic end. His sister left a chilling account of the way in which the child was treated before the overthrow of Robespierre. 'He lay in a bed which had not been made for more than six months; fleas and bugs covered him, his linen and his person were full of them. His shirt and stockings had not been changed for a year; his excrement remained in the room, no one had removed them during all that time. It was impossible to stay in his chamber because of the foul odour.' Too frightened by the threats of his gaolers to ask for anything, terrified and alone, he was left lying in his own filth in the dark, and was allowed no candles. His sister, who was old enough to understand that she must look after herself, was treated just as harshly, but managed to keep herself clean. Her situation improved a little after the death of Robespierre, when she was supplied with wood for the fire, allowed a match-box and candle, and generally treated more kindly, although she was not allowed to see her brother. The little boy, deprived of any human kindness for so long, fell ill several times during the winter. In the spring he grew worse, and died on 9 June 1795 at three in the afternoon, aged just ten years and two months. His sister wrote later: 'He had much intelligence; but imprisonment and the horrors of which he was the victim had changed him much; and even, had he lived, it is to be feared that his mental faculties would have been affected.'[28] She was the only member of her family to survive. Treated repressively and kept in ignorance of the fate of her mother, aunt and brother, she was eventually released in October 1795 in exchange for four commissioners of the Convention imprisoned in Austria. She was seventeen and had been locked away for six years. For two-and-a-half years she had been kept in solitary confinement. Scratched upon the wall of the room in which she was imprisoned were the words: 'Marie-Thérèse is the most unhappy creature in the world. She can obtain no news of her mother; nor be reunited to her, though she has asked it a thousand times.' From prison she went, rather unwillingly, to live in Vienna. In 1799 she was allowed to join her exiled uncle, the Comte de Provence, now Louis XVIII, at Mittau. From there they went to Prussia, then to Warsaw and eventually took refuge in England. She stayed with him during all his wandering years of exile. Married to her cousin, the son of the Comte d'Artois, she was described as 'pathos in person'.[29]

In its search for order the National Convention agreed upon a new constitution in August 1795. A council composed of 500 members above thirty years of age was to have the power of legislation, while 200 people above forty years of age were to form a council of elders. The old Convention was dissolved and the new Directorate inaugurated, with executive power being given to five directors, one of whom was Barras, the captain of the National Guard. Josephine de Beauharnais, Marie's former prison companion, was now living with Barras, once one of Curtius's most intimate friends. Marie thought Barras an elegant man, 'of a commanding figure, being much above the middle height, and having a handsome countenance, with very fine dark eyes. He was of one of the most ancient families in France.'[30]

It was now that Napoleon first made his mark in Paris as one of Barras's aides. Napoleon helped to suppress an insurrection in August: 'by the admirable management of his destructive discharges of artillery, he carried victory in every quarter where he appeared. . . . At six o'clock the combat was over. Bonaparte then scoured the streets, sweeping them with his artillery, wherever any resistance appeared.'[31]

With the suppression and overthrow of the Jacobins, and the untimely death of the dauphin, the old order was changing fast and Napoleon, at the beginning of his meteoric rise to power, now seized his chance.

ELEVEN

Madame Tussaud

In the middle of all this unrest, on 28 September 1795 Marie Grosholtz married François Tussaud, a civil engineer eight years younger than herself. He came from a respectable family of coppersmiths and wine producers from Macon. It is not known how they met, but François seems to have had many contacts and friends among the showmen entrepreneurs of Paris. The civil marriage was registered at the Préfecture du Départment de la Seine in Paris. Although the new civil code required the parents of the couple and four witnesses to be present at the ceremony, Marie's mother, Marie Waltner, was the only parent named on the wedding contract. The bride's witnesses were Louis Sallé, theatre owner and colleague of Curtius, and Jean François Olivier. One of the bridegroom's witnesses was a painter, M. Girard. According to the new laws, they were married in the presence of the Maire with a simple exchange of vows. At the end of the ceremony the official declared: 'Marie et François, la Loi vous unit [The law unites you].'[1]

Marie was now thirty-four, and probably hoped that her marriage to François would give her security, protection and the possibility of heirs. Their respective contributions to the marriage were very different. François brought only 7,000 francs, though he had promised 19,000. Marie brought with her three properties: 20 boulevard du Temple, valued at 19,750 francs; a house on the rue des Fosses du Temple, which was leased, and a house at Ivry-sur-Seine worth 16,400 francs. In addition to the houses, Marie's marriage portion was enhanced by the figures and curiosities in the *Salon de Cire*, and above all, by her skill as an artist.

The state of all business in Paris was poor after the prolonged revolutionary turmoil, and in spite of her new status Marie's financial problems were not solved by her marriage. On 24 Vendemaire, Year IV (15 October 1795), two-and-a-half weeks after her wedding, Marie had to borrow more money to keep the wax museum in business and this time the lender was Marguerite Salomé Reiss, a woman who lived and worked at 20 boulevard du Temple. Madame Reiss had been at the *Salon de Cire* for some years. She was named in the inventory when Curtius died, and was still living there in 1799 when the terms of the loan were amended to reduce her life annuity. In return for a loan of 20,000 assignats in 1795, Marie agreed to pay her an annuity of 2,000 livres.

There was still much poverty and suffering in France, which was on the verge of national bankruptcy. The winter of 1795 was lawless and desperate. *The Times* reported that there were 2,419 people imprisoned in Paris. There was little food, the municipal water was frozen and the markets had collapsed. 'Misery is at its height, and the dearness of goods is beyond all measure. The cold, which is now very intense, adds to our misery. Wood is scarce and at a high price. . . . What an abyss will open itself around us if the Seine should be frozen before corn and wood for the Winter are obtained.'[2] A week later it reported: 'The bread-sellers, who wanted to raise the price of a pound of bread to 40 livres, were grossly insulted, and even beaten by the mob. Some were forced to sell their bread at the price which was arbitrarily fixed by the populace; the consequence of which was, that no bread came to market the next day.' The value of the assignat kept falling.

Across the Channel, *Curtius's Grand Cabinet of Curiosities* arrived in London at the end of 1795. It is possible that the exhibition was sent over from Paris, but it is more likely that this was the touring Indian exhibition, which had finished there earlier in the year. The name of the showman in charge of the *Grand Cabinet* in London was not given, but François Tussaud was almost certainly there when it opened, as, in one of her later letters, Marie referred to a visit he made to London. It is interesting to note that the advertised *Grand Cabinet* included not only the wax figures, advertised as 'Curious Busts from Nature', but also a valuable collection of Paintings, Sculpture, Engravings, Drawings in India Ink; Battles, Sieges and Bombardments, drawn with a Pen in imitation of Copper-plate: Several pieces of curious Writing; a collection of Sculpture, and Terner's [sic] Works in Ivory; Landscapes and Profiles of the King and Queen of France, made of hair by the famous Rougin, the King's Painter in Paris.[3]

In addition to these marvels 'an ivory model of a sea port with shipping and a model of a Man of War at anchor' was advertised. 'The whole of this curious work comes under a Watch Glass.' The exhibition must have been quite large, because there were more wax figures by Mr Monstevens, modeller to the Prince of Wales; a collection of figures in rice paste and a model of a glass frigate of twenty-five guns.

At the end of 1795 the exhibition opened at New Bond Street, London, then moved on to the Old Library Room in the Guildhall, St Andrews, Norwich, from 9 to 16 January 1796. From there it went to the Town Hall at Cambridge, then up to Chester during the races in May. The rest of the tour included Manchester, at the Star Inn in Deansgate, and Liverpool, at Neptune's Coffee House; in September it went to Birmingham, New Street, opposite Mrs Bissett's Museum. The Birmingham newspapers were enthusiastic:

> Of all the exhibitions presented to the Amateurs and Artists in this Town, not one has so much merited their serious Attention as this; the great Variety of truly original Pieces, in natural and artificial Curiosities, are beyond Description: the Dying Philosopher, Voltaire &c, are Inimitable; the Glass Man of War, Sculptor's and Turner's Works in Ivory, are astonishingly fine; and in short, the Cabinet may be truly said to be composed of Curiosities the *ne plus ultra* of the Arts.[4]

The exhibition stayed in Birmingham through November and into January 1797.

In February a strange paragraph appeared in the *Birmingham Gazette*:

Mr Curtius, whose advanced Age and Infirmities puts it out of his Power to support the Fatigues of his Profession, would be very glad to find an active intelligent Man for a Partner. He would, if they could agree, set him one Half of all that concerns his Exhibition; and as soon as such a Man is acquainted with the Business, he would retire with his most affectionate Wife and youngest Child, to pass the few days he has to remain on this side of the grave, in Peace and Retirement.[5]

This Mr Curtius was obviously not Marie's uncle, who had been dead since 1794, although it is quite likely that the current manager was using Curtius's name. This was not an uncommon practice and it certainly simplified the advertising. It would have been both difficult and expensive to take the much-travelled wax figures back to Paris, and the easier option was to sell them in England. There were a number of travelling waxworks touring around the country fairs, who would have been delighted to buy a ready-made exhibition. As there is no record of the *Cabinet* returning to Paris, it is likely that a buyer was found.

* * *

Back in France, Josephine de Beauharnais asked Marie to make her portrait bust. Josephine had been living as the mistress of Barras, but now the beautiful widow had captivated Napoleon. The couple were married on 6 March 1796 in a hurried ceremony in Paris, only a week after he had been appointed General of the French Army in Italy. Immediately after the wedding Napoleon left for Italy to join his army, leaving his new wife alone in Paris.

When Napoleon departed for Italy, Cardinal Salamon wrote to the pope to warn him of the treachery of the King of Naples. The letter was intercepted, and the cardinal was once again arrested, this time charged with sending treasonable dispatches. He was eventually taken for trial to the Palais de Justice and transferred to the Conciergerie, accused of being a conspirator. While there, Salamon befriended the governor of the prison, M. Richard, who gave him special privileges including lending him the two mattresses which he had bought especially for the queen. Salamon had developed a great fear of being locked in, and Richard allowed him to have his cell door opened earlier than the regulation time. The first day that this happened, a pug dog came into the cell, jumped on to the bed, snuffed all around it and then went away. Richard told Salamon that this was Marie Antoinette's dog; when she had been moved to the Conciergerie from the Temple prison the dog was left behind and so he had given him a home. For the three months that Salamon was imprisoned there, the dog came in every morning to snuff his mistress's mattress and to look for her, but would never allow himself to be caught. After many months Salamon was eventually tried, and after an impassioned and prolonged defence was finally acquitted on 3 March 1797, soon after Napoleon returned from his triumphant Italian campaign.[6]

Marie, a covert royalist, had a wide circle of contacts, one of whom, Mary Nesbitt, was in Paris. She had left England on 5 August 1797, 'once again embroiled in spying and political intrigue'.[7] A former member of the Duc d'Orléans's circle, and a friend of Josephine, the courtesan Mrs Nesbitt was also a close friend of Mr Rose, Pitt's Secretary to the Treasury. She was believed to be acting as an agent of the British government by giving English gold to the French royalists. The gossipy *Morning Chronicle* declared:

> It is certainly no discredit to the sex that an accomplished woman is capable of playing a part so conspicuous and interesting to the fate of Nations, as that which Mrs Nesbitt had lately performed. . . . The allusions made to her acquaintance with Mr Rose are illiberal. Her intimacy with many of the more distinguished characters of the age – with Lord Thurlow and others, was no other than the society of kindred minds. An intelligent woman in the decline of years possessing the charms of conversation unrestrained by prudery, and endowed with elegant talents improved by a knowledge of the world, drew around her a select circle of friends. . . . We sincerely believe that Mr Rose cultivated the acquaintance of Mrs Nesbitt from the attraction of her mind.[8]

Three days later there were more sly allegations.

> The close connection that has subsisted between MRS NESBITT
> and MR ROSE does not in the least, as gossiping scandal would
> insinuate, impeach the purity of the Secretary of the Treasury. . . .
> Indeed for a politician there cannot be any more useful
> acquaintances than ladies of this description. They possess so
> intimate a knowledge of mankind that they are qualified to give
> very excellent hints to those who make a traffic of men, how to
> impose upon their weakness, sacrifice to their variety, or present
> temptations to their interest.[9]

Mary Nesbitt is believed to have met Marie during her journeys to
Paris, and was one of the people who helped her when she went to
England. Paris was riddled with spies. France's wars with her
neighbours and constant plotting within the government had
created a hotbed of distrust and treachery.

Many of the buildings in Paris that had once belonged to the
aristocracy, were now ruined and desolate. An English visitor, the
Revd Dawson Warren, visited the Island of Saint-Louis which was
full of beautiful houses 'now deserted and let for a trifle. All is
going to ruin. Grass grows in the streets.' He reported that the
surviving population of 600,000 Parisians were poorly fed and
poorly clad. The few public hackney carriages were mouldy,
ramshackle and unlighted, the horses broken-down hacks. Streets
were narrow and muddy; many not paved, some impassable, and
after heavy rain they became flooded. The Revd Warren had
planned to explore the city on foot, but found this somewhat
hazardous. He wrote in his journal:

> The streets of Paris are narrow and dirty. Having no pavement for
> the accommodation of foot passengers they are miserably
> inconvenient for walking. . . . The drivers of different vehicles
> which rattle through the streets shout pretty loud to give warning
> of their approach but you must scamper through the mud to get
> out of their way. In London where we have no equality, fraternity

and such hubble-bubble, the comfort of pedestrians is much more attended to.[10]

On 22 Messidor, Year VI (10 July 1797), Marie reduced her mortgage to the Horrys, but financial problems continued to trouble her. Only eight months later the Horrys demanded that a new mortgage be taken out against 'all the means, present and future of M. Tussaud and Grosholtz his wife', to safeguard their original loan. In 1799, still not satisfied with the security of their loan, they demanded once again that another new mortgage be taken out, but this time against 20 boulevard du Temple.[11]

Marie's hopes for a family were realised in September 1796 when she gave birth to a daughter, Marie Marguerite Pauline, but she was a sickly baby and died six months later at Ivry-sur-Seine. However, Marie soon became pregnant again and on 16 April 1798 Joseph Tussaud was born. Two years later, on 2 August 1800, her second son François Tussaud was born. Marie was now thirty-nine and François was to be the last of her children.[12]

Marie was in Paris in early December 1797 when Napoleon Bonaparte returned from his successful campaign in Italy to be greeted by fêtes and receptions. She observed that Napoleon, 'in the midst of these magnificent assemblies, retained his usual simplicity of appearance, and conversed mostly with men whom he considered possessed of useful talents. The invasion of England had become, at this period, a universal topic of conversation.'[13] Napoleon was appointed Commander of the Army of the Interior, but, unhappy with this post, he changed his plans and on 18 May sailed for Egypt, where the battle of the Nile in August resulted in Nelson's victory over the French fleet. Eighteen months later Napoleon, foreseeing 'the ultimate loss or destruction of his army in Egypt, and wishing to avoid sharing its disgrace', abandoned his soldiers and returned to France. Marie remembered his triumphal return. He 'was dressed in the costume of a Mameluke, in large white trowsers [sic], red boots, waistcoat richly embroidered, as also the jacket, which was of crimson velvet. He arrived about eight in the evening and the cannons of the Invalides fired a salute. His first visit was to his mother' who lived close to Marie in the Vieille rue de Temple, just above the Cadran Bleu.[14] Under the theatrical influence of Jacques Louis David, exotic costumes were much favoured by the new regime. When a five-man Directory was elected under the leadership of Barras, David designed their elaborate costumes: 'A cherry coloured cloak, white silk pantaloons, turned down boots, waistcoat of silk, à l'Espagnol, the whole richly embroidered with gold, Spanish hat and feathers.'[15]

Napoleon had not been back in Paris for long before he became aware of the instability of the government. Hungry for power, and knowing he had the loyal support of the army, he carefully laid his plans. Addressing the Council and the Directors in rousing tones he declared:

What has been done with that France which I left so brilliant? I left her in peace – I find her overwhelmed by war. I left her covered with glory and victories – I find her overwhelmed with defeats and disgrace. I left her with millions sent from Italy, and I find them dissipated, and France in misery! What is become of the hundred thousand warriors who were my companions in arms? They are dead.[16]

By a combination of bluff and bullying, and with the help of his soldiers, Napoleon first dispersed and then summarily dissolved the Council of the Five Hundred. He was then named First Consul and, as Marie put it in her memoirs: 'Here, may be considered to end the history of the revolution, which resolved itself into a government of military despotism, under the guidance of a talented but arbitrary dictator.'[17]

Napoleon, now in charge, appointed his own ministers – Berthier as Minister for War, Lucien Bonaparte for Home Affairs, Talleyrand for Foreign Affairs and Fouché as Minister of Police. Fouché had been a leading member of the disgraced Revolutionary Council, but as he possessed incriminating files and information on so many of those still in government he was too dangerous to dismiss. Marie, who knew many of those now in positions of power, had met

Talleyrand and Fouché at her uncle's house at the height of the Revolution. George Jackson, an English diplomat remarked:

> Talleyrand is considered the head of the aristocratic party, Fouché that of the Jacobinical. Talleyrand has something of severity in his manners, and from former habits is disposed to what ever partakes of refinement, even his vices. Fouché, on the contrary, is vulgar in deportment, coarse-minded, and ferocious in disposition. He is, more or less, connected with every species of malefactor, and gratifies his thirst for power and riches by the favouring of one party to the prejudice of another.[18]

Marie had already made a bust of Josephine, but in 1799, when her son Joseph was a year old, she was summoned to the Tuileries to take a likeness of the new First Consul. Told to be there at six in the morning, the only time Napoleon would be free, she was taken into a room where she found Napoleon, Josephine and Madame Grand-Maison. 'Josephine greeted her with kindness, conversed much and with extreme affability; Napoleon said but little, spoke in short sentences, and rather abruptly.' When she was about to put the liquid plaster on his face, Marie told him not to be alarmed because she would not hurt him. 'Alarmed!' he exclaimed: 'I should not be alarmed if you were to surround my head with loaded pistols.' Josephine asked Marie if she would be especially careful and particular as the bust was to be a gift for her husband, and Napoleon had only consented to have his portrait done to please her.[19] In fact, Napoleon was so impressed by the result that he made a personal visit to the *Salon de Cire*, taking with him General Masséna, one of his Mamelukes called Roustan and an aide-de-camp, to have their portraits made by Marie.

The city of Paris, where Marie had spent all her working life, was changing rapidly and many of her fellow showmen were leaving France. In October 1801 Paul de Philipsthal, whose release from prison in 1793 had been arranged by Curtius, took his phantasmagoria to London and showed it in the Lyceum Theatre in Wellington Street, just off the Strand. Upstairs there was a main room or Grand Saloon, an oblong area with two circular ends, one of which formed the stage and the other a gloomy gallery which extended along the parallel sides of the proscenium above a tier of boxes. Downstairs there was a smaller area under the western end of the auditorium, which Philipsthal converted into a theatre suitable for his phantasmagoria. The Lyceum had been built in 1765, and was used for a variety of purposes, 'from the performance of the sublime compositions of Shakespeare, to the legerdemain of Ingleby and the Dancing Dogs of Seaglione'.[20] It was in the upstairs theatre in 1785 that M. Sylvestre had delighted London with his exhibition of wax figures. Philipsthal advertised a, 'Grand Cabinet of Optical and Mechanical Curiosities', which was in three parts: Automata and other Mechanical Devices; Optical Illusions, which included 'different spectres, ghosts, or spirits of departed persons'; and lastly 'Mechanical Optical Firework', as the finale.

The inclusion of 'Fireworks', in a variety of guises, was very popular. A year earlier 'Cartwright's Grand Display of Philosophical Firework from Inflammable Air' had been the main attraction at the Lyceum. This included in the finale 'a central piece that undergoes a variety of changes and produces several thousand flames, the whole without smoke or gunpowder'. The illumination was provided by 'the most curious aeroperic branch which is lighted and extinguished in a moment'.[21] The 'inflammable air' in this case was an early demonstration of the use of gas.

The pre-publicity for Philipsthal's show was intriguing:

No more GHOSTS! What a curious age is this we live in! Formerly ghosts were supernatural, but now we are to know they are deceptions, and can be produced at pleasure. – The Phantasmagoria or Optical and Mechanical Exhibition, we understand is arrived in England. The Visionary Illusions, representing the Phantoms of Absent and Deceased Persons, is said to surpass anything of the kind ever offered to the public inspection.[22]

This was the first time that a phantasmagoria had been seen in England and it received good notices. In October 1801 it was reported that:

Mr Philipsthal's Phantasmagoria promises great profit for himself as well as scientific and useful amusement to the Public; for, considering the prevalency of popular superstition, it will afford pleasure to hear that the reign of terror must cease – as everyone will be forcibly convinced that all the horrors excited by old wives tales, of Ghosts, Hobgoblins, etc., are merely ideal and vanish into air. If anything can be said farther [sic] in commendation of this singular species of entertainment, we must add the elegant neatness with which a little Theatre has been constructed for the purpose in the lower part of the Lyceum.[23]

Seats for the performance at eight o'clock cost the public 4*s* for the boxes, and 2*s* for the pit. The show was an outstanding success. While Philipsthal terrified his audiences downstairs, upstairs in the large saloon was an exhibition of Egyptiana consisting of thirty-two painted scenes, Egyptian artefacts and 'a divertissement by Mr Lonsdale'.

In February 1802 Philipsthal was granted His Majesty's Royal Letters Patent. This was because competitors had attempted to impose upon the public 'a spurious imitation of his Mechanical and Optical Inventions', as a result of which 'his Majesty has been pleased to grant him his Royal Letters Patent, under the protection of which he has now the honour of opening his exhibition'. He also advertised that he would lend the necessary apparatus to those who wished to produce optical and physical effects in their own homes; and that he 'will produce the resemblance of any absent Friend, if the party requiring it will favour him with a previous interview'.[24]

Nicholson's *Journal of Natural Philosophy* described the show as:

[The] first distinct note in modern times when an ingenious foreigner terrified and delighted large audiences at the Lyceum Theatre. A very striking application of the magic lantern has been made this winter to the public amusement by M. Philipsthal at the Lyceum. The novelty consists in placing the lantern on the opposite side of the screen which receives the images instead of on the same side as the spectator, and suffering no light to appear but what passes through and tends to form these images. His slides are therefore perfectly opaque, except the portion upon which the transparent figures are drawn, and the exhibition is thus conducted: All the lights in the small theatre of exhibition were removed except one hanging lamp, which could be drawn up so that its flame should be perfectly enveloped in a cylindrical chimney or opaque shade.

The writer then goes on to describe how in this gloomy and wavering light the curtain was raised, presenting to the spectator a cave or place, exhibiting certain figures in relief, painted on the sides or walls. After a short interval the one hanging lamp was drawn up, leaving the audience in total darkness; this was enlivened by rolls of thunder and lightning flashes formed by the magic lantern upon a thin cloth or screen, let down after the disappearance of the light and so unknown to most of the spectators. This was followed by figures and transmutations produced on the screen by the magic lantern on the far side of it; figures apparently moving their eyes and mouths. This was achieved by the use of two or more sliders. Because there was no circle of light the figures appeared to hang in space. They could be made smaller or larger by increasing or decreasing the focus, and to move by mounting the lantern on a carriage or railway for ease of movement to and fro, which made the images appear to advance or retreat. The figures could also be made to sink into the ground or rise up to heaven. Mr Nicholson commented:

> The whole as well as certain mechanical inventions, were managed with dexterity and address, and his [Philipsthal's] gains in London have been very considerable. The figures for the most part are but poorly drawn, and the other attempts to explain the rational object, or purpose, of the exhibition, was certainly well intended, but unfortunately for his audience, his English was unintelligible.[25]

Many among the audience were terrified by the darkness and the strange sound-effects of thunder, screams and groans, which seemed to come out of nowhere as the ghostly figures rushed towards them growing larger all the time. Some of the women fainted and had to be resuscitated by their escorts. Rather like the modern ghost train, the exhilarating noise, fear and darkness of the phantasmagoria made the theatre a popular meeting place for courting couples.

As rival showmen began to show their own phantasmagoria at other theatres, Philipsthal's business began to decline. He closed the show on 7 August and returned to Paris in search of new attractions. His place at the Lyceum was taken on 10 August by the Frenchman Monsieur Charles, with his mysterious 'Auricular Communications of an Invisible Girl'. This M. Charles, another friend of Marie's from Paris, was a brother of Professor Jacques Charles, the scientist and balloonist. He had already presented his show in Paris and knew Robertson, the aeronaut and famous presenter of the Parisian phantasmagoria. The show-business world in those days was small and fiercely competitive.

The advertisements for M. Charles's show were enticing:

From an Aerostatic Globe of 18 inches diameter, suspended between two ornamental hemispheres in the middle of the room, or floating into the surrounding air, the VOICE of a LIVING FEMALE is distinctly heard as if originating in its centre, and will answer questions put by any person present, or maintain a conversation, either in a whisper or in a more audible tone; the Lady will also, if requested, entertain the Company with Specimens of Vocal Music, producing a most peculiar effect.[26]

This Invisible Girl could speak in French and English. The audience were intrigued and mystified.

Between 1793, when Louis XVI was guillotined, and the signing of the Treaty of Amiens on 27 March 1802, few English had dared to visit France. But following the signing of the treaty, which promised peace between England and France, a few English travellers dared to venture back, even though in England the treaty had received a cautious welcome. George III called it 'elusive', Lord Cornwallis 'experimental', Mr Cobbett 'infamous', Mr Wyndham 'a national death warrant' and Earl Spencer, 'a weakling'.[27]

In this new peace Marie was hoping for an influx of foreign visitors to her waxworks, but when people did at last begin to venture back, many found Paris very much changed. In April George Jackson, attached to Lord Cornwallis's peace mission, wrote: 'We have lived here for five months in a perfect maze of plots, Jacobin, military, and royalist; surrounded by spies, noting every act, and reporting every word.'[28]

Under Napoleon, now Consul for Life, Paris was released from the horror and misery of the Revolution and became a place of riotous living and self-indulgence. Much money could be made by opportunists and, as in the old days of the French court, position and power were once again used to accumulate riches. One visitor, the Revd Dawson Warren, noted that 'there was a prevailing notion in Paris that "à l'anglaise" style of dressing – dirty boots, cropped heads and large whiskers – was thought to be the way all Englishmen dressed, and was fashionable'. He was not at all impressed with the Frenchmen he met: 'Men dirty; black cropped hair; large whiskers; unshorn chins, many of them in boots. . . . This is Republican taste, and they consider it the English fashion.' He was even more horrified by 'a lady who seemed to have nothing more on than a chemise and a gown and even these left the whole breast exposed. . . . The effect this fashion must have on the morals of the country it is fearful to reflect upon. How can Fathers and Husbands allow it?'[29]

Philipsthal, now back in Paris and looking for something new, remembered Curtius and his wax figures. This might be just the attraction he needed. He approached Marie and offered her a loan to take the collection to London, with terms drawn up entirely for his benefit. She would be under his patronage, but he would take half of her gross earnings. Moreover, apart from the initial loan, which she must repay with interest, he would pay none of her running expenses. Marie, surprisingly, agreed. She knew that Philipsthal had made a great deal of money from his first London show at the Lyceum, and she saw in this rather one-sided proposal a chance to make sufficient money to repay the considerable debts she had in Paris. By 1802 the eight years' residency as a condition of the loan to Harry was nearly up. She would leave François in charge of the *Salon de Cire* in Paris, her mother and aunt would look after her two-year-old son, young François, and Marie would take four-year-old Joseph with her to England.

Meanwhile, Philipsthal returned to London and in November 1802 reopened his phantasmagoria in the much larger upstairs theatre at the Lyceum. He had also added, for good measure, 'Hydraulics, Acoustics and Aerostation'.

In order to leave France Marie had to apply for a passport to Joseph Fouché, who had been Commissioner of Police since 1799. Although notorious for his bloodthirsty activities during the Revolution, Fouché had made himself indispensable to Napoleon because of his extensive network of spies, and was living in the utmost luxury and splendour at the Quai Malaquai. His agents were numerous and had infiltrated into every organisation, making him both rich and immensely powerful. Sir Robert Barclay told the Revd Warren that Fouché 'made an income of 2,000,000 per annum, and that he presented Madame Bonaparte every month with a purse of 1,000 louis, and that he had all the gaming houses in his pay'.[30] The Revd Warren noted that a spy was uncovered among the servants with the British delegation.

Fouché, of course, was aware of Marie's past, her associations with the court of Versailles and her secret trips to the Madeleine cemetery. She knew him well from his visits to Curtius, and described him as 'rather a good looking man, thin and sharp featured, somewhat above the middle height'. At first he refused to issue her with a passport, saying 'it was contrary to the laws of the country then existing to allow any artists to leave France'. Eventually he agreed to sign her passport, no doubt after the added encouragement of a bribe.

So it was that in late 1802 Marie, who had not ventured outside Paris for thirty-five years, set out with four-year-old Joseph to join Philipsthal in London. She showed considerable courage.

TWELVE

'Everyone is astonished by my figures'

Britain was bursting with *émigrés* who had brought with them their strange foppish ways. In France they had been denied the most basic of human rights, had had their property sequestered and, by decree, were banished from their homeland. Most of them still thought it unsafe to return home. Many were living in straitened circumstances and although some still kept up appearances, the reality was bleak and depressing. *Emigré* society was a hotbed of gossip, intrigue and scandalmongering. Their invasion was seen as a mixed blessing.

In 1802 London was small and very crowded. The city spread from Leicester Square in the west to Bishopsgate in the east. Regents Park in the north was in the country, and timber yards lined the southern shores of the Thames, beyond which were mainly fields. The streets of the city were narrow and dirty, not unlike those of Paris, but in England there had been no revolution. Many of the English were living in poverty but they were not living in fear. One can only imagine how Marie must have felt on arriving in this strange city. In Paris she had lived surrounded by loyal friends, including her mother, her aunt and her husband François. Now, aged forty-one, Marie Tussaud had left those familiar surroundings and was alone in an alien world. When she arrived she spoke no English, only French and German, and her sole companion was her four-year-old son Joseph.

It is not known how long Marie planned to stay in England, but she told her husband she would return to Paris when she had made sufficient money to pay their debts. She took with her thirty-five portrait figures and 'an Egyptian Mummy, proved by Hieroglyphics to be the body of the Princess of Memphis, who lived in the time of

Sesostris, King of Egypt, around 2528, 1491 years before Christ, being actually 3,328 years old'. Other attractions were 'The shirt of Henry IV of France in which he was assassinated by Ravaillac, with various original documents relative to that transaction; a small model of the original French guillotine with its apparatus; and a model of the Bastille in Paris in its entire state.'[1] She took all these by ship to London, packed securely into crates. No doubt there were breakages, but Marie was well equipped to make the necessary repairs. Once arrived, she had to find accommodation, set up her exhibition and display the figures. Marie found herself lodgings at 2 Surrey Street, and her boxes were probably unloaded at Surrey Stairs, a wharf at the end of the street just upstream from Blackfriars Bridge. Surrey Street is just south of the Strand and opposite the church of St Mary's. To the west was Somerset Place and beyond that the French Church. Close to the church was the Lyceum Theatre. Judging by Philipsthal's later behaviour, it seems unlikely that he gave her much help on her arrival, though he may have had an agent or interpreter to help with the transfer of the wax figures from the boat to the lower rooms at the Lyceum Theatre. Although Philipsthal had loaned her enough money to get to London, he made no mention in his phantasmagoria advertisements of the new attraction installed downstairs. Marie, with no experience of touring and no English, would have found it impossible to place advertisements herself. Philipsthal did not choose to do so. There is mention in a Lyceum advertisement on 7 December 1802 of the addition of 'A Cabinet of Wonders', which could have referred to Curtius's 'Cabinet of Curiosities', and there is also a cryptic note in the Lyceum Theatre's book of cuttings on 4 January 1803: 'Lower Theatre. Egyptian Mummy. Adm. 2/-.'[2]

Marie had enough experience with the *salon* in Paris to know that she must include some British celebrities in her exhibition. The ideal opportunity came soon after her arrival when, in February 1803, the traitor Colonel Despard was publicly hanged and then beheaded for attempting to seize the Tower of London and assassinate George III. Marie, taking advantage of a situation which had become all too familiar to her, made a death-mask of Despard's head after his execution, and put the figure on display. While in London, she also modelled the Duchess of York and Sir Francis Burdett, a well-known politician. He had spent some time in Paris at the beginning of the Revolution; as he frequented the same circles as Curtius, he had probably already met Marie. Marie also modelled 'from life' the Duchesse d'Angoulême, whom she had known as a child at Versailles. Indeed, having spent eight years at Versailles, Marie must have had a number of acquaintances among the *émigrés*.

Philipsthal advertised on 18 March that he was now under the patronage of the Duke and Duchess of York. He needed all the publicity he could find, as there were now several other phantasmagorias in London all competing for public attention. There were also many other rival attractions. Panoramic scenes were especially popular. By clever use of lighting and perspective, viewers standing on a central raised platform in a circular room could really believe that they were part of a battle or cityscape painted on huge panels around the walls. Sometimes a moving panoramic scene would unroll before their eyes. Philip Astley's Circus was still popular. Not only did Astley put on his magnificent equestrian shows in the 44-foot central ring of his amphitheatre, but he also diversified into spectacles of every description. At the end of the evening the performers moved up on to the stage for a melodrama or pantomime, the show often not finishing until after midnight. Later, when his Westminster Amphitheatre was destroyed by fire, Astley moved to the upstairs theatre at the Lyceum.

To attract the pleasure-loving Londoners it was not enough just to entertain; it was imperative to show them something new. Shows and spectacles were well patronised, and some were very skilful, with moving clockwork automatons that could answer questions, play chess and enact simple scenes apparently without human interference. Theatrical scenery became more elaborate, especially with the advent of the designer Philippe Jacques de Loutherbourg, who achieved wonderful and innovative effects with lighting. This was helped by new discoveries such as the Argand Lamp, which Curtius had used in Paris, and which gave a much more intense light than wax candles or the old type of oil lanterns. The effect could be varied by the use of coloured transparencies placed in front of the lamps. It was not until 1826 that the invention of limelight intensified the light still further.[3]

There were many other attractions in London at that time. Science and scientific discoveries were a great source of entertainment, and lectures on magnetism, electricity and the movement of the planets were given in the guise of sensational performances. Friedrich Winzler, a German from Brunswick, arrived in London in 1803. Having changed his name to Frederick Winsor, he floated a company for the promotion of gas lighting and hired the Lyceum Theatre in early 1804 for a public demonstration. The show was an unmitigated failure. Members of the audience were overcome by the fumes of the impure coal gas; some fainted, while others developed blinding headaches, sore throats and running eyes, and all remarked on the choking smell. Mr Winsor was denounced as a charlatan.[4]

The pursuit of knowledge was popular, and the collecting of souvenirs became a fashionable pastime for travellers. The 'Grand Tour' of the eighteenth century had often resulted in mixed collections of relics: stuffed animals, birds, geological specimens, pictures and artefacts of all kinds – and many of these became the basis for the popular Cabinets of Curiosities so favoured by the Georgians.

Marie's waxworks was beginning to attract some attention, but in April 1803 she suffered a setback. Philipsthal, irritated by his dwindling receipts, announced that he was leaving London and would be taking his show to Edinburgh. Marie, according to the terms of her agreement, and deeply in his debt, was told she must go with him. The few letters she wrote to her husband reveal both her loneliness and her resentment towards Philipsthal. Her writing, bold but unformed, lurches across the paper and the words run into one another. Her spelling and grammar are a confusing mix of German and phonetic French, with no punctuation. According to her grandson Victor Tussaud, her speech was just as idiosyncratic, and once she had learned English she spoke it with a strong French and German accent.

25 April 1803. From 2 Surrey Street, the Strand, London
Marie to François Tussaud, Boulevard du Temple No. 20, Cabinet
de Curtius, Paris.
My friend, my dear friend and my dear friends,

I received your letter with great pleasure. Nienie [her nickname
for Joseph] and I cried with joy and sadness at not being able to
embrace you, but now it is Tuesday and we leave next Thursday.
The Cabinet has been shut since Saturday and all is now in boxes.
M. de Philipsthal treats me as you do, he has left me all alone. It is
better so, as he is angry about everything. Do you remember the
arrangements that you made with Stieber to ship all our boxes
and belongings, nobody told M. Tenaviel, the agent for
Edinburgh. M. Philipsthal is annoyed with M. Charles about this.
Mr Philipsthal remains behind until his action with the Baron is
finished. He is no longer with the Cabinet. I must now travel
alone. As soon as I arrive in Edinburgh I will write to you and
give you my address. I implore you my love to reply to me at once
as your letters are my only consolation in a place where I know
no one. I will end by embracing you a thousand times, all my love
to my dear Francison [her son, François], mother and aunt and
dear Charlot. Give our love to Madame Vienne. Nicnie is very
well and hugs you with all his love and sends you a thousand
kisses. I am for life your wife.
Tussaud.

In another hand at the bottom of this letter is written:

Mr Wright, my solicitor sends M. Tussaud his greeting and begs
him to visit at his leisure the gentlemen whose addresses are given
below, to ask them why they have not replied to Mr Wright.
Mr Ferris, No. 126 rue la Verrerie, Paris – Negotiator and Agent.
Mr Adrian Carpenter, 307 boulevard de la Madeleine, Paris –
House salesman.
Mr Ferris, having received power of attorney and other
documents of Madame Courette, which were posted on to him in
January last, wants to know what has been done in the matter.[5]

George Wright, Marie's London solicitor, was asking for some clarification of her properties in Paris. At her request he drew up a document dated 26 April 1803 which gave François full power of attorney over all her property. She authorizes:

the said François Tussaud her husband . . . to whom she gives full power, to borrow what seems good on the best items he can, all the money he requires and to compel his said wife to join with him completely in paying the capital and interest laid down in any transaction and to agree and sign all obligations affecting all or part of these payments. Of the said Madame Tussaud giving of a power of attorney and notably a house in the country in her possession at Ivry, near to Paris, a house situated in Paris, 84 [sic] boulevard du Temple, proved to be hers; to renew all obligations, sell to any person not bankrupt at the best price, encumber, stipulate and condition as he deems fit, all or part of the said power of attorney, handle available sums of money, at the required time receive all money due to the said Madame Tussaud from whatever title and whatever cause.[6]

Why Marie gave François such sweeping powers is unclear. There were money problems in Paris and Tussaud was buying, selling and subletting Marie's property in a bewildering series of transactions. How much she knew of what was really happening we will never know. One of the reasons she had undertaken the long and arduous journey to England was to try to make enough money to pay off their debts, but Curtius's *salon* in Paris was no longer the place it once was. Without Marie's management and skills, the waxworks in Paris seemed doomed.

In London, Marie had packed up her exhibition and was ready to travel to Edinburgh. Mr Charles, whom she had known in Paris, became her adviser and confidant. He went ahead of her to Edinburgh and opened his show, 'The Invisible Girl', on 14 April 1803 at 63 South Bridge Street, opposite the College. He boasted in the *Edinburgh Evening Courant* that it was:

174

the only True Original and the most Incomprehensible Experiment that has ever been Witnessed in the World. The Invisible Girl, induces the inventor thereof, Mr R. Charles, to hope that the curious in Scotland and the Amateurs of Surprising Performances in particular, will receive much gratification in paying attention to an effect so extraordinary of the Acoustic Arts as seems to be the result of magic. This living Aerostat and its incomprehensible Voice, forms a most impenetrable puzzle to the inquisitive Mind, at the same time that conjecture is equally excited by another singularity attending the LADY of the BALLOON, who, though herself invisible to the keenest eye, seems to be in the midst of the Assemblage, and sees everything that passes in the room; this Mysterious Incognita seems to be in possession of every hint, thought and action of the company. In speaking, even in a low voice, the sound is heard by the young lady, who answers immediately all questions in French or English, Sings agreeably, and holds a conversation on any subject.[7]

Mr Charles went on to inform the public that the experiment had received great attention in Paris by the visits of the Consuls of the Republic and members of the National Institute. He added that he 'was truly sensible of the flattering approbation by which he was honoured by His Royal Highness the Prince of Wales, Monsieur, and the most distinguished personages and Philosophers in England and Scotland'. The secret of the Invisible Girl was revealed in an early *Encyclopaedia Britannica*: 'Charles, a Frenchman, exhibited a copper globe, carrying four speaking trumpets, which was suspended in a light frame in the centre of a room. Whispers uttered near to this apparatus were heard by a confederate in an adjoining room by means of a tube passing through the frame and the floor, and answers issued from the trumpets in a loud tone.'[8] There is a diagram in Robertson's memoirs illustrating how the apparatus worked.

With Mr Charles now in Edinburgh, Marie had a good friend to assist her while she was establishing herself. His help was invaluable. He placed two advertisements on the front page of the

Edinburgh Evening Courant on 7 May 1803, one for his show, the Invisible Girl, and one for Marie's Composition Figures which:

> Will open on Wednesday next the 18th instant at Bernard's Rooms, Thistle Street. Accurate Models from life of Bonaparte, First Consul of the French Republic, Madame Bonaparte, Cambaceres, Le Brun, Moreau & Kleber, plus numerous other distinguished characters of the French Revolution, accurately modelled from life by the great Curtius of Paris. The particulars of which are explained by the handbills of the day. Admission 2/-.

Once the exhibition had opened, more attractions were added to the advertisement: 'An Egyptian Mummy 3,293 years old. Accurate models of the Guillotine and Bastille and a vast number of other curiosities fully specified in the handbills.'[9]

The day after Marie arrived in Edinburgh, she wrote to her husband in Paris to tell him of her adventures:

> 11 May 1803
> My dear friend, my dear Franciscon and my dear mother and my aunt.
> I hope this finds you in good health like us. We are all well.
> I told you we left London on the 27 April and arrived in Edinburgh on the 10 May in good health and good company. There were 36 passengers and dozens of people were ill through the bad weather. The sea was terribly rough. We saw three storms which lasted three days and everyone had to go below deck. The boat rolled in a terrifying manner, and the captain who had made the voyage many times said he had seen nothing like it. Monsieur Nienie was not at all afraid and made friends with the captain and with everybody. The captain wished he had a child like him for he had the courage of Bonaparte. He said he was one of the best sailors and that he would like to train him and said he would be a tribute to France. Everyone liked him and nicknamed him 'Little Bonaparte'. The captain told me that I was obliged to settle the remainder of the fare. I told him that I was having an argument

with Monsieur Philipsthal, who did not want to give me any more money as he said he had paid for the journey. When I had threatened to return to Paris and he saw I was serious, he offered me ten pounds. It is always thus with Monsieur. He asked M. Tenaviel to pay the expenses from the bank when we arrived, but he had no money. If I had not found Mr Charles we would have been obliged to let everything go. Mr Charles lent me 30 pounds to pay for everything and we had to pay 18 pounds for all the figures and my voyage to M. Tenaviel who had made the arrangements. I have taken a very nice room which is furnished and decorated for 2 pounds a month and I am lodging at the same house with very pleasant people. The landlady speaks very good French which is a strong attraction for me. Mr Charles will remain with me for the opening. I hope the Salon will be ready in a week. Mr Philipsthal will come to Edinburgh when his business is finished with M. le Baron. I have a German man to help me, supplied by the Baron, a strong, honest man, who speaks French and German and English. M. le Baron is no longer with M. Philipsthal, who is now all alone with his phantasmagoria which annoys him. We must take care of ourselves. We are in a pretty little town set in mountains covered by snow. I still have a bad head, as though I am still on the sea. I think I have found a successor to Charlot, 'un damsel dan valle chamber', who has spent all her life in France. She is very friendly and we spend our free time in my rooms so I feel I were in Paris again which consoles me greatly. Nienie is fêted like a prince and spends all day at the château, playing with a little French boy. My friends, I send my best embraces to my mother and my husband and my dear Franciscon. I am too far away to see you, but I remain your wife, Maria, and miss being with you and to embrace you. We send you thousands and thousands of embraces.
I am your wife for life.
Tussaud.[10]

Marie had taken rooms with Mr and Mrs Laurie at Barnard's Rooms, 28 Thistle Street, New Town, Edinburgh, where she also hired a large room to show her figures. Now marooned in Edinburgh, she must have been concerned about the obvious fragility of the peace with France, reported daily in the newspapers. She did not speak English, she had no experience of touring and she was quite alone with Joseph. She was desperate for news from her husband and family. When the Treaty of Amiens collapsed at the end of May 1803, two weeks after she had arrived in Edinburgh, communication between Edinburgh and Paris became more difficult:

26 May 1803.

My dear friend, my dear friends, my dear Franciscon

We are well. This is the third time I have written to you without an answer. Maybe I have not received your replies, but remember that I am your wife and that you are the father of my children – my dear children. If both Franciscon and my mother were with me I would rest more easily and it would be better for me and Nienie. I hope that at the present time you are in good health. I opened the Salon on the 18 May at three o'clock in the afternoon [*atrouserlaprimitie*]. On the first day I took 3 pounds and 14 shillings [*chilin*], the next day 5 pounds; on the third, 8 pounds and 9 shillings; the fourth, 9 pounds 12 shillings; the fifth, 7 pounds 12 shillings; the sixth, 5 pounds 5 shillings; the seventh, 7 pounds thirteen shillings, and the eighth, 13 pounds 6 shillings. All this is good for the Salon and I hope to make money in this way. Everyone is astonished by my figures, the equal of which no one has seen here, as good as the ones I have made. Everyone likes Monsieur Nienie. The greatest fear for me is a tirade from Philipsthal, who has no time for me because he believes I have many friends in Edinburgh. He appears to be worrying all the time how he can get me to give him money. He is known as a 'ranter' by everybody. [The next part is indecipherable.] . . . He is surprised because everybody is on my side. I am liked as much here as I am at home, and not treated as a foreigner. I ask everyone for help.

She says that she and Nienie are happy but working very hard:

20 The fight for the Bastille on 14 July 1789, and the capture of the Governor, M. de Launay, by Berthault/Prieur. (*Photothèque des Musées de la Ville de Paris*)

21 The killing of M. Foulon on 23 July 1789. Artist unknown. (*Photothèque des Musées de la Ville de Paris*)

22 Trundling wheelbarrows across the Champs de Mars, to build an amphitheatre to celebrate the first anniversary of the fall of the Bastille. Artist unknown. (*Phototèque des Musées de la Ville de Paris*)

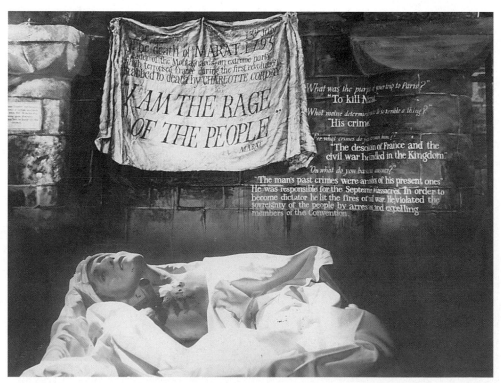

23 Tableau of the murdered Marat, at Madame Tussaud's waxworks. 'I am the rage of the people.' (*Madame Tussaud's Archives*)

24 The Conciergerie Prison. (*Author's Collection*)

25 Tableau of a young Marie Grosholtz at work on a guillotined head. (*Madame Tussaud's Archives*)

26 Guillotined heads of Marie Antoinette and Louis XVI on pikes, as displayed at Madame Tussaud's waxworks. (*Madame Tussaud's Archives*)

27 The Bristol Riots: saving the wax figures on Sunday 30 October 1831, by William Muller. (*Madame Tussaud's Archives*)

28 The Bazaar, Baker Street, in 1835. The Exhibition's first permanent home. (*Madame Tussaud's Archives*)

29 Madame Tussaud aged 77 by E. Hervé, frontispiece from the second edition of Madame Tussaud's *Memoirs*, 1838.

30 'I dreamt I was waltzing with Madame Tee', by Cruikshank from the *Comic Almanack*, 1847. (*Madame Tussaud's Archives*)

SEASON OF 1846.

M^{ADAME} TUSSAUD & SONS

Have the high gratification to state that THE GROUP of the

ROYAL FAMILY AT HOME!

CONSISTING OF

Her Gracious Majesty, Prince Albert, and their Four Lovely Children, the Prince of Wales, the Princess Royal, the Princess Alice, and Prince Alfred,

HAVE GIVEN COMPLETE SATISFACTION TO THOUSANDS. The novelties for the present season consist of a

Magnificent Display of Court Dresses,

OF SURPASSING RICHNESS,

Comprising TWENTY-FIVE LADIES' AND GENTEMEN'S COSTUMES, intended to convey to the **MIDDLE CLASSES** an idea of **REGAL SPLENDOUR**, a most pleasing novelty, and calculated to convey to young persons much necessary instruction. Amongst them will be noticed the FULL DRESS of His Majesty

LOUIS PHILIPPE, AS LIEUT. GEN. OF FRANCE

As King of the French, worn by himself on all public occasions, with the Grand Star, Cordon, &c., of the Legion of Honour.

The truly beautiful

GREEK WARRIOR COSTUME,

Of surpassing workmanship, conveying an idea of a GREEK OFFICER in full Costume, of matchless beauty, and a curiosity for the ladies, as a specimen of NEEDLEWORK. The Ladies' Dresses comprise such as are Worn at Court by the Highest Classes. The Collection now contains upwards of ONE HUNDRED AND TWENTY PUBLIC CHARACTERS. Also,

THE MAGNIFICENT

CORONATION ROBES of GEORGE IV.

Worn and designed by himself, and which cost upwards of £18,000.

THE RELICS OF NAPOLEON,

OF SURPASSING INTEREST. The GOLDEN CHAMBER containing the Camp-bed on which he Died, the Coronation Robes, the Cloak of Marengo, and the highly celebrated MILITARY CARRIAGE, taken at Waterloo. The magnificent Rooms fitted up for the purpose, at a great expense. The recent Novelties are

THE NATIONAL GROUP OF EIGHTEEN FIGURES,

IN HONOUR OF THE DUKE OF WELLINGTON,

The Group of the House of Brunswick,

CONSISTING OF FOURTEEN CHARACTERS;

Showing the whole of the British Orders of Chivalry, never before attempted ; consisting of the Robes of the Garter, Bath, St. Patrick, Thistle, and Guelph, with their Orders, &c. ; the whole producing an effect hitherto unattempted.

"THIS IS ONE OF THE BEST EXHIBITIONS IN THE METROPOLIS."—*Times.*

Bazaar, Baker-street, Portman-square.

Admission, **1s.**   Children under Eight Years, **6d.**   Napoleon Rooms and Chamber of Horrors, **6d.**

OPEN FROM ELEVEN IN THE MORNING TILL DUSK, AND FROM SEVEN TO TEN.

G. COLE, Printer, Carteret Street, Westminster.

31 Poster for Madame Tussaud's 1846 exhibition. (*Madame Tussaud's Archives*)

32 The Sleeping Beauty being examined by a Victorian gentleman. (*Madame Tussaud's Archives*)

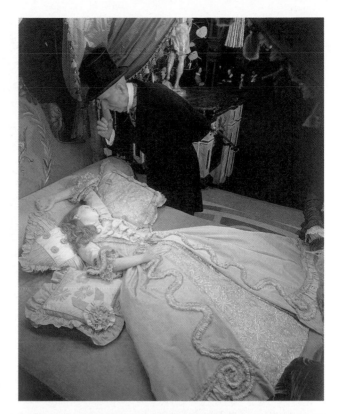

33 The Duke of Wellington contemplating the tableau of Napoleon's deathbed. Print from the painting by Sir George Hayter. (*Madame Tussaud's Archives*)

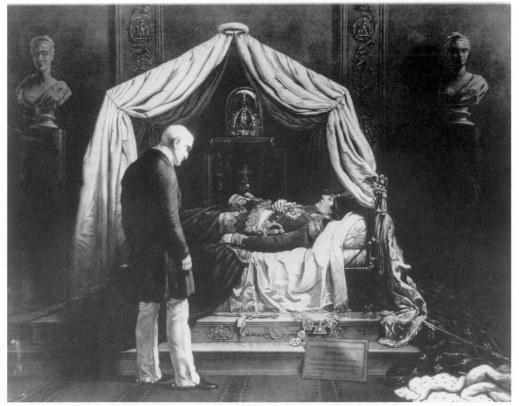

34 Sketch of Joseph Tussaud. Artist unknown.
(*Madame Tussaud's Archives*)

35 Photograph of Francis Tussaud. n. d.
(*Madame Tussaud's Archives*)

36 Figure of
Madame
Tussaud, among
her own models
of the French
royal family.
(*Madame
Tussaud's
Archives*)

We haven't a moment to even take a meal. He is a very hard worker and keeps his head down – sometimes we have been too tired for supper. We have promised ourselves a trip to the country [*kambain*], on Sunday to try and find some wild honey. We will pass the day in the pretty countryside with some kind people. M. Philipsthal is jealous of this and wants us to mix with no one. He is my enemy and only wishes me harm, but I hope to be done with him in six months' time. He is not doing well, his business is very bad and he has only the Cabinet upon which to rely.
I am for life your wife.
Tussaud.[11]

Only three days later, on 29 May, she wrote to her aunt Madame Allemand, who was also living at 20 boulevard du Temple. Marie was concerned about letters not reaching her and asked her aunt to write to her by way of Hamburg if the Channel was closed. She wanted to let her know that all was well and she was making money:

We are in a good place here and people are very friendly and I hope to do well. On the ninth day we took 14 pounds and seven shillings; the tenth day 11 pounds and 17 shillings; and on the twelfth 13 pounds 14 shillings. The cabinet gives much pleasure in this town. The Salon is open from 11 in the morning until 4 o'clock in the afternoon and from six o'clock until 8 o'clock.

She had made a portrait of Joseph and told her aunt that his portrait which was on display was much admired by the ladies, who wanted to know if the picture was like his absent father. She planned to stay in Edinburgh for a further three months. 'If all goes well I hope to pay M. Philipsthal from the time his share was started, what he has spent – his expenses. I shall pay him interest from the start. If this does not suit him, I shall take action, because the laws of Edinburgh are fair. Following upon the payment he will be without defence.' She was worried about her legal position and had consulted a lawyer, the brother of the owner of the house. She told Madame Allemand they were very honest people and would lend her £1,000 if she needed it. She hoped then to be free of M. Philipsthal: 'I have good friends at my side and if he thinks that I am afraid of him he is mistaken.' She continued:

> If not, I shall try the magistrate as I am sure of my case and I will fight this case myself since for a very long time I have done everything for myself without M. de Philipsthal. I am in a difficult position. By this bad agreement I alone have had to pay expenses and buy my materials out of my half of the receipts of the Cabinet – and everything went to him. He is not content to pay the expenses of the Cabinet which comes from my skills and we will not be friends. He believes I cannot work without him.

Marie concluded: 'Mr Charles has ended all this for me and has given me very good advice. He will himself find the money, I hope to be finished with the bad business.'

Marie was enjoying her new life and her new-found status in Edinburgh, where everyone took her for a great lady and wanted to help her, unlike the despised Philipsthal, whom Marie resented deeply. 'Everyone looks on M. Philipsthal with his Phantasmagoria as a charlatan.'[12] But she was desperately missing three-year-old Franciscon whom she had not seen for over four months. The collapse of the Treaty of Amiens on 23 May meant that she was now living in a country at war with France, and the papers were full of anti-French propaganda. The suddenness of the resumption of hostilities caught several English tourists on the wrong side of the Channel, and the *Edinburgh Evening Courant* reported: 'He [Napoleon] has seized and imprisoned all our countrymen and women in France!!!' Any British subject there aged between eighteen and sixty 'shall immediately be considered prisoners of war'. As a French national in Scotland, Marie may well have feared for her own safety.

She was delighted to receive a letter from François on 18 May telling her all was well at home, and replied on 9 June 1803 from Edinburgh:

> I like it here very much, and as well as the people and the very good friends I have found here, our affairs go well. For example, today is

the 18th day our Cabinet has been open and we have taken 190 pounds and 1 shilling. We hope that it will continue, and in July we will have the fair and the horse races which will last for two weeks. Everyone will come to the capital from the country and we hope during the time of the fair, to take twenty pounds a day.

She was still very concerned about her position with Philipsthal, and was hoping to earn enough money so that she could pay off the loan, plus whatever interest was due. 'If this is not convenient, and if he demands an exorbitant rate of interest, I have decided to bring an action and dissolve the partnership with him, to free myself from his domination, which to me is insupportable.' She was hoping that some of her more influential friends would help her. The letter continued: 'As you complain about my writing I have used the hand of the interpreter who explains the models and who you know. He is the Swiss with whom you once went to the opera in London. He wishes to send you his best wishes.' Mr Charles also sent his good wishes, and Marie told François that she had repaid the money which Mr Charles had lent her when she first arrived in Edinburgh. 'Mr Charles has done some very good business here, he has suggested joining with me – but once I have got rid of Philipsthal, I do not want any more associations, no matter with whom. I have had a very unhappy experience, and besides I am better off on my own.'

She told him she was surprised that he had asked her to return home at such a dangerous time, especially before she had settled her debts with Philipsthal. 'It is very fortunate that I made the journey with all our belongings, since the greater part of the heads have been broken, and I have had to remake them. I hope to keep my word which I gave you, not to return home without a well filled purse.'

But Marie was still feeling homesick and cut off from her family:

You have told me, beloved, nothing of what is happening at home; if you have taken a turn at cooking – or if you have altered the Salon because I am not ready to return. I would strongly urge you to take my place at home, to work hard for the children, and to change the Salon while I am not there to argue with you. I urge

181

you too most earnestly to take care of my dear mother, my aunt, my dear Franciscon and my sister. Nienie and I join in sending our heartfelt love. My dear friend remember me. My only desire is to learn all your news and I implore you to see that all your letters reach me. If they come by Hamburg, send them to someone you know. I repeat my address is with Mr Laurie, Bernard's Room, New Town, Edinburgh.
Once more farewell beloved, Your wife, Tussaud.[13]

Marie must have been torn between her promises to her husband to return 'with a well filled purse', and the isolation and loneliness of her life in Scotland. However, it was becoming increasingly difficult to return to France, even if she had wanted to. When hostilities had resumed in May, a state of panic swept Britain and the most improbable stories began to circulate. Napoleon was building a Channel tunnel to march his soldiers under the sea to defeat England and invasion by hot air balloon was imminent. In response, watchers along the coast were waiting for flotillas of boats carrying troops to emerge from the mists, and Martello towers were hastily built for defence.

The editorial in the *Edinburgh Evening Courant* of 11 June called for action:

> By the latest intelligence from Paris it appears to be the general opinion of the people in that capital, that Bonaparte in consequence of the severe agitation of his irritable temper . . . is absolutely disordered in his intellects. Every day some extraordinary proof of this state of mind is confidently expected to burst forth, that will justify even those who appear to be his friends, in taking some decisive measures for placing the Government in other hands.

Two months after Marie had opened her Cabinet of Curiosities in Edinburgh, Philipsthal arrived. His advertisement announced the opening of his 'wonderful performances' at Corri's Rooms, James Square, with 'Two Elegant Automatic Figures, as large as Nature', which both moved as though alive; 'A Self Defending Money Chest', with four small cannon to shoot any person trying to force it open; 'A Mechanical Peacock', which ate, drank, cried, unfolded its tail and answered questions from the audience; and 'A Cossack in Miniature', which danced. To these would be added 'several original outstanding and unparalleled experiments in the Science of Optics, of which he is the sole inventor and which were brought out of his native country, Germany'. And, of course, the phantasmagoria.[14]

The first night was a disaster. His apparatus failed, the special effects didn't work and the audience were not at all impressed. The next day he published an apology in the *Edinburgh Evening Courant*, but it was too late. The public had lost interest, and there were many other more reliable exhibitions to go to. He closed his show a month later.

Marie received two letters from François in July, but waited until she knew her financial position before she replied. She sent him news of the current situation regarding her debt to Philipsthal. It seems that out of her takings he had paid for the wages of two men to assist her, and also the rent, tickets and advertisements for the two-and-a-half months she had been in Edinburgh. These outgoings amounted to £118 18s, leaving a net profit of £301 12s to be divided between Philipsthal and Marie. She also had to pay him £41 18s for the expenses of the journey north. It appears from her letter that she no longer trusted Philipsthal, and deeply resented the financial hold he had over her:

We have had plenty of arguments arriving at this settlement of the account, as it has been he who has paid everything, who has organized, and who has done everything. I have been forced to accept his accounts as he placed them before me.

I am in a very difficult situation, hardly able to exist with him, as he treats me like a slave. I have made all possible efforts to break the association. I have shown our agreement to different lawyers who say there is not the least chance of it being broken legally. The agreement is entirely in his favour and at his disposal.

183

There is only one happy solution for us with him and that is to separate, and he will have none of it.

Marie told François that she didn't want to go on to Glasgow with Philipsthal as planned; she would prefer to stay in Edinburgh where she was still making money. She was desperate to find some way 'out of this mess, so that I can, after making some suitable arrangements, stay in a town where I can busy myself with my own business and not be worried by his affairs and his phantasmagoria'.

Mr Charles was proving a good friend, but she was still undecided whether or not to accept his help:

> Mr Charles has again asked me to join with him and to leave my tyrant, and he is willing to settle the debt, in the event of Philipsthal being willing to make the break. I am not at all sure what to do, as I am afraid of falling between Charybdis and Scylla. If I see the smallest chance of doing so, I will do so as quickly as possible and avoid with all my skill an arrangement as tyrannical as that with Philipsthal. There is nothing else to be done in such a situation.
>
> In spite of the crisis don't be anxious and don't be upset – I have every hope of overcoming all my difficulties with the aid of the Almighty. I will write again in a few days, as soon as I am certain of Philipsthal's plans, and also when I hear from the lawyer, and decide what to do about Mr Charles.

Marie was pleased to hear that everyone was well in Paris and wrote in return that five-year-old Joseph 'is learning English quickly, and has started to read and takes lessons every day. As for myself, I am reasonably well for a woman harassed with anxiety and fear.' She was missing all her family and sent them 'a million kisses'.[15]

* * *

Philipsthal left Edinburgh at the end of July leaving Marie to manage on her own; she did not hear from him again until

December. Her exhibition was doing well. She was a resourceful woman, and Edinburgh was a safe place to settle after the perils of the Revolution. There were many things to do in the summer. The Edinburgh Races were held on the sands at Leith; a Pipers Competition was advertised at the Theatre Royal with Highland Reels; a Card Assembly took place at the New Assembly Rooms in George Street; and the Grand Panorama of the French Capital was showing at North College Street.

It was at this time that the British government, under the leadership of Pitt, decided they needed to raise more money for the renewed war against Napoleon and so introduced the contentious Window Tax, which caused considerable outrage. In September the *Edinburgh Evening Courant* noted: 'sky-lights, cellar lights, staircase or passage lights, are all to be included. Windows giving light to more than one room or landing place, shall be charged as so many distinct windows as the number of places given lights to.' Many people living in large houses bricked up their extra windows to avoid paying the tax.

Marie stayed in Edinburgh until the end of September, and then went on to Glasgow to the New Assembly Rooms in Ingram Street, arriving on 1 October. She exhibited in Glasgow for three months, staying until the beginning of January 1804. Her next letter was written from her Glasgow address at Mr Collon, Pastry Cook, Wilson Street, and was dated 10 October. It had been three months since she had heard from Paris and she wrote to her aunt, 'so it is possible you have forgotten me'. She was beginning to rely more and more on five-year-old Joseph who 'speaks English like a native and replies with ease. He is my interpreter.'

Marie was bitter about Philipsthal whom she had not seen for three months:

We are not good friends with this scoundrel. I did wrong not to take the opportunity when he wanted to take all that I had made – £500 – as in my case I had paid him £100 in Edinburgh in the belief and hope that I should be finished with the monster who has neither scruples nor honour. He knows very well when I am on my own, that I shall pay him the rest at the earliest opportunity as I promised him in Edinburgh. Unfortunately I have lost his answer which he wrote to me. People are not taken in by his phantoms, that is why he has fallen out with me. . . . We made £600 in four months in Edinburgh, where I took a lot of money. I am very pleased, and have good friends. I have been in Glasgow since the 1st of October and all goes well. The first receipts amount to £40, which more than pays our expenses, and I hope to do still better – there are still plenty of towns.[16]

Two months later she wrote again to her husband:

Our Cabinet has been fairly successful here until this week, which has fallen off. I plan to close three days after the New Year and go to Greenock, eight leagues from here – but after that I do not know where I shall go, and will tell you later. I will not give you all the details of our receipts. Suffice to say I have received £250. M. Philipsthal is at the moment in Dublin with M. le Baron and his entourage. Today I received the news of his arrival. I am alone with my dear Nienie and my interpreter.[17]

At the end of 1803 Philipsthal had endured a wild and stormy crossing to Dublin. Much of his apparatus, including the magic lanterns, was lost when his ship was wrecked, although luckily most of his slides were saved. He had to commission a new lantern after his arrival from Mr Clarke, a Dublin optician, and this delayed the opening of the phantasmagoria. Marie wrote: 'According to his plan I must follow him to Dublin very shortly – but I have still not decided. At least it will not be this winter during the bad time of year.' The Irish Sea was notoriously dangerous, especially in the winter season, and Marie was not a good sailor. She had heard reports of a French invasion in the south of Ireland which worried her: 'I will not go there until I am sure that there is no danger for myself and for my Cabinet, and when peace has been re-established in that country. While we are waiting we will exhibit in some Scottish towns, and there are some quite large ones, and the time will be spent in this country in perfect peace.' She was still homesick and relying heavily on Joseph: 'The only thing I miss for my complete happiness is I need to embrace all our dear family. Nienie wants to see his dear Franciscon again and to talk to him in English. He is making great progress in that language and is very busy at his lessons which he takes every day.'[18]

Marie was still reluctant to go to Ireland, though she seemed to realise that it was inevitable, and so in January she travelled to the sea port of Greenock to wait for better weather.

18 January 1804.

Glasgow. We leave tomorrow for Greenock – all our things are packed. M. Philipsthal is in Dublin, as I have told you he is not yet open again, and I am afraid to go and join him. I am very undecided, above all about travelling at this time of year. If I must go, it will not be until the better weather comes. Send me your news more often. I will write as soon as I am settled in Greenock. Will you address your letters for the time being to Madame Henniker, George Street, New Town, Edinburgh. . . . My friend I hope it will not be long before I am with you again. I live for that happy moment and am tormented by not seeing you. Let me know if you are doing any work. As soon as my Cabinet is opened I will write to you. In the meantime goodbye, goodbye.
I am for life your wife.
Tussaud.[19]

Philipsthal eventually managed to have his equipment repaired and opened his phantasmagoria at the Little Theatre, Capel Street, Dublin, on 23 January 1804.

It was then that Marie, after only a short stay at Greenock, unwillingly set sail to join him in Ireland.

THIRTEEN

'Joseph and I must go on our way'

In early 1804 Marie landed in Dublin. She was a poor sailor and did not enjoy the journey, as she told her husband in a letter she wrote after her arrival. 'Me and my son are lucky to be alive. We endured a terrifying crossing. We struck a storm and three vessels which left port with us were sunk beside us in five minutes. You can well imagine my losses. I had to make good what I had lost. When I think that I made the decision not to make the journey during the winter as you know.' She had opened her exhibition in the Shakespeare Gallery, near Grafton Street: 'I hope to be quiet here and am just making some portraits of famous people in the town for my salon, which is drawing big crowds. Everybody is very pleased. I have come to the slack season, but everybody makes me think that I shall make a lot of money in the winter.'[1]

The Ireland to which Marie travelled in 1804 was oppressed by poverty and divided by religion. The majority of the population were Roman Catholic, as was Marie, but they were ruled by English Protestants, many of whom were absentee landlords. The Act of Union uniting Britain and Ireland had become law on 1 January 1801, but was bitterly opposed by many, especially the followers of Henry Grattan. Martial law was imposed. The Catholics had few rights, and although Pitt had campaigned vehemently for Catholic emancipation George III refused to sanction the Bill, and it did not become law until 1829. Ireland had long been considered the back door into England, and with the renewal of war with France in 1803 British fears of invasion increased. Regiments of English soldiers were garrisoned throughout Ireland and billeted in the towns. They provided an enthusiastic audience for Marie's waxworks. The Irish, too, many of them sympathetic to France, were attracted to the exhibition of historical figures. She found a ready audience.

Shortly after her arrival she was finally able to escape from the clutches of M. Philipsthal. A story handed down in the family explained how she managed to do this:

During Madame Tussaud's stay in Ireland, although an exceedingly careful and strictly economical woman, she unfortunately found it necessary to borrow, and she got into the clutches of a money lender named Philipps [Philipsthal].[2]

While exhibiting in Dublin, among the celebrities who visited her collection was the distinguished and eminent lawyer, Curran. It was only natural that there should ensue an animated and sympathetic conversation between the witty advocate and a lady who had so much to relate concerning the French Revolution, and the many notabilities of the period with whom she had been familiar. Before taking his leave, however, the penetrating and astute lawyer, apologising to Madame Tussaud for the liberty he was taking, begged to be informed of the reason for her apparent discomposure.

Nothing loath she informed him of her sad position, and greatly to her delight he requested to see her papers, and finally said he would see her through her troubles. When Philipps [sic] knew that the great Curran was conducting her affairs he speedily came to terms, and promptly dropped the proceedings he had already commenced, and Madame Tussaud had little difficulty in making most satisfactory terms, and getting quit of him. When, however, she thought of her bill of costs, it was with fear and trembling she asked for them, and greatly to her gratification she was informed by the generous hearted Irishman, that the pleasure of assisting a lady, and a foreigner in distress was a sufficient recompense in itself.[3]

Marie could hardly have found a better champion than John Philpot Curran. A famous Irish judge, he had been called to the Irish bar in 1775 and was a follower of Grattan's party. He supported parliamentary reform and Catholic emancipation, and defended the leaders of the United Irishmen conspiracy when they were brought to trial. Famous as an orator, he was a fierce champion of justice and equality and refused to be intimidated. In Marie's advocate Philipsthal had more than met his match, and at the end of May 1804 he announced that he was leaving Dublin for England. He was briefly sighted over the next few years travelling around the English countryside, quite often with new additions to his show. There is a record of a christening of two children at St Luke's Church, Chelsea, on 13 August 1819, the parents being Paul de Philipsthal and Mary his wife. It seems that he died in 1830, for in May 1830 a benefit performance was held in Wakefield for the widow and children of 'the late Mr Philipsthal'.[4]

When Marie wrote to François in June from 16 Clarendon Street, Dublin, she berated him: 'You have not written sir, everyone is asking often.' By now the early enthusiasm of her first letters had abated, and although she seemed more settled still she missed her family and especially her son Franciscon. She was immensely proud of six-year-old Joseph, whom she relied upon as her interpreter:

My friends be patient, because I suffer so far from you, and I press you against my heart, and my dear Franciscon who will no longer know his poor mother and his proud Englishman [Joseph] – he really is English, everyone believes him to be because he speaks English so well. He is learning very well and at the moment he is taking piano lessons from one of my friends who is very fond of him. He is a child of great promise and unequalled intelligence, and everyone likes him. I hope, my friends, that you are caring for my poor Franciscon. Have no fears for us as all is well, I have no fear. M. Tussaud I hope you are taking care of my mother, aunt and Franciscon and that on my return I shall not find anything with which to reproach you.

Marie was paying rent of £25 for a six-month lease, and taking an average of £6–7 a day which was quite enough to cover her expenses, especially as she no longer had to worry about

Philipsthal's loan. She had now added the busts of the Rt Hon. J.P. Curran and the Rt Hon. H. Grattan to her exhibition, and planned to stay in Dublin 'until March and then I shall go to Limerick, Cork and Belfast, which are very good towns in which to exhibit. From there I shall return to Scotland, until we are once again at peace.'[5]

* * *

In Paris, unbeknown to Marie, François was gambling with her property. On 26 Floréal, Year XIII (16 May 1804), the Horrys insisted that a further mortgage be taken out to safeguard their loan of 20,000 francs, on 'the goods present and future on husband and Grosholtz and especially fixed assets at Ivry-sur-Seine'. In order to settle part of the loan, the house at Ivry-sur-Seine was sold by François to Jean Paul Carré and his wife Jeanne Marguerite le Colley, for the sum of 16,997 francs. On his acquisition, M. Carré was to pay 8,998 francs to the Horrys to discharge part of François Tussaud's debt. The outstanding amount of 3,415 francs and 91 centimes was lent to François by a lawyer, Louis Désiré Pelet, thus finally settling the Horrys account. François also borrowed 5,000 francs from Pelet at 5 per cent interest. As surety for this, he mortgaged 20 boulevard du Temple, 'the house of Anne Marie Grosholtz inherited from Matte Philippe Guillaume Curtius'.[6]

Marie now had little left of her inheritance from Curtius. François was deeply in debt, and in October 1804 a writ was taken out by the lawyer M. Pelet, seeking the payment of interest on his loan. The property at 20 boulevard du Temple was let to a showman named Colley, possibly the brother of the woman who had bought the house at Ivry-sur-Seine. Although Marie was named in all these transactions she was not consulted. The power of attorney she had given François in 1803 allowed him to do as he wished with her property.

Marie's next letter to François was written nine months later, in March 1805, the year in which Napoleon abandoned the confusing Revolutionary calendar. She had still not heard of François's transactions. The British blockades of French ports meant that mail from France was erratic and unreliable; indeed, the letter she had just received from François had taken five months to arrive. She told her husband that seven-year-old Joseph no longer spoke one word of French. She was doing well in Dublin, taking about £100 a month.

> They come in crowds every day from six o'clock until ten o'clock. My cabinet is well known as there one can see portraits of men both famous and notorious. I am very proud of it – I hope to receive a great deal more. I have plenty of courage. My cabinet is always in demand and that is, no doubt, why I have had a letter asking me to visit the towns in the vicinity. I leave for Cork, which is about 100 miles south.

Still desperately missing five-year-old Franciscon in Paris, Marie thought that she should remain in Ireland for the sake of both her children:

> I hope by working hard for my children to give them a good start in life and make them into men that a father and mother may be proud of – this is the wealth we can give them. There will then be no cause to reproach me for harm I have done. I have no regrets, for my enterprise is more important to me than returning to you, now that I have finished with M. Philipsthal.
> Adieu – adieu, Joseph and I must go on our way.
> I hope that you are looking after my mother and my aunt well so that I may not reproach you.[7]

Over the next three months, now that the summer had come, Marie began her travels around Ireland. Her next, and last, letter to her husband was sent from Waterford on 20 June 1805. She wanted to reassure him that all was well with Joseph and herself.

> Have no doubts that I shall do well for the time being, and I hope to succeed as I now work for myself and my children. I am going to make money with my Salon. It is probable that I will visit 2 towns and I will do better as I am now quite alone. There are

about fifty towns, but everything is dear and they are so far apart from each other. I am planning to spend the winter near to a big town, and from there go on to the north where there is a big town with a large population. . . . I have been invited to go, and I can make a lot of money as there is an Exhibition there – and it would be impossible in this town here.

You ask me if I speak English; I speak enough to carry on my business. I have to speak English as my son does not speak a word of French and I live with English people. I do not speak as well as our son, because everybody takes him for an Englishman. He does not even know how to say *'bon goure'* [sic] in French. When he comes back to Paris, I hope that he will learn French quickly. I wish I had my beloved Franciscon here with me to give him the same chances as his brother. I should be happy if he had the same chance as him.[8]

When she wrote this letter to her family, Marie was still planning to return to France, though probably not until the hostilities had finished. In the meantime she kept travelling:

We make our way by land and sea. For 13 days we endured a very heavy storm at sea and everybody was ill. It was a very bad crossing, but by merciful providence we are here safe and sound. Your son is a very good sailor. He is happy at sea and wants to be a traveller.

Goodbye, write a little when it is possible. We cannot write to you, my friend, about our plans until we know them.

I am for life your wife. Tussaud.[9]

This is the last letter we know of from Marie Tussaud to her husband François.

The three years she spent travelling around Ireland were to set a pattern for the next thirty years of her life. Moving from one town to the next with her wagonload of 'composition figures', she stayed in each for as long as the Cabinet could attract visitors, then packed up and moved on again to the next town. Like so many itinerant showmen, she lived her life on the road. Marie tells her husband that she speaks enough English to carry on her business. Her grandson Victor remembered that even in 1845 she spoke heavily accented English, reflecting her German and French origins. In 1805 she is recorded as having been to Kilkenny, Waterford and Cork, but then we lose sight of her until she reappears in Belfast in May 1808. The Napoleonic wars dragged on until 1815, during which time the British continued to blockade the French coast, effectively preventing travel between England and France. In those thirteen years the marriage between Marie and François Tussaud became no more than a paper record at the Hôtel de Ville.

* * *

From the time Marie left Paris in 1802, François seems to have been speculating by selling and leasing property in Paris. He took out mortgages in October and November 1805 on various houses. He was issued with a second writ by the lawyer, Pelet, in September 1806, which he paid, and throughout 1807 there are numerous leases, mortgages and an assortment of documents which show that he was more interested in managing theatrical property than running the *Salon de Cire*. His main interest in the wax museum was as a possible source of income, for he had no wax modelling skills himself. Although he asked Marie to return to him in 1805, soon after she had settled her debt with Philipsthal, France and England had been continually at war since 1803 and Marie had refused. She knew that life would be hard if she returned to her old existence in Paris in a France consumed by Napoleon's ambitions, and she could see there might be a better future for herself and her family if she stayed in Britain.

During this time Margeurite Salomé Reiss was managing the *Salon de Cire* for François. It was she who, in 1795, had lent Marie money for the business, in return for an annuity of 2,000 livres. Now François, heavily in debt and unable, or unwilling, to pay her annuity, used the power of attorney given to him by Marie, and in 1808 signed the *Salon de Cire* over to Mademoiselle Reiss in cancellation of all his debts to her. The closure, dated 19 September 1808, stated that 'François Tussaud cedes to Mademoiselle Salomé Reiss all the objects comprising the salon of figures known as the Cabinet of Curtius. These objects include all the wax figures, all the costumes, all of the moulds, all the mirrors, lustres and glass which she may deem fitting. M. Tussaud herewith renounces any right in this regard.'[10] Thus, without consultation, he disposed of the last of Marie's French inheritance. It was this act, above all others, that created the final rift in the Tussaud marriage. She never forgave him.

* * *

Marie returned to Scotland from Ireland at the end of July 1808, and set up her exhibition in the Mason's Hall in Greenock. This was the first time she advertised under her own name:

> By permission of the Magistrates
> Madame Tussaud, Artist
> Of the Grand European
> Cabinet of Figures
> Modelled from life
> Respectfully informs the Ladies and Gentlemen of Greenock and its neighbourhood that she has arrived in this town on her way to London, and purposes Exhibiting for a short time in the Mason's Hall, commencing Monday first. Greenock, 28 July, 1808.[11]

She stayed in Greenock until the end of August, then went on to Glasgow for a few months before returning to Edinburgh in January 1809. On 27 January 1809 Marie advertised in the *Edinburgh Star* that she was opening in Edinburgh at 48 South Hanover Square: 'Madame Tussaud's Grand European Cabinet of Figures. The great concourse of company constantly attending these rooms, is the surest proof that it deserves the attention of the public.' The exhibition was opened by the Right Honourable William Coulter, the Lord Provost, and the newspaper declared it to be 'truly elegant and will doubtless make a fashionable winter's promenade'.

During Marie's stay in Edinburgh, a Grand Military Promenade and Festive Ball was held at Corri's Rooms on 17 February 1809, under the distinguished patronage of 'Her Grace the Duchess of Buccleuch, Her Grace the Duchess of Gordon, Lady Caroline Douglas, the Countess of Buchan, the Countess of Montgomery and Lady Duncan'. The Duke of Buccleuch was then Lord Lieutenant and High Sheriff. In 1977 a note was found in an old dressing-up box in Selkirk, addressed to 'Their Graces the Duke and Duchess of Buccleuch and Queensbury'. It seems that Marie had loaned some figures for the Military Promenade and Festive Ball, perhaps to decorate the Assembly Rooms. In the note:

> Madame Tussaud presents her duty to her kind patrons . . . and her friends in general on this side of the border especially the Co. Dumfries. She begs to say that she has no objection to the wax figures being sold which she believes can be easily managed, more especially the duke of Marlbro' which cost her very dear, *but* she herself had never had any difficulty in selling but she will send a Messenger for *all* the Jewels which she desires may be delivered to her without fail.[12]

No costumes, figures or jewels were found with the letter. We know from later advertisements, when she was exhibiting in Bath, that she rented out costumes for Fancy Balls. It is quite possible that she would also provide appropriate wax figures for special occasions such as a grand Military Parade.

Marie exhibited in Edinburgh for nearly four months. In March she introduced the scandalous figure of Mrs Clarke, the mistress of the Duke of York. She had been accused of using the duke's name to sell military appointments, then pocketing the money. Her trial was the sensation of the season and the *Edinburgh Star*, which reported it in minute detail, printed 'the gallant Duke's Love letters, and other Interesting Papers never before published'. The love letters, peppered with pet names and baby talk, created much mirth when read aloud as evidence in the parliamentary inquiry. Marie advertised the new figure of Mrs Clarke in bold letters on her poster. As she had learned in Paris, it was important to keep the figures in her exhibition topical to attract the public.

By March the news must have reached Marie in Edinburgh of her husband's disposal of Curtius's *Salon de Cire* to Mademoiselle Salomé Reiss. It would have been a devastating blow, even to someone of Marie's strength of character. François had betrayed her; she was separated from her mother and nine-year-old son Franciscon, and all her plans for working for the future of the two boys were thrown into confusion. Every possession in Paris that Marie cared about had been mortgaged, sold and lost. There was now no future for her there. She would have to stay in England. Perhaps reflecting this loss, there is a significant change in the newspaper advertisements over the next few months. By the end of March they cease to mention her name; they become smaller and lack the push and enthusiasm she had always displayed. The exhibition of 'composition figures' was offered only under the small headline of '48 South Hanover Square'. It seems likely that this was when she went south, leaving the exhibition in charge of one of her assistants, possibly Mr Knight.

Marie spent much of 1809 in London, where she 'modelled from life' George III and Queen Charlotte. This is when she is believed to have rented Effingham Lodge, at 65 Central Hill, Norwood, from Mrs Nesbitt, whom she had known in Paris.[13] Mrs Nesbitt had returned from her travels by 1803 and between 1806 and 1810 was busy enlarging her home, Park House in Norwood. On 5 May 1810 she wrote to Lord Auckland, asking him to allow her more time to pay the back rent she owed him.

For the next few years Tussaud's exhibition travelled around England. It remained at Hanover Square in Edinburgh until 9 May, during which time Marie was in London. By the end of 1810 she was back in Edinburgh and showing her figures at the Panorama in Leith Walk, not far from the Botanical Gardens. A gold watch was repaired for her in September by the Edinburgh watchmakers James Ritchie & Sons.[14] From there she moved down to Newcastle in June 1811. Marie's passage around the towns of England and Scotland in these early years is largely unrecorded. There are occasional advertisements in the local papers, sometimes with a review of the show, but only if she stayed in one place for long enough. Moving the exhibition from one place to another was a slow and sometimes dangerous business. Public roads were poor, and only maintained by so many days of enforced labour from village to village. When the faster mail coaches came in and the turnpike roads were opened, the stretches of road between the toll gates were kept in good repair by the coach companies. However, the rest of the roads became a quagmire in the winter. Travelling was hard and laborious, only improved after 1815 when Macadam began to construct roads made of crushed stone.

Marie, who was now fifty-three, followed the punishing schedule of all travelling showmen – packing up, moving on, setting up anew, advertising, selling tickets, closing the show, then packing up and moving on again. Charles Dickens's novel *The Old Curiosity Shop* describes a travelling waxworks show and its proprietor Mrs Jarley, 'the delight of the Nobility and Gentry and the patronised of Royalty', who sounds remarkably like Madame Tussaud. Mrs Jarley explains that:

> The exhibition takes place in assembly-rooms, town halls, large rooms at inns, or auction galleries. There is none of your open-air wagrancy [sic] at Jarley's, recollect; there is no tarpaulin or sawdust at Jarley's, remember. Every expectation held out in the handbills is realised to the utmost, and the whole forms an effect of imposing brilliancy hitherto unrivalled in this kingdom.[15]

A surviving account book for the years 1811 to 1813 holds an invaluable day-to-day record of Marie's exhibition, and gives a good picture of their daily life, with lists of their 'Disbursements and Disappointments'.[16] Inside the front cover of the small, well-thumbed book are three names: Joseph Tussaud, Mr Knight and Madame Tussaud. On the opposite page are two names and addresses: Mrs Henniker in Edinburgh, who had been Marie's contact address when she left for Ireland in 1803, and below that, Mr Henniker of Wine Street, Bristol. Mr Knight's role was unspecified, but he was probably the show's manager. As Joseph was only thirteen in 1811, Marie would have needed the assistance of a manager and some male employees to help with the work of moving and setting up the figures.

The account book starts on Monday 2 December 1811 at North Shields, where the company stayed for eight weeks taking a total of £118 5s 6d. There Marie paid £3 16s for music lessons for Joseph and £3 6s for a music book. She also paid a German master 11 guineas. The next town they visited was Hull, where they arrived on 13 March 1812 and exhibited at 4 Market Place. A printer, Mr Peck, was paid the sum of £18 18s 6d for 100 posting bills and 4,000 handbills, their only form of advertising. They stayed for sixteen weeks in Hull and on 8 June Marie paid £2 12s for Joseph's piano lessons, now a regular part of his education. Apart from the earlier entry for a German master, there is no mention of any other schooling. They seem to have hired wagons to transport the figures from one town to the next, because at the end of their visit to Hull was written: 'coach hire for Sunday, 12/- and 15/-'. In her early days of travelling around the British Isles, Marie hired covered wagons, common stage wagons; it is possible that as she became more successful she bought her own wagons but this seems unlikely, especially as her stay in some towns was for several months. Some of her expenses included repairs to wheels and payments to drivers and assistants. Occasionally, payments for the costs of re-gilding occur, probably for props and scenery.

Sometimes she took lodgings in the places where she exhibited and it seems likely that she and Joseph travelled between engagements by stagecoach, while the assistants travelled in the wagons with the figures. She opened in York on 16 July 1812 in the Dancing Room at Goodramgate. By now she had sixty-nine figures, and more handbills were ordered from Mr Peck. She stayed in York for about six weeks and then went southwards to Leeds for two months, where they exhibited in rooms opposite the Hotel Briggate. Here Joseph took piano lessons from Mr Mills. On Monday 16 November, after staying for seven weeks, they 'left the house in Briggate' and paid £1 4s to hire a coach to Manchester where they opened on 2 December 1812. From Manchester they went to

Liverpool, where Mr Muff was Joseph's piano teacher, then to Birmingham for six months, then Worcester and finally Bristol on 30 June 1814. In Bristol Marie exhibited in the Assembly Rooms and it is likely that she and Joseph stayed in Wine Street with Mr Henniker, whose name appears in the front of her account book.

It can be seen from the account book that Marie employed several assistants to help with jobs such as setting up the figures, driving the wagons from one engagement to the next, taking care of the costumes and carpentry. While they were in Leeds, William was paid 15s a week, Mr Knight was paid £1 and William's wife, who may have helped with the costumes, only 10s a week. According to Marie's grandson Victor, it was Marie's idea to pay wages to her employees on a Friday evening instead of the usual Saturday, 'having observed that in some instances the men spent their money too freely in public houses to the detriment of their wives and families and she considered they were less likely to abuse the opportunity on Friday than on Saturday'.[17]

When they reached Hull in March 1812 Mr Knight was still with them but William and his wife had been replaced by Richard Fuller and a new woman, Rebecca, who was paid 7s a week. On 10 May an extra man, John Martin, was engaged for 12 guineas a year. It was customary to have someone from the waxworks to name and explain the various figures to the visiting public. Dickens's Mrs Jarley offers little Nell just such employment and tells her:

'The duty's very light and genteel, the company particularly select,' . . . and so well did Nell profit by her instructions . . . that by the time they had been shut up together for a couple of hours, she was in full possession of the history of the whole establishment, and perfectly competent to the enlightenment of visitors.[18]

Young Joseph, with his perfect English and knowledge of the business, would almost certainly have been the guide for Madame Tussaud's exhibition, and doubtless was more than 'competent to the enlightenment of visitors'.

By now Marie had seventy figures, and as the exhibition changed and grew so did the staff. She already employed three men, and another new man, John Lamp, joined them in Manchester. Mrs Jarley's waxworks employed only two men, and when reaching the place of exhibition:

> The chests were taken out with all convenient dispatch, and taken in to be unlocked by Mrs Jarley . . . They all got to work without loss of time, and very busy they were. The stupendous collection were yet concealed by cloths, lest the envious dust should injure their complexions. . . .The two men being well used to it did a great deal in a short time; and Mrs Jarley served out the tin tacks from a linen pocket like a toll-collector's which she wore for the purpose, and encouraged her assistants to renewed exertion.[19]

There are occasional entries in the account book for blue starch, dyeing and washing, and also for transparencies and lamps, and even rush lights for 1s 3d. Marie, trained by Curtius, knew the importance of good lighting for the figures and it was always a major expenditure. At the beginning of the tour, when she was in North Shields, she bought 120lb 'candels' for £5 7s 6d. The following Monday a further £3 6s 7d was spent on more candles. The total expenses from shutting in Leeds to opening in Manchester were £30 14s. This constant moving from one assembly hall to the next was expensive, especially in the setting-up costs. In that first week they spent £23 7s 4d, which included 18s 4d worth of green baize, 2lb of pins for 16s and the costs of a glazier, a mason and a carpenter for £9. In Leeds they bought 21 lb of mould, candles and some spun hair.

There was also the expense of food and lodgings for her growing workforce. At the beginning of the tour, when they stayed for eight weeks in North Shields in December/January, four carts of coals were delivered and a considerable quantity of food and drink. Meat, bread, butter, tea, coffee, sugar and milk were listed, as well as four bottles of wine and two bottles of rum. There were a number of people to feed, and they ate well. Their shopping lists included mutton, beef, porter, oysters and eggs. In April they bought oil, vinegar and 'sallad'.

The cost of clothes was also noted, not only for Joseph and herself but also for the figures. When Joseph was fifteen, in January 1813, he was fitted out with new clothes: a pair of pantaloons at £2, a waistcoat and new gloves for £1 2s 6d and a pair of top boots for £2 12s. There was also 3s 6d worth of 'macassar oil for Joseph's hair' and unspecified 'expenses for the Ball' of 14s and 11s respectively.

While she was at Manchester, Marie 'modelled from life' the Prince Regent and the Duke of York. The account book notes that clothes were bought for these new figures. Stockings, breeches and some dummy shoes were bought for £1 6d, also coats for 3 guineas. Lace and muslin cost £2, and a hat, gaiters and boots were also purchased. More materials were bought to the value of £4 7s, a figure for £3 5s, and more lace, boots and wax.

An analysis of these accounts shows that the expenses of the exhibition were high in relation to the entrance fee of only 1s. Although Marie probably covered her costs, the profits must have been small. She had to keep moving, needing to find new venues.

In December 1814 Marie took her wax museum to Bath for the first time and advertised her arrival in the *Bath Journal* of 5 December.

Madame Tussaud, Artist. J. Tussaud, Proprietor, most respectfully informs the Nobility, Gentry, and Public of Bath and its vicinity that the Grand European Collection of Figures, as large as life, consisting of Eighty-Three Public Characters, which has lately been exhibited in Paris, London, Dublin etc., is now open for Public Inspection in the Great Exhibition-Room and various other Apartments, at No. 2 Westgate Buildings.

Now sixteen years old and well trained by his mother, Joseph was playing an increasingly important role in the running of the exhibition. However, although he was growing up, Marie was determined to remain in control. This was the only time his name appeared as 'proprietor' on an advertisement.

The Westgate Buildings are in the lower part of the entertainment centre of Bath and within sight of the Theatre Royal, where the revival of 'Mother Goose' was 'hailed with the most cheering and unequivocal marks of applause. Grimaldi puts the house in good humour the instant he presents himself, and by a thousand whimsical pranks contrives to keep the audience in an incessant roar of laughter and applause till the fall of the curtain.'[20]

The height of the Bath season was in the winter, when the fashionable came to take the waters and to be seen at all the right places. This was the Bath of Jane Austen's novels, when the theatres were full and the libraries and Assembly Rooms well attended. Balls were frequent and a daily list of arrivals was published in the *Bath Journal*. Madame Tussaud's waxworks, with her parade of the famous, was an entertainment not to be missed.

Marie kept travelling and kept adding new figures to her exhibition. From Bath in 1815 she went into Devon and Cornwall. When she took her exhibition to Portsmouth, she advertised a new portrait of Napoleon taken, she said, while he was a prisoner on the *Bellerophon* at Torbay awaiting deportation to St Helena. Napoleon had escaped from Elba at the beginning of 1815, landed in France near Cannes and had forged northwards for 100 days gathering an army all the way. Louis XVIII fled from Paris when Napoleon entered the city on 20 March. Napoleon then travelled north with all speed, determined to crush the allied armies, but was finally defeated at Waterloo and taken prisoner. It is quite possible that Marie saw him when he was imprisoned on the *Bellerophon*, citing her earlier meeting, but it is perhaps more likely that this portrait was made from memory.

On leaving Cornwall Marie travelled back to London via Salisbury, Newbury and Reading, and by September 1816 was installed in the Magnificent Mercatura at 29 St James's Street, London. Here she was able to stay for eighteen months. To borrow from Dickens's novel, *The Old Curiosity Shop*:

When the festoons were all put up as tastily as they might be, the stupendous collection was uncovered, and there displayed, on a raised platform some two feet from the floor, running round the room and parted from the rude public by a crimson rope breast high, divers sprightly effigies of celebrated characters, singly and in groups, clad in glittering dresses of various climes and times, and standing more or less unsteadily on their legs, with their eyes very wide open, and their nostrils very much inflated. And the muscles of their legs and arms very strongly developed, and all their countenances expressing great surprise. All the gentlemen were very pigeon-breasted and very blue about the beards; and all the ladies were miraculous figures; and all the ladies and gentlemen were looking intensely nowhere, and staring with extraordinary earnestness at nothing.[21]

Joseph, now eighteen, began to look for other ways to earn money. First he advertised himself as a teacher in the art of wax fruit modelling, for a fee of 3 guineas, and shortly afterwards added a new advertisement for 'a profile machine' with which he could make silhouette portraits at a cost of 2s.[22] An ingenious structure still in use today, the *camera lucida* consists of a right-angled prism mounted on a brass rod, the base of which is clamped to the table. Looking through an eye-hole the artist sees a clear reflection of his subject on the paper, and an accurate silhouette portrait can be made by drawing around the outline. The apparatus was simple, lightweight and could be used in full daylight, unlike the *camera obscura* which was more complex. The *camera lucida* was ideal for a travelling show like the waxworks exhibition.[23] Joseph would have had plenty of time to perfect his use of the profile machine as the waxworks stayed in London for eighteen months until early 1818. During this time the new Waterloo Bridge was opened, named to commemorate the decisive battle. It must have been a relief to both Marie and Joseph to remain in one place for more than a few weeks. It offered them a chance to renew old friendships and time to replace and repair some of the wax figures, but above all it gave them a much-needed respite from the rigours of the road.

FOURTEEN

Tussaud & Sons

At the beginning of 1818 it was time for Marie, Joseph and the other members of the travelling exhibition to move on. They went first to Rochester. There is a story concerning this visit which was to be retold many times in various guises, as part of the publicity and promotion for the exhibition. At the Rochester exhibition, a lady visitor, 'after making her observations on the several Figures', came to one of an officer:

> 'Well, Sir,' said she, with great naiveite [sic], 'and pray who are you?' To her great surprise and confusion the supposed model bowed very politely, and replied, 'My name, madam, is Captain B——, of the —— regiment, and very much at your service.' On recovering herself the lady wittily observed, 'I beg pardon Capt. ——, for my mistake, and must confess that in the involuntary compliment which I have paid to the Exhibition, I cut rather a sorry *figure* myself.'[1]

By the middle of November 1818 Madame Tussaud had arrived in Cambridge with her collection of 'Whole-length Composition Figures' consisting of 'Ninety Public Characters' to open at the Concert Room at the Black Bear Inn in Market Street. The advertisement in the *Cambridge Chronicle* warned that it would be 'Positively for a very short time'. On 4 December the reporter for the newspaper wrote:

> There is something peculiarly interesting in a good exhibition of this nature. A gallery of paintings, or a cabinet of medals, affords but a faint resemblance, at the best, of the illustrious dead; but in

a well executed display of figures the characters of the past and the present day are brought before the eye, with all the force of the *actually* erect and almost speaking image in its proper costume. – We cannot recommend a higher, or more rational treat than an Inspection of the Collection now open to the public in the Concert Room.[2]

On 11 December, as the reporter noted, the exhibition was still drawing crowds:

We have been highly gratified by the numerous specimens of talent displayed by the respectable *Artiste*. The resemblance to the human face divine in the portrait models is admirable; the ground colour of their flesh – the varied tints of nature – the lustre of the eye – the anatomy of the head, are managed with a skill which cannot be surpassed. *Voltaire* is inimitably fine; the emaciated philosopher and poet seems to breathe, and when contemplating his singularly expressive face, the spectator almost fancies that the lips are open and are about to address him. . . . We strongly recommend a visit to the Concert Room to the preceptors and others having young persons under their care, as a view of the Figures will awaken in their minds a desire to open the pages of history and biography, and be the means of their deriving much useful knowledge, as well as rational amusement. The *coup d'oeil* will be found particularly pleasing when the room is lighted up in the evening.[3]

Dickens's Mrs Jarley also recommended her exhibition to young people and waited upon the boarding-schools in person, 'with a handbill composed expressly for them, in which it was distinctly proved that wax-work refined the mind, cultivated the taste, and enlarged the sphere of the human understanding'.[4]

A correspondent to the *Cambridge Chronicle* on 25 December was moved to verse:

'Tis a common opinion, and justly believ'd,
That sight, of all senses, is soonest deceiv'd:

If a doubt should exist, the most obstinate mind
A perfect conviction might easily find.
While Tussaud's collection of Figures remains,
Which from all ranks and ages due praises obtains.
Its merits elude all the force of the pen;
Give beauty to women, true spirit to men.[5]

The exhibition closed a few days after Christmas and in the New Year headed north again up the east coast of England, first to Norwich, Lincoln, Newark and Nottingham, then across to Derby, Sheffield, Wakefield, Leeds and Manchester. The exhibition continued to be successful despite the poverty and unrest in the north, culminating in the infamous Peterloo Massacre which took place at St Peter's Field in Manchester on 16 August 1819.

Early in the next year, on 29 January 1820, George III died. He was a tragic figure who for some years had been living in his own mad world, confined in a wing of Windsor castle. Neglected by his family and forgotten by his people, he talked incessantly, but his only companions were his keepers and servants. He was succeeded by the Prince Regent, now George IV. Coronation scenes were always popular with the public and in October Marie, now based at the Exchange in Manchester, advertised that: 'The Magnificent Throne got up by Messrs Petrie and Walker of St. Ann's Street which has been some time in preparation, is now ready for inspection.'[6] It was essential that her display stayed up to date, and by December she had 'a likeness of His most gracious Majesty King George IV, taken from a bust executed by an eminent artist within the last three weeks'. This bust was 'Universally allowed to be one of the best likenesses ever taken'.

In 1821, while Marie was exhibiting in Liverpool, Napoleon died on St Helena. One of the first tableaux she had created for the Assembly Rooms was that of Napoleon's Coronation, based on her old friend Jacques Louis David's famous painting. Many years before, she had known and modelled Napoleon, Josephine and David from life, in Paris. Now Napoleon and Josephine were dead, and David was an old man living in exile in Belgium. As David had used her death-mask of Marat in 1793 to create his famous picture, now Marie, twenty-eight years later, used his painting of Napoleon's coronation to create a much-admired tableau.

Towards the end of June she announced in the *Liverpool Mercury* that the exhibition would have to close as she was taking it to Dublin. This was to coincide with the visit of George IV to Ireland in August, as part of his coronation celebrations. In July she advertised that, owing to the postponement of her departure, the exhibition would remain open. This was her usual trick to attract more visitors, and she also announced a new full-length portrait of George IV in his coronation robes. It was a common publicity ploy, also used by Dickens's Mrs Jarley, who 'commanded an announcement to be prepared, to the effect that the stupendous collection would only remain in its present quarters one day longer'. The next day the exhibition remained closed, but the following day another announcement was produced:

> wherein it was stated, that, in consequence of numerous enquiries at the wax-work door, and in consequence of crowds having been disappointed in obtaining admission, the Exhibition would be continued for one week longer and would re-open the next day. . . . Mrs Jarley sat in the pay place, chinking silver moneys from noon to night, and solemnly calling upon the crowd to take notice that the price of admission was only sixpence, and that the departure of the whole collection, on a short tour among the Crowned Heads of Europe, was positively fixed for that day week.[7]

Beside the figure of George IV, Marie had a model of Queen Caroline, his estranged wife. She was barred from the coronation ceremony when the doors of the abbey were shut in her face, and she was humiliatingly turned away. The annuity of £50,000 awarded to her by Parliament was no compensation, and the public were outraged and saddened by her unexpected death at the beginning of August. The *Liverpool Mercury* reflected the thoughts of many of its readers:

The sacrifice is at an end! The agony of the victim has subsided in death! Caroline, Queen of England is no more! – The most persecuted woman of the present day, after having displayed a strength of female fortitude of which there are few parallels in history, has expired in the midst of a people who admired and loved her, but neglected by those whose duty it was to protect and honour her. At twenty-five minutes past ten on the evening of Tuesday last, died Caroline of Brunswick! A woman of whom it will be said, to the disgrace of the country, that her sorrows began almost with the first step that she set upon our shore.[8]

Marie had booked passages for herself, Joseph and her party on the *Earl Moira*, sailing from Liverpool to Dublin to arrive there in time for George IV's coronation visit. It was to be a terrifying voyage. When they set sail from Liverpool on 8 August, a wild storm wrecked their vessel with severe loss of life. The ship struck first on Burbo Bank and then on Wharf Bank, where it went aground. Local papers later reported that the captain was drunk. When the passengers realised the captain was too inebriated to navigate, they demanded that the ship return to Liverpool, but he refused to turn back, insisting there was no danger. The waves were monumental and crashed on to the deck, tearing it apart and washing many of the passengers overboard.

One tremendous wave which struck the weather bow, carried off from ten to fifteen poor souls at once. Men, women and children, who seemed to be in the greatest agonies, were now washed away, and every succeeding wave appeared to mark its victims; the survivors had scarcely time to breathe between each. One man jumped overboard and was for some time seen struggling towards the shore, supported on a trunk or box.[9]

Rescue craft put to sea but only about 50 passengers were saved out of an estimated 100 or more persons on board, including a crew of 6. The captain was one of those who drowned. The rescued passengers were put ashore wherever a landing could be made along the coast.

From a privately published family record, *Annals from our Ancestors*, comes the story of what happened to Marie and her party:

One stormy evening Mrs Ffarington [the author's great-aunt] and her two daughters, Susan and Mary Hannah, with some guests staying in the house were sitting after their dinner in a room called the morning room, a comfortable apartment leading off the hall in the front of the house, Worden, Preston. They heard footsteps on the gravel outside and heard the bell ring and one of the servants go across the hall to the door. A colloquy seemed to be taking place amidst a babel of voices which no one could understand. Mrs Ffarington's curiosity was aroused and she went to the door herself where she found the butler being addressed in voluble French by a party of people outside. She brought them inside and found them to be a little company of foreigners who had suffered shipwreck on their way to Dublin. The leader of the party was Madame Tussaud, a middle-aged lady who had fled from Paris during the Reign of Terror, after having been a favourite of the Royal Family and suspect in consequence, and having been forced by the Communists to exercise her art of wax modelling on the decapitated heads of many of their victims. She brought some of her models to London and started an exhibition there afterwards touring with them about the country.

The shipwreck cast her and the survivors of her party on the Lancashire coast and all her possessions went to the bottom except one small box which the unfortunate companions carried between them when they all started to walk to Preston which they were told was the nearest town. Darkness fell on them and they struggled along in the rain and wind soaked to the skin and caked with Lancashire mud. They mistook their road and instead of arriving at Preston they found themselves at the lodge gates of Worden. How they got past the lodge I don't know, but they arrived at the house as described and were taken in and housed. Supper was got ready and dry clothing and they turned out to be such charming and interesting people that their stay was prolonged for several days. The small box contained miniature models of various historical figures, and Madame Tussaud announced her intention of setting to work at once on fresh life-sized models of those that had been lost. Mrs Ffarington took her upstairs to a room where a number of old chests were kept, full of old costumes which had belonged to former members of the family, and presented her with a good many of these to clothe her new figures and help her restart her exhibition. In addition to this Mrs John Mathew [Mrs Ffarington's step-sister] at North Shields also became interested in Madame Tussaud and gave her a quantity of valuable old Venetian lace.[10]

This story is interesting for several reasons. Unless Madame Tussaud kept a store of moulds for the heads somewhere in England, it appears that she could remodel them at will from miniatures. If this is so, then many of the 'authentic models' are made from what she remembered, rather than from original casts. This in no way belittles her collection, for she was in every sense an artist, but it gives an insight into her working methods and adds another dimension to the exhibition. If she did keep a store of moulds in England and only travelled with a certain number of her figures, then where was this repository situated? The story also shows her indomitable courage and energy. Her ability to brush off this major disaster and set to work immediately on a new display demonstrates why she was so successful. It is interesting to note the version of her own past history that she told to her hostess. As a royalist and an unwilling victim of the Revolution, she would have received a warm welcome in England.

* * *

At the same time as this drama was taking place in England, 21-year-old François Tussaud set out from Paris to join his mother and elder brother, whom he had not seen for nineteen years. François, brought up by his father and grandmother, Madame Waltner, seems to have tried a variety of occupations, none of which suited him.

Apprenticed initially to a grocer, he disliked the occupation intensely and so he was removed and articled to an architect, a profession he enjoyed. However, his father decided that the cost of completing this training was more than he wished to pay, and instead put him to work with a maker of billiard tables. Here he learned carving and wood-turning but, finding this less than satisfying, he decided to try his luck in England.

Francis, as he now called himself, landed at Dover and set out to walk to London. He had bought a supply of cheap ship's biscuit to feed himself and an old military knapsack which contained his clothes. The first night he slept under a haystack, but was woken early in the morning by some farm labourers who, because he spoke no English, thought him to be a foreign deserter. When he was taken in front of the mayor of the nearest town, he explained his situation to the French-speaking official and was immediately freed. Eventually he arrived in Liverpool at the time of the shipwreck, and was horrified to hear of the supposed drowning of his mother and brother. He was about to return to Paris, when a message arrived to say that they had been saved. His son Victor said:

> The meeting was of a most affecting description, both overcome with emotion were unable to speak for some minutes. She was delighted to receive him, and placed him at once in all respects on an equal footing with Joseph, who, greatly to his credit received and greeted him with utmost cordiality. Thus mother and son were reunited for the first time since their separation after a lapse of so many years.[11]

After the shipwreck, Madame Tussaud and her party, now with the welcome addition of Francis, returned to Liverpool and remade their lost figures with all speed. It seems likely that, as they were going to Ireland for a special coronation exhibition, they had only taken part of their collection with them and had left the rest in Liverpool. The exhibition was reopened and remained in Liverpool from August until the end of November 1821. They exhibited over Christmas at the Exchange Rooms in Manchester and from there embarked on a major tour of the north-west of England, staying in towns sometimes for a few weeks and sometimes for a few months. Over the next year and a half Marie exhibited at Preston, Warrington, Blackburn, Chester, Shrewsbury, Kidderminster, Birmingham and Coventry, where she stayed for three months. Francis, although he had a passport, still had to report from time to time to the magistrates in the towns where they stopped. The war against France had only recently ended and all foreigners, especially Frenchmen, were objects of suspicion. Francis observed to his son Victor that 'it was much in the same manner as a ticket of leave man has to report himself to the police'.[12]

From Coventry Marie went south to Cheltenham and Bristol, where she stayed from August to the end of the year, then at the beginning of 1824 Madame Tussaud's Cabinet of Curiosities staged a triumphant return to Bath. She announced her arrival in the *Bath Chronicle* of 17 January:

> Positively for a short time. Will be opened in a few days of which due notice will be given. In the New Bazaar, Quiet Street. Which will be splendidly fitted up to represent the Throne Room, Carlton Palace. Forming a gallery of upwards of 80 feet in length. A Magnificent Promenade, splendid Coronation Groups. Which have lately been viewed in Liverpool, Manchester, the Theatre Royal, Birmingham, Assembly Rooms, Cheltenham and in the Pavilion, Bristol, by 136,000 persons. Madame Tussaud. Artist to the late R. H. Madame Elisabeth, sister of Louis XVI, niece to the celebrated Courcis of Paris, patronised by his R. H. the Duke of York and her late R. H. the Duchess, by His Majesty Louis XVIII, by the late Royal Family of France, and by many of the first families of the Kingdom, hopes for a share of that patronage which will be her pride to merit.[13]

She advertised the two magnificent coronation groups of George IV and Bonaparte, 'both got up at an immense expense, and such as has never failed of giving general satisfaction'. Also a 'splendid group representing Mary Queen of Scots abdicating the Crown of

Scotland'. This group was copied from a celebrated picture in the Palace of Edinburgh, and was almost certainly the same group described by Charles Dickens some years later in his magazine, *All the Year Round*:

> The figure of John Knox . . . is advancing upon the unhappy Mary Queen of Scots (with whom he is supposed to be arguing) on the outside edge, threatening to 'crush her', not only metaphorically but practically, if she does not promptly yield to the force of his reasoning. The whole of this group is well worthy of attention, for is not Martin Luther blazing away at this injured lady on one side, while the Reverend Knox is skating dead at her on the other? Lord Darnley and John Calvin are standing behind her in different stages of intoxication, while the Queen of Scots herself is smiling feebly, and slipping slowly off her chair, in obvious idiocy produced by the noisy gentlemen on either side.[14]

Ignoring such mocking comments, 'Madame Tussaud assures the Nobility, Gentry, and the Public, that nothing shall be wanting to render the Collection worthy of support; and she therefore looks forward to the patronage of those Ladies and Gentlemen to whom the merits of the Collection are known. There will be a PROMENADE, accompanied by a Military Band, every day from 1 till 3, and from 7 in the evening till 10.'[15] Francis Tussaud later told his son Victor he believed that his mother, brother and himself had the distinction of being the original promoters of promenade concerts. The novelty of a band to accompany the evening promenade was started in about 1819, continuing later with the introduction of an orchestra and occasionally singers. Both Joseph and his brother Francis were skilled musicians, and these concerts gave the visitors the pleasure of listening to classical and popular music while strolling through the gallery.

The price of admission to the exhibition was still 1s, or you could take a subscriber's ticket for 5s which allowed unlimited access. The public were informed that 'the expense of this Establishment was upwards of £40 per week'. It was open every day from eleven in the morning till dark, and from half past six till ten at night, and, most important of all in a Bath winter, had 'fires kept night and day'.

The New Bazaar, now a restaurant, is an imposing 80-foot-long colonnaded hall on the first floor above a row of shops in Quiet Street. The space is well lit by lofty Georgian windows at each end and the walls ornamented by pillars and scalloped niches. It must have looked magnificent when filled with Madame Tussaud's elegant wax figures backed by mirrors and illuminated by numerous candelabra and oil lamps to show off the groups to their best advantage. Those of the *ton* who were in Bath were there to be seen as well as to see. The exhibition provided an ideal place to promenade elegantly, warmed by the ever-burning fires.

Madame Tussaud's Bath was an exciting place. The *Bath Chronicle* and the *Bath Herald* presented weekly a list of new arrivals, whose names were printed in order of precedence, with dukes at the top and majors at the bottom. All new arrivals to the city were asked to enter their names and addresses in the Bath Guide to ensure that they received suitable acknowledgement. There were other attractions in Bath that January. A Subscription Concert at the Assembly Rooms on 24 January was advertised for Subscribers, Nobility, Gentry and the Public. At the Theatre Royal Mr Sinclair presented 'Guy Mannering or, the Gypsy's Prophesy', and for light entertainment for the second half there was a Highland Fling by the Misses Giroux. On 28 January Monsieur Barnett, Professor of Magical Illusions, promised to perform 'a great number of Feats of Illusion. Among which Dancing and Speaking Money will answer any question the company may propose.' His show was such a success that he repeated it on 4 and 6 February and offered to produce a variety of Novel Experiments 'and repeat the Extraordinary Disappearance of a Person, there being rendered instantly invisible'.[16]

In February Wombwells' Royal National Menagerie arrived in Bath in two large touring wagons and opened in Dorchester Street. The menagerie included: 'A most beautiful HORSE WITH HORNS. That Extraordinary Animal the QUAGGA. The enormous yet sagacious MALE Elephant. The only male Elephant in England, who does tricks. And a multitude of monkeys, birds, and smaller animals.'[17]

Madame Tussaud continued to advertise weekly in the *Bath Chronicle*, as this encouraged favourable reviews. On 31 January one review ran: 'The charming exhibition of Madame Tussaud is one of the chief objects of attraction at present in our crowded city. It is honoured with the unqualified approbation of its numerous and fashionable visitors, and cannot fail but be delightful to all.'[18] And another, on 14 February, claimed that:

> The impression produced by this exhibition is totally different from other branches of the imitative art. In an assemblage of Statuary, we admire the conception, we are astonished at the sublimity of the forms before us, but the actual animation of the figures we contemplate never occurs to us. The pretensions of the Artist in Composition are not of so lofty a nature; perfect resemblance alone is aimed at, to form the boundary of the sculptor: but here, art, assisted by the colouring of nature, is added to the identical costume of real life; so that the work produced, with the exception of motion, is more than a resemblance, it is our neighbour himself: and while we walk through the silent ranks, our eyes unconsciously avoid their full gaze, as we involuntarily shrink from the steady observation of so large a company. Such are the impressions produced by this collection, universally allowed to have no equal in this kingdom, and which must be seen to be appreciated.[19]

As Mrs Jarley says: 'I won't go so far as to say, that, as it is, I have seen a wax-work quite like life, but I have certainly seen some life that was exactly like wax-work.'[20]

Four years after the coronation of George IV, coronation scenes were still popular and drew the crowds. A rival to Madame Tussaud's tableau opened in the Masonic Hall, York Street, at the end of February. Marshall's Original Panorama of the Coronation, Procession and Banquet had come direct from the Great Rooms, Spring Gardens, London. 'Marshall's Peristrephic Panorama has one view of the Coronation, and 5 views of 40ft each of the procession', its advertisement announced. 'The 7th view is the Banquet. The Panorama moves. A Full Military Band, drums, trumpets, etc. will perform the Coronation Music during the movements of the Panorama.' The admission charge of 2s for a box was a little higher than Marie's, though it was possible to sit in the gallery for 1s.

One of the main attractions for Bath society that winter was the Grand Fancy Dress Ball to be held in the Assembly Rooms at the end of February. The *Bath Chronicle* was awash with advertisements from costume suppliers such as Mr Solomon, Tailor and Habit Maker, 19 Charing Cross Road, London, who 'offers to forward to the Nobility and Gentry of Bath his Wardrobe of Fancy Ball dresses'. Dresses were also offered by J. Nathan at 20 New Bond Street who had 'A Parisian Repository at 14 George Street'.

Madame Tussaud, not a woman to miss a business opportunity, took advantage of the growing demand and inserted her own advertisement in the *Bath Chronicle*:

In consequence of the numerous applications for costumes which Madame Tussaud, Artist, has been honoured with from the Nobility, Gentry and Visitors to her Exhibition, she has the honour to inform them, that early in the ensuing week, of which due notice will be given, she expects an assortment from London, which will rival in brilliancy and propriety any hitherto offered for such occasions, comprising, Costumes of every nation; and which she has no doubt, from their elegance and the modest charges she purposes making for them, will meet the approbation of those who intend to honour her with their patronage and support.

It was not only costumes that were available in Bath. A 'Fashionable Wig and Choice Perfume Warehouse' at 6 Milson Street offered 'Gentleman's Dress crop Perukes and Ladies' ditto. Ladies' Grecian Head Dresses, Ladies' Fronts à la Madona or à la Coburg. Ladies' Frontlets or Ladies' Bandeaus.' Prices for these ranged from a high of £2 8s for a Grecian headdress, to a low of 5s for a Frontlet. Most important of all: 'The above articles are all warranted to retain their curl in any climate.'[21]

The Fancy Ball, as it was called, took place at the Assembly Rooms on Friday 27 February, and 'was graced by upwards of 500 persons of rank and fashion. Shortly after 9 o'clock, groups of well dressed figures presented themselves at the doors for admission.' The list of costumes described by the *Bath Chronicle* was long and eclectic, though how many were supplied by Madame Tussaud is impossible to know. There were many peasant costumes of varying nationalities, a Cinderella, a Mary Queen of Scots, a Fairy Sylph, a Mameluke, several Hindoo [sic] ladies and a Fair Star to mention but a few.

> The dancing was carried on with spirit; and after the country dance, quadrilles, waltzes, and sarabands, gave occupation pleasant enough. At one o'clock the Banquet was served. Breakfast was sumptuously served at five; after which till seven o'clock the next morning, none seemed to know that the day must end the pleasures of the night; indeed could the musicians have toiled on, it is probable that dancing would not have ceased till midday.[22]

A timely advertisement offered a welcome cure for a multitude of ills. 'Dr Solomon's Cordial Balm of Gilead. Relieves those persons, who by an immoderate indulgence of the passions, have ruined their constitutions.' The symptoms of this ruination were many: 'Affections of the Nervous System, Obstinate Gleets, Involuntary Emissions, Excesses, Irregularity, Obstruction of Various Evacuations, Weakness, Total Impotency, Barrenness etc.' This 'Cordial Balm' was a universally popular panacea and household remedy. When Marie was exhibiting in Liverpool in 1813 she had obtained permission to make a life-mask of the famous man himself, but Dr Solomon had panicked when she spread the plaster over his face and refused to let her continue. However, she did manage to make a model of him, and such was his fame that she exhibited his figure in the collection for many years.

Bath, at the height of the season, was the place to be, and Marie and her sons remained there, lauded by the *Bath Chronicle* and enjoyed by 'the first set', for nearly three months. They finally packed up and moved out on Saturday 3 April. There were several modes of travel open to them, by stagecoach, wagon, private carriage or on horseback. But all travelling was slow, even by the most modern transport. 'The *Shamrock*, a new light post coach, carrying only four inside passengers' took fifteen hours to reach London. The stagecoaches could take days. Marie and her sons may themselves have travelled by coach, but the increasingly large exhibition would have to be laboriously packed into large, slow wagons to be transported on to the next venue. From Bath the wagons lumbered east, calling at Cirencester, Oxford, Northampton, Peterborough and Stamford, reaching Cambridge in the autumn. The *Cambridge Chronicle* was happy to announce their arrival on 29 October 1824:

The Entirely New Exhibition has just come from Oxford, where it was visited by nearly 10,000 persons. Madame Tussaud, Artist, has the honour most respectfully to announce to the Nobility and Gentry of the University and the Town of Cambridge, that by kind permission of the Worshipful the Mayor and Magistrates she will have the HONOUR TO EXHIBIT her collection of COMPOSITION FIGURES in the Town Hall where she hopes to meet with patronage and support; and she begs to announce, that in testimony of her gratitude for so distinguished a favour, the whole of the amount taken on the first day's receipt, will be given, clear of every expense (with the approbation of the Mayor), for the benefit of Addenbrookes Hospital.[23]

Earlier that year there had been a smallpox outbreak in Cambridge, and Addenbrookes had supplied free vaccine for those wishing to be inoculated. Marie had learned that it was good for business to donate the first day's money to a local charity. The exhibition ran in Cambridge until 18 December.

In January the following year the Tussauds took their exhibition to the Assembly Rooms in Colchester, and then exhibited in eight different places in Essex, Norfolk and Lincolnshire. On each occasion the advertisements followed a pattern. Thanks were given to the local dignitaries, then an announcement made that the opening day's profits would be donated to a local hospital or a worthy cause. Any new figures or tableaux of topical events were given prominence in the advertisements. When attendance began to flag, another announcement was made that, owing to a future booking, the exhibition must close in a week or two. This created renewed interest and boosted the number of visitors. A further announcement was then made that, owing to popular demand, the exhibition would remain *in situ* for a further few weeks. Finally with a flourish of gratitude and thanks, the exhibition moved on to its next port of call, and the carefully planned scenario would start all over again. It was a formula that proved very successful, and one they stuck to throughout their travelling years.

Marie was now sixty-three, and had been on the road for twenty-three years, but she wasn't yet ready to settle down.

FIFTEEN

'The most unqualified approbation'

Marie had by now become accustomed to life on the road. Travelling with the wax figures, as she and her sons did, would have been arduous in those days of badly maintained highways, and dangerous too, with the ever-present threat of footpads and highwaymen. However, by her own hard work this indomitable woman had succeeded in making her exhibition one that was known and welcomed the length and breadth of the British Isles.

Heading north once again Marie continued to show her figures until she reached Edinburgh on 7 January 1828 for her last return visit. Here she exhibited for nearly four months in Gibbs Great Room, Waterloo Place. On 10 January, believing that the fame of her exhibition had preceded her, she placed a very small advertisement in the *Edinburgh Evening Courant*: 'Splendid promenade. Patronised by the Right Honourable Earl Provost and Magistrates of Edinburgh. Now open at the Carlton Convening Hall, Waterloo Place.' But this time her waxworks was not the only one in town. In the same paper on the same day a very much larger rival advertisement challenged her supremacy: 'Springthorpe's Extensive Collection of Composition Figures containing nearly two hundred noted Characters. All habited according to the age in which they lived. Admittance Ladies and gentlemen one shilling Children half price Descriptive Catalogues 6*d*.'

Stung by the competition, Madame Tussaud and her sons immediately sprang into action. On 14 January they inserted another advertisement in the *Edinburgh Evening Courant*, challenging the usurpers:

PATRONIZED by the Universities of Oxford and Cambridge.

Madame Tussaud, Artist, begs leave to solicit the attention of the lovers of Fine Arts to the merits of her exhibition, now open, as above-mentioned. Certain of the approbation of those who will honour her with a visit, she fearlessly relies on the liberality of the inhabitants of Edinburgh, knowing that merit has only to be known to meet with their support; and she trusts, therefore, that any prejudice excited by the view of other Exhibitions will be done away with by a personal inspection, as on any visitor expressing the least dissatisfaction, the Admission money will be returned.

As a result of this spirited attack, Springthorpe's Extensive Collection of Composition Figures retired defeated, and by 11 February Madame Tussaud announced triumphantly: 'As her visitors have already amounted to several thousands, she fearlessly states, that in no one instance had anyone expressed any other feeling but that of the most unqualified approbation.'

The winter of 1828 was severe in Edinburgh, and on 19 January the snow lay two inches deep. The *Edinburgh Evening Courant* advertised many other attractions to tempt people out. At the Theatre Royal there was Italian opera. On another day Mr Vandehoff performed *Hamlet*, and Mrs Siddons 'gave, as she always does, a beautiful and affecting portrait of Ophelia'. The tragedy was followed, on the same night, by the pantomime 'Mother Goose', 'which excited in no ordinary degree the merriment of the audience'. In February Mrs Siddons was appearing as Desdemona in *Othello*. For those who preferred more exotic entertainments, the Chinese Salon in Princes Street was offering:

Two Chinese Ladies, the only Female Natives of the 'Celestial Empire' ever seen in Europe. These most interesting and elegant objects of public curiosity are natives of the city of Congscc-Langlin-foo in China. Their very diminutive feet, scarcely exceeding three inches in length, and finger nails of nearly the same extent, are with them the most significant tokens of personal consideration and rank. Their dresses are according to the richest costume of their country.[1]

And in the Royal Amphitheatre, Ducrow, who had once worked for Astley's Circus, was astounding audiences with his equestrian and gymnastic performances.

During this stay in Edinburgh Marie modelled Sir Walter Scott, one of the most popular authors of the time, and advertised this on 18 February: 'Last week but one. New Addition. Portrait resemblance of the celebrated Sir Walter Scott.' As always there was an extension 'by popular demand', and Madame Tussaud finally moved on in April to the west coast of Scotland, where she showed in the Old Assembly Rooms, Assembly Street, Dumfries, from 22 April until after the Whitsuntide Fair on 31 May. Advertising in the *Dumfries and Galloway Courier*, 'she proposes, with the wishes of her visitors, to postpone her departure till after the Whitsuntide holidays, in order to afford her Country Friends an opportunity of viewing her collection'. From Dumfries Marie went down to Preston, then to Liverpool, where in 1829 she created a sensation by introducing a tableau of Burke and Hare, the body-snatchers. The case aroused a ghoulish interest as the details emerged of the lucrative trade practised by the duo, who murdered more than sixteen victims and then sold their bodies – for sums ranging from £8 to £14 – to anatomy schools starved of suitable cadavers. Marie first modelled Burke from sketches made at the trial in Edinburgh. Joseph modelled Hare, who saved himself by turning king's evidence, then Joseph took a death-mask of Burke who was hanged on 28 January.

Marie's next incentive for a new tableau came while she was exhibiting in Shrewsbury, in the great Assembly Rooms. Early on Saturday 3 July 1830 George IV died, weakened by a life of over-indulgence. The tableau of George IV's coronation was supplanted by that of the new king, William IV, surrounded by six figures standing under a magnificent canopy.

Although Joseph had been with his mother since she first arrived in England in 1802, and Francis had joined them in 1821, Marie still kept a firm control over the running of the exhibition. Both her sons had become skilled wax modellers, and were active in everything to do with the exhibition. Both were musicians, and played in the orchestra, and Francis was also a sculptor. They were now married 31-year-old Joseph had married Elizabeth Babbington, and their first son, Francis Babbington, was born in 1829, while 29-year-old Francis was married to Rebecca Smallpage, and in 1831 they, too, had a son, Joseph Randall. Marie was to see many more grandchildren. Joseph and his wife would have three children, and Francis and Rebecca, nine. Victor, who passed down many anecdotes about the early days of the waxworks, was Francis's third son, born in 1842.

Marie, accompanied by her ever-increasing family, continued to zigzag down the country until she reached Bristol, arriving on 3 September 1831. A few days later their exhibition opened at the Assembly Rooms in Princes Street. This was a time of great unrest throughout Britain. The Reform Bill, aiming to increase the franchise, had been thrown out by the House of Lords. The people were insistent that they must have greater representation, and the bishops and lords were just as insistent that they would not forgo their exclusivity by extending the franchise. When the Bill was overthrown, there were numerous riots and acts of violence around the country. Angry protesters broke the windows of Apsley House, the London home of the Duke of Wellington, who was against the Bill. When Marie first arrived in Bristol all seemed reasonably calm, but on 22 October, the 'Last week but two' of her show, Marie announced that the exhibition would be 'unavoidably closed for one day only, on Thursday next, October 27, in consequence of the Assembly Room being required for a public meeting, and will be re-opened at the usual hours on the following day, Friday'. This public meeting, which concerned the Reform Bill, was the forerunner to the terrifying Bristol riots which started on Saturday 29 October 1831 and engulfed the town. The riots disrupted the community, destroyed lives and property, and sent entertainers fleeing for safety. Once again Marie found herself at the heart of an uprising.

Four editions of the *Bath Journal* were printed on 31 October, as it tried to keep up with the unfolding drama:

Saturday, very riotous proceedings marked the day in Bristol. The arrival of Sir Charles Wetherell, the Recorder, being expected by 10 o'clock several thousand persons had assembled at Totterdown awaiting his approach. At half-past ten his arrival was announced, he was attended by 4 or 500 special constables, with bludgeons or staves. The moment he came within sight of the population, execrations, yells and groans were uttered, loud and deep. Several volleys of stones were thrown. Dense masses of people thronged all the road. The Recorder reached the Guildhall, and proceeded to open the Commission, but from the groans and yells not a word could be held. Sir C. threatened in vain to commit; the noise increased. Constables were then sent into the body of the Hall to seize the offenders. The people then began coughing, so that still not a word of the Commission could be heard. When concluded, three tremendous cheers were given for the king which was echoed by the thousands outside. Afterwards Sir C. proceeded to the Mansion House, amidst continued groans. The mob entered the Mansion House. Another volley of stones was thrown, fortunately without injury. Two or three windows were broken. A slight scuffle now ensued between the mob and special constables, and two or three were taken into custody. A general rush was then made by the people to the Quay, where they armed themselves with bludgeons. The crowd increased, more windows were broken. At five o'clock the riot act was read; immediately after which every window, frames and all, in the Mansion House was smashed to pieces. The town was one scene of disorder, noise and confusion, loud huzzaing from the people, and soldiers riding up and down.

The riots went on all night and into the next day. Sir Charles, who had taken refuge in the Mansion House, managed to escape in disguise, by a back way. 'The crowd broke into the Mansion House but were repelled. On Sunday morning they assembled again in Queen's Square and once again broke into the Mansion House and entered the cellar and drank, or spilled the wine.' There were people rolling about in the street intoxicated with spirits. 'Business is at a

225

stand. Female chastity has no protection, the violation of every Law, characterises the insurgents.' A company of soldiers had just arrived and 2,000 more special constables were sworn in. The Mansion House was fired, as was the Bishop's Palace. The hated Tollbooths on the Princes Street Bridge were smashed. The County Gaol was broken into, the prisoners freed and then the gaol set alight; the same thing happened at the Bridewell prison.

The third edition of the *Bath Journal* was issued at eleven o'clock. 'At this hour when our informant left, a great part of Queen's Square was burnt to the ground – fully three parts much damaged – only one side of the square was left entire. The populace would not allow a fire engine to come near them.'[2] Madame Tussaud only just managed to save her collection from the fires in Queen's Square. Felix Farley's *Bristol Journal*, reported the situation:

> It was stated that among other places the Assembly Rooms were marked out for destruction containing at the time their valuable collection of figures. These at an immense risk of injury, were partly removed as hastily as circumstances would permit. The house in which Madame T. lodged on the opposite side of the street was among the number that became ignited from the firing of the West side of the Square, and we regret to hear that the lady's constitution received a severe shock.[3]

Once the Assembly Rooms had been marked for burning, Joseph, Francis and the assistants only just had enough time to get the figures out to safety before it was torched. Eventually, after several days of fierce fighting, the rioters were brought under control. Many of the buildings were looted before they were fired and valuable furniture and paintings lost. Twelve people were killed and many more injured.

The Tussauds were not the only entertainers to be affected by the riots. Ducrow's Company, famed for their equestrian feats and *poses plastique*, arrived in Bristol during the week of the uprising, on the night of Saturday 5 November, having engaged the theatre for a month. There was still fighting in the streets. They armed themselves and stood by all night to repel the rioters, but the situation was so dangerous that they left Bristol late the next day, at about eleven o'clock in the evening. Marie, who had survived many such uprisings in Revolutionary Paris, had certainly not expected to be confronted by revolution in England, but she refused to be intimidated. Having saved her wax figures from destruction, she packed up and went to Bath, arriving on 14 November, a little earlier than expected.

Back in Bath for the third and last time, Marie, now aged seventy, opened her exhibition in the Masonic Hall, York Street. She advertised in the *Bath Herald*: 'By permission of the Worshipful the Mayor, Madame Tussaud and Sons have the honour to announce that their splendid exhibition which in 1822 [1824] met with the most flattering reception from the liberal public of Bath will be open for inspection.' New figures included Lord Brougham 'in his Coronation Robe', His Majesty William IV, Mr Canning, Louis-Philippe and Charles X (her one-time friend Comte d'Artois, brother to Madame Elisabeth).

On 19 November the *Bath Herald* reported:

The Masonic Hall is now the abode of perhaps the most singular assemblage of Characters that ever were seen familiarly mixed under the same roof. . . . The arrangement is admirable and the light effective. The approbation of the entire kingdom has been bestowed most unreservedly upon this most interesting collection, and we doubt not that it will be as extensively patronised here as it has been in the other cities where it has been exhibited.

The exhibition remained in Bath over Christmas and continued to receive fulsome praise from the *Bath Herald*:

We conceive it to be no little merit in Madame Tussaud's Figures that rational beings, greatly aware that they are entering upon a collection of Effigies, should be unable to distinguish between the imitation and the reality till they observe the want of motion. In the coronation group of Bonaparte, the principal figure reminds us forcibly of the celebrated picture by David, the imposing attitude of the chief personage placing the diadem on his own brow, brings to mind the commanding spirit of the Exile of St Helena, once the ruler of half Europe. The good old Lady's effigy of herself is an excellent specimen of the fidelity of the art. – We were grateful to observe a numerous company enjoying the Promenade, enlivened by the excellent quadrille band.

There were other worthy entertainments to brighten up the Bath season. In the Bazaar Rooms in Quiet Street, Mr Lloyd was offering a 'Morning Course of Four Astronomical lectures, illustrated by the DIOASTRODOXON, or Grand Transparent Orrery'. Another more famous celebrity, Signor Paganini, was appearing in the Bath Assembly Rooms. Following a tour through Europe, 'astonishing the world with his matchless performance on the fourth string alone',[4] Signor Paganini had begun his English tour to much acclaim at the King's Theatre in London in June 1831. It was rumoured, quite untruthfully, that he had been a political victim, locked in a dungeon for twenty years, and that he had acquired his amazing dexterity by playing all day long on a broken violin with only one string. Although his concert in Bath was reviewed by the *Bath Chronicle* with less approbation than Tussaud's exhibition, and was reported as having an 'indifferent success, the house not being even half full', Marie added the figure of Signor Paganini to her exhibition. When she closed her show at the Masonic Hall on 14 January 1832, Mr Lloyd took her place with his Dioastrodoxon.

Once again Marie set off on tour. She made a last circuit across to Oxford, down to Portsmouth and then east to Canterbury and Dover. From there she headed west to Maidstone and then Rochester, where she exhibited in the converted theatre from 24 September to the beginning of November, and so, finally, reached London, arriving at the Green Man, Blackheath, in December 1833, and taking £344 in a few weeks. Over the next eighteen months, between December 1833 and March 1835, she remained in London, moving from one location to another. From Blackheath she went to the London Bazaar in Gray's Inn Road, where she took the

Assembly Rooms on the first floor for six months.[5] Although most of the newspaper reviews were adulatory, one is more honestly critical and probably gives a truer picture of the figures in the exhibition:

> This art of working in wax has been applied with great ingenuity to some imitations of nature, more especially of anatomical preparations. It has never been brought, however, to copies of the human countenance. In general the vapid velvet face with its gazing but unspeculating eyes, is consigned to the perruquier's window, without any remonstrance or regret on the part of the lovers of *virtu*. In the productions of Madame Tussaud and her sons, a bold attempt is made to overcome the blemish which has hitherto almost rendered their art contemptible. In many of their heads there is evidently a laboured effort to be true to their models, while in the management of the eyes they have also succeeded in imparting to the glass something of meaning. The large room in which this exhibition is displayed has been prepared for it with great care and expense. One end is occupied with a representation of the coronation of his present Majesty, in which there are seven figures, viz., the King, the Queen, Earl Grey, the Chancellor, the Duke of Wellington, the Archbishop of Canterbury, and the Bishop of Norwich. In this, group we may not call it, but set of figures, we cannot praise the skill of the artists. That of the King alone appears to produce a *vraisemblante* effect. The other end of the room is occupied by a similar subject, representing the coronation of Bonaparte. This is better than its companion. The two Mamelukes in particular are well executed and their costume picturesquely arranged. The countenance of the Pope is not successful, nor has the expression of Napoleon the sternness which it bears in David's picture from whence this is copied. Round the sides of the room are disposed smaller groups and single figures; some on platforms, some on pedestals, and a few on the floor. Amongst these some are well worthy of notice. The Princess Charlotte comes nearest to perfection of any figure in the exhibition. Her face is rather too handsome; but it has a

startling semblance of life. We cannot say much for the other members of the Royal Family. Mrs Siddons as Queen Catherine is a good copy from Marlowe's picture and would give a strong notion of the great actress in this celebrated part. The John Kemble, in Hamlet, is in every way inferior; the face is much too attenuated, and the figure deficient in size and stateliness. . . . The decoration of this apartment and the costumes are very rich, and, where the whole is aided by the effect of lamplight, it becomes highly interesting; the mellow artificial illumination throwing a deeper tone over the flesh colour to the figures, and rendering the glare of the glass eyes less remarkable. Those, therefore, who visit this exhibition in the evening, will see it to most advantage besides having the pleasure of hearing the musical efforts of Messrs. Tussaud and the Fishers. We shall, in concluding, remark that there are figures of Burke and Hare, the murderers, in this collection, and with almost the reality of life about them. They should be got out of the chief room, and into that ghastly apartment in which the masques of Robespierre, Carrier, and the figures of Marat, Stewart, Holloway and Corder are kept.[6]

Charles Dickens, who visited Madame Tussaud's a few years later, was likewise not impressed by the figure of John Kemble:

We are told by the pamphlet, that 'whether we view him as an actor or an author, we shall find that he possessed wonderful talent'. It being extremely difficult to view this gentleman as an actor in the present day, we are compelled to content ourselves with viewing him in wax, the result of which scrutiny is, that whether he was possessed of a wonderful talent or not, he was certainly possessed of very wonderful legs; of a wonderful power of keeping upright upon them; and of a presence, generally calculated to affect the spectator with profound depression.[7]

Today, particularly in Madame Tussaud's and the recently refurbished Musée Grevin in Paris, where some of the earlier wax figures are exhibited alongside their modern equivalents, it is interesting to compare the realistic results obtained from modern materials with the smooth waxiness of the nineteenth-century figures.

During their six-month stay at the London Bazaar, from 26 December 1833 to June 1834, the exhibition earned £1,103 in admission fees. When the lease ran out, they moved to the Lowther Rooms off the Strand, where they exhibited from 20 June to 15 August. During that time Marie took £202, but the various expenses for setting up the rooms came to £120, so the overall profit was small. It was not easy during this time in London to get a long lease on a suitable hall. As the number of figures increased, and they built more elaborate settings, the cost of moving the exhibition from one venue to the next became higher. According to Victor Tussaud, his grandmother had a very personal system of accounting. Such items as money for rent, gas and insurance were put aside and accumulated until the payments became due. After paying wages and incidental expenses, the balance, if any, was divided by two. Whatever this sum, one half was used for improving the attractions of the exhibition, and the other half divided between the Tussauds in three equal shares. There were many weeks when the Tussauds' income was very small.[8] This must have been especially difficult for Joseph and Francis with growing families to support.

From the Lowther Rooms they moved to Grove House, Camberwell, for two months, then went on to the Mermaid Inn at Hackney, then back to the London Bazaar in Gray's Inn Road at the end of December 1834.

Francis, with his architectural knowledge, had become skilled at building new sets for the exhibition. For the latest move he had designed and built a 'Magnificent and Unequalled Portable Decoration, superior to any ever exhibited representing a Golden Corinthian Saloon'. According to the records, this wonderful setting cost more than £1,000; and would certainly have enhanced the exhibition, but it must have added greatly to the cost of the constant moving. Ten new lamps were bought that year for £23 10s, which sum included repairs to twenty-eight other lamps and hire of a further twenty-four lamps for six months. They also bought one gross of lamp cottons for 8 guineas. On 29 December the new and elaborate presentation displayed the coronation groups and tableaux to wonderful effect. The critics were impressed. During the three months they stayed at the London Bazaar, however, the Tussauds' profits were small.

While Marie was exhibiting in London she was approached by the Dean of Westminster, who was concerned about the condition of the collection of wax effigies in Westminster Abbey. Made to commemorate various sovereigns throughout the ages, they had been carried in their funeral processions. Many were very old, and had fallen into a dirty and dilapidated condition, and were known as 'The Ragged Army'. The Dean, according to Victor, said to Madame Tussaud:

> Madame, I have called on you with reference to our figures at the Abbey which are in sad need of repair. I therefore beg of you to be so good as to undertake their necessary renovation and make them fit for public inspection.
>   'Sare,' said the old lady in her usual blunt and abrupt manner, 'See you sare, I have a shop of my own to look after, and I do not look after other people's shops.'[9]

Marie, always keen to take every opportunity to promote her own exhibition, could evidently see no useful purpose in repairing wax figures for the Dean of Westminster.

There was to be one last move for Madame Tussaud. In March 1835 she took her exhibition to The Bazaar at the corner of Baker Street and Portman Square. Once again, the cost of moving the figures, props, costumes and scenery was considerable. The building into which they now moved was large, and had once been the living quarters and stables of the Royal Life Guards Regiment. When it ceased to be a barracks in 1820 it was used for a variety of other purposes, and became known simply as The Bazaar. At the beginning of the nineteenth century bazaars were promoted as venues where it was acceptable for women to keep stalls and sell goods. They usually had a doorman for security and to give some protection against unwelcome harassment, and, as in this case, the premises could also be leased for exhibitions.[10]

Madame Tussaud's exhibition was shown in a large room on the top floor, once the guards' mess room. Underneath this exhibition room there was a residence, at 58 Baker Street, where the family could live. The rooms were adjacent to the Panklibanon Iron Works, which sold household ironware of every variety, and an open space at the back was used as a show place for the sale and display of carriages.[11] It was also used as a cattle market. When Marie and her sons moved into Baker Street they had no intention of making it their permanent home. They regarded it as merely another exhibition space where they would stay for as long as the business was good. Joseph and Francis, with their growing families, may have found the constant moving difficult, but the exhibition was their life.

Having stayed at Baker Street for sixteen months, in September 1836 Joseph went down to Brighton in order to book the Town Hall for their next move. While he was negotiating the deal, the death occurred, in Manchester, of the much-loved opera singer Madame Malibran. Only twenty-eight, she was very beautiful and had been married for just a few months to the celebrated violinist M. de Beriot. Her husband was so shocked by her sudden and unexpected death that he fled, leaving others to arrange her funeral. The newspapers seized on the story, and for a while they were full of little else. Francis Tussaud immediately made a model of the singer in her most famous role, that of Lucia di Lammermoor. The response from the public was overwhelming. People thronged to Madame Tussaud's to look at the beautiful likeness of the tragic singer. Attendance doubled, and Joseph was recalled from Brighton. It was then the Tussauds realised that if they selected the right figures they would not need to travel the country. They could do just as well by staying in one place. A long lease for the first floor of the Baker Street gallery was thus negotiated with Mr Boulnois, the proprietor.[12]

For many years her friends and family had pressed Marie to write down her still vivid memories of her early life, including her experiences in Paris during the revolutionary years. But she was not a writer, and anyway she was always too busy. But now, possibly because she was getting older, or possibly because she was now settled in one place, she allowed a family friend, Francis Hervé, to copy down her reminiscences. He had previously written a rather wordy travel book, and was happy to oblige. He explained in the Preface that he would do so:

> because of the very pressing importunities of her friends, she alleging it would appear both vain and presumptuous in her to imagine that she was of sufficient importance to excite any interest in the public mind. . . . She has been prevailed upon to give as accurate an account of what occurred during her residence in France, comprising a period of more than thirty years, as her memory will permit, and which may be considered as totally unbiased by any political prejudice.

He thought her personal descriptions of the different characters were likely to be far more accurate than those generally given by other authors, 'Madame Tussaud, from her profession, naturally becoming a more accurate observer of physical appearance than others usually are'.[13]

Because little was known about Marie's colourful history, and the waxworks at Baker Street was becoming a fashionable place to visit, the book was very popular when it was published in 1838. The first edition of the *Memoirs* had a picture of a young-looking seventeen-year-old Marie as a frontispiece, while the second had a contemporary picture by E. Hervé of a rather severe-looking Madame Tussaud aged seventy-seven, wearing a very frilly white cap. The book attracted many people to the exhibition, all curious to see the lady herself sitting behind the small table in the entrance hall, taking money from the visitors as they arrived.

In *All the Year Round* Charles Dickens noted that Marie's exhibition had become so famous, that:

> Visitors from the country go to see these waxworks if they go nowhere else; tradesmen living in the neighbourhood put 'near

Madame Tussaud's' on their cards; the omnibuses which run down Baker-Street announce that they pass that lady's door as a means of getting customers; and there is scarcely a cab horse in London but would make an instinctive 'offer' to stop as he went by the entrance.[14]

Marie the woman had made her exhibition so successful that she had now become synonymous with Madame Tussaud's the waxworks.

SIXTEEN

'Your wife for Life'

Marie, now settled successfully in London, thought she had left her old Paris life far behind. She had never returned to Paris, and had had no communication with François for over thirty years. Little is known of his life during that time, apart from a few old files which record various financial transactions. One document, dated 21 September 1831, concerned the death of Madame Anne Françoise Lemel, his '*demoiselle de confiance*', who had looked after him at 36 rue des Fosses du Temple. He paid 50 francs for her funeral expenses. Other correspondence clearly shows that his finances were still causing him problems. After the death of his mother, François had had a disagreement with his brother over an inheritance he had not received but which he thought was due to him. But when his sister, Madame Bacheville, died in August 1839, she left him a legacy of 2,078 francs.[1]

The *Salon de Cire* was still in the boulevard du Temple and still trading under Curtius's name, although there were no longer any connections with Marie. A visitor who had known it in its heyday found it largely unchanged:

> For sixty years it has remained the same, it has neither gained nor lost anything. It is humble and modest with its little entrance, its Barker at the door and its two lamps. As for its wax sentry, he is a joker; I have known him for forty years. I have seen him as a soldier in the French Guards, a Chamborant hussar, a Grenadier of the Convention, trumpeter of the Directoire, Consular guide, Polish Lancer, Chasseur of the Imperial Guard, drummer of the Royal Guard, Sergeant of the National Guard; last Sunday he was the Municipal Guard. . . . When you enter the salon, you find it

exactly as it was originally, dark and smoky. The new figures have relegated the old figures to the back, as the king who arrives at Saint-Denis causes his predecessor to descend into the tomb in order to take his place on the last step of the vault. However, you will find there, as you will at the door, faces which you recognise. How many good or evil celebrities! How many heroes, scholars, virtuous persons, villains, the Sieur Curtius has passed in review since the opening of his museum. I believe, however, that they have more often changed the clothes than the figures. . . . The thing which has certainly not changed its place is the great table setting where the kings are united together. We have seen Louis XV and his august family; the Directoire and his august family; the three consuls and their august family, the Emperor Napoleon and his august family; Charles X and his august family and now today we see Louis-Philippe and his august family. . . . I will refrain from speaking of the fruits which form the dessert. I can confirm that the apples, pears, peaches and grapes set out on this august table are the same as those which I saw there thirty years ago. I do not think they have ever been dusted since.[2]

Marie must have been shocked and dismayed when, on 6 April 1840, François unexpectedly re-entered her life. Having already disposed of Marie's inheritance in Paris, François, it seems, was now seeking her cooperation to claim a further inheritance which didn't belong to him. Again in financial trouble in spite of the legacy from his sister, he had decided to try to obtain Curtius's unclaimed inheritance from Mayence. The money had been left to Curtius and his brother Charles some fifty years before by an uncle, but Curtius, the sole legatee after the death of his brother, had been unable to obtain the legacy before he died. The money would probably have come to Marie, as Curtius's only heir, but she had made no claim. Now François, discovering this untapped legacy, saw an opportunity, as Marie's husband, to make an application for it and he made enquiries in Mayence. He was told by the Department of Foreign Affairs that he needed documents to prove his legal right to the money. These included deeds and evidence stating the name and position of the successors of G. Curtius, and the will of G. Curtius, if in existence, and the deed of distribution of the estate. He also needed a revised power of attorney from Marie giving him the authority to deal with that part of the money which should have gone to Charles Curtius. It was about this power of attorney that he contacted his estranged wife.

François sent a letter to Marie via an acquaintance in London, the Widow Castille, who delivered it personally. The response, as she told him, was not encouraging.

> All the same I must say sir that she appears to hold against you certain very grave reasons for dissatisfaction since in the first place she seemed not at all pleased to hear from you and told me that she had transferred all her possessions to her sons. These children have married English girls. In passing I may tell you that she has lived in London many years. You can write to her at this very short address – Madame Tussaud's, as your wife is very well known in London. It is impossible to describe the beauty and richness of the exhibition – in all my life I have never seen anything more magnificent.[3]

On 27 August 1841 Joseph and Francis sent their father a sharp letter:

> Sir,
>
> Madame Tussaud and ourselves do not wish to have any correspondence with you. We believe that you have enough to live comfortably for a man at your time of life. Meanwhile we hope that Providence will provide for you, and that the Eternal God will pardon you for your infamous behaviour. The exhibition is our property.
>
> F. Tussaud and Joseph Tussaud.[4]

It would seem their annoyance was justified. As the Widow Castille had pointed out, the success of the exhibition was of their own making. In 1842, probably as a result of this unwanted letter from their father, Joseph and Francis applied for their Denization Documents (naturalisation), which was granted on 26 August 1846. This was an important step. There was a real possibility that, in the event of Marie predeceasing François, their father would inherit the London waxworks. In law a woman's property passed to her husband upon marriage – a situation which was not to change until the Married Woman's Property Act was passed in 1882.

Meanwhile, François persisted with his claim, but without taking proper legal advice. In early February 1843 the lawyer in Mayence wrote rather tetchily: 'I beg you sir to seek the help of a Solicitor in your affairs and be more business like, and not try the patience of a man about to enter his eighty-sixth year, who is looking after your interests.' He wrote again three weeks later:

The members of the Administration of the Public Funds recognise nobody but Philippe Guillaume Curtius with whom to negotiate anything, and that if Philippe Guillaume Curtius is no longer alive his successor must establish his bona fides by a death certificate, of which he must apply an exact copy certificate by the Paris authorities, and the Chargé d'Affaires of the grand Duchy of Hesse.

If you want to establish your title in this matter, you must obtain a proxy from your wife, who has been residing in London since 1803, and supply a certified copy. Consult a solicitor who will tell you that the demands of the administration are reasonable.[5]

It is not known how much Marie knew of François's attempts to claim Curtius's inheritance, but she was rightly suspicious of his intentions. She must have feared he would try to claim the London waxworks, because on 13 July 1844 she had her solicitor draw up Articles of Partnership between herself and her sons. She was now eighty-three and, reluctant though she still was to cede responsibility to anyone, she was, understandably, still very wary of François. She wanted to ensure that it was her sons who would inherit the business in which they had all worked so hard.

Joseph wrote to his father on 5 October: 'After very careful consideration mother cannot maintain the power of attorney which you request, and having sought advice from our lawyers, they have recommended that she has nothing to do with it, since it would constitute a grave injustice to her children. . . . It is all in your interest and not ours.' By 30 December 1844 the Tussaud brothers were getting annoyed with their father:

In the last letter we received from you, you reproached us for not writing (what kindness have you shown us to date?) Our reply is that it is forty-four years since our honoured mother left Paris, and she has received no money from her business. As you well know, when you marry someone well endowed with this world's goods and property, she has a right, not only to a share of the profits, but in the management of half that property. You left mother in debt and difficulty in London, all of which she overcame by hard work and perseverance, without asking from you one *sou* from your own pocket. Up to the present time you have not sent any money to help her. On the contrary you have sent her no details of her business, and the profits from that business, of which you, alone, have had the benefits for many years. We believe, with mother, that she has no reason to have any regard for you who have treated her in such a way. I can assure you that every time that you write, mother becomes ill, and above all, when you write that you will come and see her. It is too ridiculous for words when you speak of your qualities as a husband.[6]

By the following March, Francis, who had been brought up in Paris, was beginning to feel sorry for his father who, now in his late seventies, was having problems with his sight and with walking. The brothers had unsuccessfully tried to negotiate a financial settlement with their father. Francis wrote:

I have learnt that you do not wish to make any settlement. As a result I have begged mother and my brother to leave things as

they are at present. You must remember that my brother and I have a fairly large family – and although you are our father, we must look after our interests and think of them. . . . Send me all your news and write to me at my house.
10 Shaftesbury Avenue, New Road, London.[7]

He received no reply and the next month wrote again, rather anxiously:

I wanted to know how you were. We do not wish to hurt you in any way, particularly at your age – we think our proposition is to your advantage as well as our own – but you have deemed it otherwise – much to my annoyance. You think also that we are working against you as far as mother is concerned. I can assure you there is not the slightest truth in that. She is quite at liberty to think and act for herself and it is nothing to do with us if she has not the slightest desire to see you.

Mother is fairly well although she grows thinner every day. I hope that she will be spared to her friends for some time – although I am not her favourite, my brother Joseph is, as he has been with her since his childhood. I hope that you will write to me at my home.[8]

Francis had lived with his father until he was twenty-one, and was evidently seeking to reassure him that he was not forgotten. It seems that Francis and Joseph had their quarrels, which is not surprising as their upbringing had been so different, and Francis may well have felt excluded from the close relationship between Joseph and Marie. For a few months François refrained from writing, but then in 1846 he received several demand notices for land tax on property he owned at 73 rue des Fosses du Temple, and he wrote again to his sons asking for a loan. They agreed to lend him the money, but with the stipulation that it must be repaid within the year as they were 'counting on this sum for a new addition to the Exhibition. We will lend it to you free of interest. We only require a proper receipt from you and hope that you will be prompt with it.'[9]

241

In spite of his constant demands for money, Francis and Joseph decided to visit their father in Paris. Marie was horrified, and told Joseph that if he tried to see his father or have anything to do with him she would never forgive him. 'Such was the enmity between the old lady and her husband that she was always in dread that he might someday make his appearance and claim her Exhibition and all she possessed.' However, because Francis had lived for so long with his father she could not forbid his visit. Francis told his son Victor that because of Marie's opposition, Joseph waited outside while he talked to his father, but Joseph's 'curiosity to see his father being great, he was enabled to do so by standing on a chair and looking over a screen, unperceived by the feeble and rather deaf old gentleman with whom [Francis] was conversing'.[10]

Following the visit for a few years there was silence from François in Paris, though Francis wrote to him again on 14 March 1848, worried about his safety during the Paris uprising. The year 1848 witnessed revolutions throughout Europe. In Paris King Louis-Philippe was forced to abdicate and was replaced by a president, Louis-Napoleon, later to become Emperor Napoleon III.

Francis wrote:

I hope that you are in good health and that this scrimmaging has not worried you. When you have reached your age you don't want to have anything to do with politics. . . . Please write as soon as possible and let me know how your eyes and legs are. With the advancing years recovery is not so quick. Mother is beginning to grow very feeble and at times she is very ill as she suffers from asthma which allows her no rest at night, and as the climate of England is a damp one it does not help. Her legs are bad like yours, and she has bunions that hurt her when she walks. She asks to be remembered to you.

I am not on speaking terms with my brother.

Maybe Marie was softening towards her husband, or perhaps Francis was just being polite to the old man about his mother's concern. There was obviously still some strife between the brothers, possibly about the running of the exhibition or possibly about how to handle their father. But they must have made up their quarrel because on 29 June they wrote a joint letter to him, as they were still concerned about how he was managing in the disturbances. They begged him to write as soon as possible, 'because the worry and uncertainty is making mother ill. . . . May the Almighty watch over you.'

In the early autumn Joseph found time to visit his father. The purpose of the visit was to see how the old man was managing, and to try to sort out better accommodation for him in Paris. When he returned to London Joseph wrote to his father to say that Francis had agreed to the move. 'With regard to the apartment on the boulevard, I have spoken to my brother and he will be pleased to share half the extra rent with me, since he thinks you will be much better in every way living there.' He was now also concerned about his mother, who had been very ill since his return, but he hoped that she would soon be better. He ends his letter: 'I shall always remember with a great deal of pleasure my latest visit to you. My brother joins me in sending you all our love and best wishes.'

It was the last time Joseph saw his father, who died on 15 December 1848. The previous day François Tussaud, 'being established in a room on the second floor lit by a window overlooking a courtyard, such room being part of an apartment occupied by M. Tussaud in a house in Paris, rue des Fosses du Temple 36, has made and dictated to the lawyers . . . a last will and testament in the presence of witnesses'. Wishing to acknowledge the kindness 'she lavished on him', he left the sum of 5,000 francs to the Widow Bertrand, 'living with me in her capacity of companion help'. He wanted this to be a first charge on the estate.

The final settlement of the estate was complex. The respective amounts brought by François and Marie to their marriage are listed, and Marie was by far the greater contributor. Though they lived together for the first seven years of their marriage, François gave her no financial help once she had left France. The winding-up of the estate revealed that Marie had the right to approximately 69,000 francs, and Joseph and Francis the right to 20,500 francs, to be divided between them. It is not known if they received their legacy, though Joseph and Francis did pay Madame Bertrand her 5,000 francs. There was no mention of the inheritance in Mayence.

* * *

Seven years earlier, in 1841, Marie and her sons had begun to collect Napoleonic relics for an ambitious exhibition which opened in specially prepared new rooms in March 1843. The exhibition included Napoleon's travelling carriage, taken after his defeat at Waterloo. The carriage, given to the Prince Regent as a gift, was sold for £2,500 in 1816 to the collector William Bullock, who then exhibited it in his Egyptian Museum at Piccadilly in London, and also took it to various country venues. This relic was an object of great interest and proved an excellent investment, making more than £26,000 for Bullock. The carriage then disappeared, but in 1842, following some information gleaned from a casual conversation, Joseph found it in a repository belonging to Robert Jefferys in Gray's Inn Road, 'a respectable coach manufacturer, who took the carriage in part payment of a bad debt'.[11] Realising its potential, he bought it. Considerable refurbishment had to be made to the neglected vehicle, but once cleaned Napoleon's Carriage became the centrepiece of the Tussauds' very successful Napoleonic exhibition. Just as it had once earned a fortune for Mr William Bullock, so it now did for Madame Tussaud. Charles Dickens thought the Napoleon relics:

> in some instances very remarkable, and are authenticated on good authority. The carriage taken after the battle of Waterloo is especially interesting, and, with its huge wheels and immense strength and solidarity of construction, is highly suggestive of the rough roads which have to be rattled over in the course of a campaign. The contrivances of which it is full, for the Emperor's convenience, are very curious. The visitor to this part of the Tussaud collection, is allowed to get into the carriage, and sit there if he chooses, examining the inside of this very interesting vehicle at his ease.[12]

The Duke of Wellington was another frequent visitor. He, of course, had a very personal interest, and always wanted to know when anything new was added to the Napoleonic Rooms. He would spend hours looking at the wax effigy of Napoleon and became such a well-known figure that Joseph commissioned a painting of the scene by Sir George Hayter.

In 1842, when Marie was eighty-one, she modelled a self-portrait for the *salon*. Her great-grandson, John Theodore, described her as:

small and slight, and her manner was vivacious. Her complexion was fresh, her hair dark brown with never more than a sprinkling of grey, and her soft brown eyes were keen and alert when her interest was aroused. She was a great talker, her conversation was replete with reminiscences, and, moreover, she was blessed with a faultless memory.[13]

The model of the diminutive, bespectacled old lady was placed among the other figures, and as she still sat in the entrance hall it sometimes caused visitors to wonder if they were seeing double. Charles Dickens remembered her well, 'sitting at the entrance of her own show, and receiving the shillings which poured into her exchequer. She was evidently a person of marked abilities, and of a shrewd and strong character.'[14] Tussaud's exhibition was now so well known that when Phineas Barnum, the American showman, came to London in 1844 with his show, which included the famous 25-inch-high midget Tom Thumb, he offered to buy Madame Tussaud's exhibition to take to New York. Neither Marie nor her sons were interested in selling and so he returned to America in 1846 without it. As a legacy of his interest, the exhibition for many years showed a model of Tom Thumb, together with one of his original costumes.

As is still true today, to be modelled and placed in Madame Tussaud's exhibition meant that you were a person of some consequence, or, in the case of the Chamber of Horrors, of some notoriety. When in 1845 the London exhibition received a clandestine visit from the Count d'Orsay, a close friend of Charles

Dickens, his likeness, too, was added to the ranks of the famous. The popular count was deeply in debt and the bailiffs were after him, and so for fear of being arrested he was unable to leave Gore House where he lived with Lady Blessington. But he had painted a portrait of a member of the royal family, and it was essential that he check the proofs before it was engraved. He would have been safe to venture out on a Sunday, as all debtors were immune from arrest on that day, but the engraver refused to work on Sunday and so d'Orsay was obliged to visit him on a weekday. D'Orsay's friend Sir Edwin Landseer suggested he make the visit but with his face well muffled. The count reached Landseer's house safely and together they successfully called on the engraver. They count then became somewhat reckless and asked if they could visit some place of amusement together. The chose Madame Tussaud's exhibition. They much enjoyed it, but the count became anxious when he realised that they were being followed by two strangers. His heart must have missed a beat when one of the men asked 'Have I the honour of speaking to M. le Comte d'Orsay?' 'I am he', came the reply. 'Then, if M. le Comte will be so very kind as to allow me, Madame Tussaud presents her compliments, and she will be greatly honoured if M. le Comte will give her some sittings and will permit us to add his illustrious figure to those already in our establishment.' The count, relieved and delighted, agreed willingly. And Madame Tussaud, never one to miss an opportunity, had another well-known face to add to her collection.[15]

Inevitably, as Marie grew older, she grew more frail. She was happy at the end to leave the running of the exhibition to her two sons, and she seldom went out, preferring the company of her family. Marie's grandson Victor remembered seeing her:

> seated in her room in front of a small table on which she usually had a dozen or even more large silver watches. She used to amuse herself by winding them up every night and regulating them if required. They were of the kind used by old-fashioned countrymen which require such an effort on the part of their owner to produce from a deep fob. She used to call me little

Christmas as I was born the latter end of December, and it was her custom to give me a bright half sovereign on Christmas Day and a similar gift on New Year's Day, also oranges and cakes, most powerful aids to my naturally retentive and tenacious memory. I need scarcely say that my brothers and sisters also received presents according to their ages.[16]

Marie remained in reasonably good health to the end of her life. After only a few days of illness, during which she was confined to her bed, she died at 58 Baker Street on 15 April 1850, surrounded by her family. She had not made a will, but summoned her two sons before she died. 'See you,' she said, 'I leave all I have to you to divide equally, and do not quarrel.' After a while she turned to Joseph who could not restrain his tears and said: 'See you, Joseph! Why do you cry? I have lived all my life an honest woman. Are you afraid to see an old woman die?'[17] According to John Theodore Tussaud, her great-grandson, she 'brought cheerfulness and geniality to bear upon the tasks that lay before her, and therein lay the secrets of her triumphs. She was diligent and attentive to her business, devoted to her family, and attached to her friends.'[18]

There were obituaries in several newspapers, including *The Times*, the *Illustrated London News*, the *Annual Register* and the *Gentleman's Magazine*. All briefly related her life story. *Chambers Book of Days* reported:

Many who are no longer in their first youth must also have a recollection of Madame Tussaud herself, seated in the stair of approach, and hard to be distinguished in its calm presence, from the counterfeits of humanity which it was the business of her life to fabricate. Few, however, are aware of the singularities which marked the life of Madame Tussaud, or of the very high moral merits which belonged to her. She had actually lived among the celebrated men of the French Revolution, and framed their portraits from direct observation. It was her business one day to model the horrible countenance of Marat, whom she detested, and on another to imitate the features of his beautiful assassin,

247

Charlotte Corday, whom she admired and loved. . . . Escaping from France, she led for many years a life of struggle and difficulty, supporting herself and family by the exercise of her art. Once she lost the whole of her stock by shipwreck on a voyage to Ireland. Meeting adversity with a stout heart, always industrious, frugal, and considerate, the ingenious little woman at length was enabled to set up her models in London, where she had forty years of constant prosperity, and where she died at the age of ninety, in the midst of an attached and grateful family, extending to several generations.[19]

Marie was buried in the grounds of the Roman Catholic chapel at the corner of Cadogan Gardens and Pavilion Road, Chelsea. There seems to be no record of the funeral, but the weekly account book, under the heading 'for Mother's funeral', records some of the costs. A total of £35 was paid for the ground at the cemetery and the funeral clothes supplied for the staff came to £86. This included six new black suits for menservants, four black silk bonnets for Martha, Harriet, Davis and Kemp, and six ditto grey straw for domestics. There was also an allowance for a cab for the servants on the day of the funeral.[20]

The small cemetery where Marie was buried closed in 1855. When the chapel was demolished some years later, all the coffins were removed to vaults beneath the new church of St Mary's, built in 1879, at the corner of Cadogan Street and Draycott Terrace. Later still, most of these coffins, including those of many of the Tussaud family, were moved again to their present location at St Mary's Catholic Cemetery, Kensal Green. Marie's coffin, however, was not moved but remains in an unmarked location in the environs of St Mary's, Cadogan Street, in the nave of which is placed a memorial tablet.

An unfounded but persistent story in the London underworld claimed that Marie had been buried adorned with priceless jewels given to her as gifts by the crowned heads of Europe. In a strange twist, some half a century or more after her death, the newspapers reported that thieves had broken into the Tussaud family tomb at

Kensal Green with the intention of stealing this jewellery. Four men were named: Charles Asquith, Jim Christy, Joe Brown and a man named Read. These would-be grave robbers set off one night armed with the necessary tools and entered the graveyard by climbing a wall. They found the tomb, in an elaborate chantry chapel with a belfry above, and managed to break in through a small barred window. Three of them entered while Christy, the oldest member of the gang, remained outside to keep watch. Once inside the small chapel the men's lamps revealed a flagstone covering the stairs leading down to the vault. When they raised it, a heavy nauseous atmosphere rose from below. Joe Brown wanted to leave at once, but Asquith, the ringleader, told him not to be so stupid – 'Dead 'uns can't bite you.' He led the way down into the vault where they found five coffins. The name-plates were in French which none of them could read. They attacked the first coffin but found nothing of value in it. Asquith then went on to the next one, and ordered Read to help him lift it down, but Read, stepping backwards, tripped over the lid of the first coffin and fell heavily. The noise was terrific and the three robbers, already unnerved by the atmosphere, froze. They heard footsteps outside approaching the steps and feared they were discovered, but it was only old Christy, who told them he was spooked by the graveyard and wasn't going to stay. Asquith told Brown to go up the steps and tell him off, which Brown did. As he turned to go back down to the vault, Brown slipped; to save himself from falling, he grabbed hold of a rope, which turned out to be the chantry bell rope. The bell tolled – and kept on tolling. The men, believing this to be a supernatural manifestation, fled from the tomb as though pursued by vengeful ghosts. Scrambling frantically over the cemetery wall they found themselves on the bank of Regent's Canal (the Grand Union Canal). The water was black, cold and evil smelling, but driven by fear Asquith, Christy and Brown flung themselves in and managed to get across. Read, who couldn't swim, refused to try, and they had to abandon him on the far bank.

Belief in the 'dead man's curse' is strong in the underworld. Two months later the body of Read was taken from the canal. Jim Christy died within a year in the mental ward of the workhouse.

Asquith was caught on his next job, served five years' penal servitude and died barely a week after his release. Joe Brown survived, but was caught for another offence and served twelve years in Parkhurst.[21] If Marie had been alive, no doubt Asquith, Christy, Brown and Read would have joined their fellow rogues in the 'Separate Room', renamed by *Punch* in 1846 as the Chamber of Horrors.

* * *

After the death of their mother, Joseph and Francis continued to expand the museum. In London in 1851 the Great Exhibition filled everyone's thoughts. The main exhibition was to be held in the breathtaking Crystal Palace, built under the inspirational guidance of Prince Albert. Many new visitors were expected in London from all over the world and the Tussaud brothers decided to almost double the size of their premises in anticipation of the increased attendance. Again Francis's architectural skills were utilised. The Chamber of Horrors was enlarged, as until 1851 it could only hold about a dozen figures with very poor access by a narrow staircase. Now, new space was created and new rooms were also added to the main exhibition, which 'were decorated with great taste, and elegance, and exhibited a charming old world look. To quote the words of a lady of title, "The rooms seemed to suit the figures, and the figures the rooms".'[22]

After an initial lull at the start of the Great Exhibition, people thronged to London, and the Tussauds' gamble paid off handsomely. The rooms were crowded with visitors and by the end of the year, they had not only recouped their outlay but had earned a considerable sum. Francis told his son later that it was not until then that he and Joseph had any money to call their own. They had truly been living from hand to mouth.[23]

Marie's two sons did not outlive their mother by many years. Joseph died on 15 August 1865 aged sixty-eight, and of his three children only one daughter, Louisa, survived him. She was not interested in the business and, needing money, sold her share to the two other partners, Francis Tussaud and his eldest son, Joseph Randall. Francis's large family consisted of five daughters and four sons, Joseph Randall, Francis Curtius, Victor and John Theodore, who died aged eighteen. The three older boys were already busy at work in the exhibition when their father died in 1873, aged seventy-three, and all were skilled modellers. The waxworks continued to thrive at the Bazaar, but when problems arose with the lease the Tussauds decided to build their own premises. They found a suitable site in Marylebone Road, not far from the Bazaar, and a magnificent new exhibition hall began to rise on the site, to be completed in 1884 at a reputed cost of £80,000. There the exhibition remained for forty successful years under the management of the Tussaud family. But in 1925 a disastrous fire, probably caused by an electrical fault, swept through the building, feeding greedily on the wax figures with such ferocity that it was impossible to extinguish it. By the time it had burnt itself out most of the figures had been destroyed. Out of the 467 models, only 171 were rescued. The building was ruined, most of the paintings burnt and all that remained of the Napoleonic Rooms was a charred axle from the Waterloo coach.[24] The Tussauds, however, still owned the site and most of the moulds stored in the basement had survived. So, with a tenacity worthy of Madame Tussaud herself, a new company was formed and in 1926 rebuilding started. Baker Street was reopened in 1928. There continued to be a member of the Tussaud family working in the exhibition until 1967, when Bernard Tussaud, Marie's great-great-grandson, died.

To visit Madame Tussaud's is still a nostalgic trip. Those who today take their children there for a special treat were once, years ago, taken there by their own parents. Some of the original models, especially those of the French royal family and the guillotined heads, provide a continuous historical link from 1793 to the present day. As Dickens said prophetically in 1860: 'Madame Tussaud's is, with the whole population of this country, something more than an exhibition: it is an institution.'[25]

APPENDIX

The History of Marat's Bath

An interesting story appeared in 1885 concerning the bath in which Marat was assassinated on 13 July 1793. The odyssey of this historical object is as bizarre as the object itself.

After Marat's assassination, the bath disappeared. It was not listed in the inventory of his house after his death, and it appears almost certain that his widow, Simonne Evrard, sold it to her neighbour, who was a journalist. Some years later it was rediscovered by a Justice of the Peace, when he was called to an apartment in the rue de l'Ecole-de-Médecine, next door to the one formerly lived in by Marat. Following the death of the apartment's owner, the journalist, the Justice of the Peace had to make an inventory of the contents before placing seals on the doors. Among the items listed in the inventory were a library of books, two spheres, an old box, a surgeon's instrument and, of special note, the bath.

In 1795 there had been a surge of anti-Marat sentiment, and the Convention had passed a decree that the bust of Marat from the rue Montmartre should be destroyed along with the urn containing his ashes. When Marat fell from favour, the journalist had prudently stored the bath away, and then forgotten about it. The bath was of a design common in 1773, when water was expensive and had to be heated by kettle. Entirely enclosed up to the chest, the bath was made of brown leather, now almost black, in the shape of a sabot. A low leather stool was placed inside the bath, where Marat could sit and write, and under the wooden step at the side of the bath was kept the heating apparatus.

After the journalist's death his belongings were sold, and the bath was bought by the royalist M. de Sainte-Hilaire, perhaps because he thought it would be useful. He took it to his family home at Sarzeau, a little village in the south of Brittany. On Monsieur de Sainte-Hilaire's death in 1805, all his possessions passed to his daughter, Mlle Capriole de Sainte-Hilaire, who lived well into her eighties and died in 1862. Having no heirs she left all she possessed to the *curé* of the little village of Sarzeau, where she was still living.

Twenty years later a journalist from *Le Figaro*, intrigued by stories he had heard, unearthed the curious history of this bath, which he set down in an article published on 15 July 1885. It was then the *curé* realised that this strange old relic might provide a means for him to make a lot of money with which he could help the people of his parish. He offered it for sale first to the director of the Musée Carnavalet, the museum for the history of Paris. The director, an expert in these matters, hoped to buy the bath for the museum, but the absence of any firm provenance and the high price asked by the *curé* of Sarzeau led him to abandon the plan. The *curé* then contacted Madame Tussaud's waxworks in London via the English government. The Tussauds, well aware of the historical value of the piece, offered to pay 100,000 francs for the famous bath. Delighted with this, the *curé* thought of all the good he would be able to do for his parish with the English gold, and wrote to accept the offer. Sadly, however, owing to simple human error all these philanthropic plans came to nought. The letter of acceptance, left by the *curé* in the presbytery to be collected by the postman, was somehow mislaid and so never reached the Tussauds. Not realising this, the *curé* refused other, far more modest, offers but heard no more from Madame Tussaud's. They, having received no reply to their offer, thought it had been rejected. Some time later a reasonable offer was received from Phineas Barnum the showman, but the *curé* considered that to be undignified. No major collections in America, England or Europe now seemed to be interested in the bath of *l'Ami du Peuple*.

Eventually, fearing that he would never sell it, the *curé* accepted 5,000 francs from the Musée Grevin, which had first opened in Paris in 1882.[1] There it can still be seen today. This bath, in which Marat was stabbed in 1793, is now over two hundred years old, and is the very same bath which young Marie Grosholtz sketched for David's famous painting and for her own acclaimed scene. This bloodstained relic is the only real artefact in the Musée Grevin's dramatic tableau of the death of Marat.

Notes

Abbreviations
MTA – Madame Tussaud's Archives
MTM – Madame Tussaud's *Madame Tussaud's Memoirs and Reminiscences of France*

Chapter 1: 'A great crowd of curious people'

1. Born Strasbourg, 4 October 1743.
2. Born 18 February 1716.
3. MTA.
4. *Madame Tussaud's Memoirs and Reminiscences of France*, ed. Francis Hervé, Saunders & Ottley, London, 1838, p. 4 (MTM).
5. MTA.
6. Ibid.
7. *Encyclopaedia Britannica*, 9th edition, 1875, Vol. XXI, p. 24–6.
8. MTA.
9. Louis Sebastien Mercier, *Le Tableau de Paris 1782–1788*, tr. and ed. Helen Simpson as *The Waiting City*, Harrap & Co. Ltd, London, 1933, p. 207.
10. MTA.
11. The Opera was situated near the northern boundary of Paris between the Porte Saint-Denis and the Porte Saint-Martin, near 20 boulevard du Temple, where Curtius now had his main wax museum. Within five minutes' walk to the south-west was the rue des Fontaines (Desfontaine), which led directly to the Prince de Conti's palace in the Temple. Here many of the prince's protégés were housed (1777 map of Paris).
12. Salvador, *Le Boulevard du Temple et ses célébrités depuis soixante ans*, Massin, Paris, n.d., Bibliothèque Nationale de France.
13. Mayeur de Saint-Paul, *Le Chroniquer désoeuvré ou L'espion du Boulevard du Temple*, London, 1782, pp. 135, 136.
14. MTM, p. 17.
15. *Encyclopaedia Britannica*, 9th edition, 1875, Vol. XXI, p. 26.
16. MTM, p. 12.
17. Ibid.
18. Ibid., pp. 11, 12.
19. Théodore Faucheur, *Histoire du*

Boulevard du Temple, Paris, 1863, p. 39.
20. Ibid., p. 49.
21. Robert M. Isherwood, *Farce and Fantasy, Popular Entertainment in Eighteenth Century Paris*, Oxford University Press, Oxford, 1986, p. 200.
22. Mercier, *The Waiting City*, p. 70.
23. Ibid., p. 46.

Chapter 2: 'The royal family is a spectacle'

1. Madame de la Tour du Pin, *Memoirs*, 1853, tr. by Félice Harcourt, Harvill Press, London, 1969, p. 26.
2. Madame Campan, *Memoirs of the Private Life of Marie Antoinette, also Memoirs of Madame Campan*, Henry Young & Sons, Liverpool, 1917, 3 vols (Vol. 1 with F. Barriere), Vol. 3, pp. 272, 275.
3. Ibid., Vol. 1, p. 24.
4. Ibid. p. 19.
5. *The Ruin of a Princess, as told by the Duchess of Angoulême, Madame Elisabeth, sister of Louis XVI, and Cléry, the King's Valet de Chambre*, tr. Katharine Prescott Wormeley, London, 1913, p. 15.
6. MTM, pp. 31, 33.
7. Madame Campan, *Memoirs*, Vol. 1, pp. 211, 243.
8. Ibid., p. 19.
9. Madame de la Tour du Pin, *Memoirs*, pp. 71, 72.
10. Madame Campan, *Memoirs*, Vol. 1, pp. 85, 86.
11. MTM, p. 61.
12. Ibid., p. 40.
13. Ibid., pp. 30, 31.
14. Madame Campan, *Memoirs*, Vol. I. 2, p. 37.
15. Madame Campan, *Memoirs*, Vol. 2, pp. 54, 55.
16. Isherwood, *Farce and Fantasy*, p. 200.
17. MTM, pp. 125, 126.
18. Ibid., p. 13.
19. Ibid., p. 56.
20. *Encyclopaedia Britannica*, 9th edition, 1875, Vol. IX, p. 716.
21. MTM, p. 13.
22. Ibid., p. 15.
23. Madame Campan, *Memoirs*, Vol. 3, p. 261.
24. MTM, p. 56.
25. Ibid., p. 21.
26. Ibid., p. 26.
27. *Ruin of a Princess*, p. 19.
28. MTM, p. 22.
29. Ibid., p. 24.
30. Ibid, p. 50.
31. Ibid., p. 23.
32. Ibid., pp. 41, 42.
33. Ibid., p. 53.
34. Ibid., p. 52.
35. Quote from *Madame Elisabeth* by M. Trouncer, London, 1955, p. 102.
36. Ibid., pp. 126, 127.
37. From *The Life of Marie Antoinette* by Montjoie, as recalled by Madame Campan, Vol. 2, p. 61.
38. Madame Campan, *Memoirs*, Vol. 3, p. 131.

39. MTM, p. 40.
40. Ibid, p. 56.

Chapter 3: 'Seduction had its Code'

1. MTM, p. 102.
2. Ibid., pp. 127, 128.
3. Ibid., pp. 128, 130.
4. *Diaries and Correspondence of the Rt Hon. George Rose*, ed. Revd Leveson Vernon Harcourt, Richard Bentley, London, 1860, Vol. 1, p. 41.
5. Bachaumont, *Mémoires Secrets*, Paris, 1783.
6. Almanach National de France, 1793.
7. Etienne Gaspard Robertson, *Mémoires récréatifs, scientifiques et anecdotique du Physicien aeronaute E.G. Robertson*, Paris, Rignoux, 1831–4.
8. *Encyclopaedia Britannica*, 9th edition, 1875, Vol. I, p. 188.
9. MTM, p. 38.
10. Ibid., p. 39.
11. Ibid., p. 67.
12. Ibid., p. 36.
13. Madame de la Tour du Pin, *Memoirs*, p. 73.
14. Arthur Young, *Travels in France During the Years 1787, 1788, 1789*, ed. Jeffry Kaplow, New York, 1969, p. 12.
15. Ibid., p. 76.
16. Madame Campan, *Memoirs*, Vol. 2, p. 82.
17. Ibid., pp. 129–37.
18. Ibid., Vol. 1, p. 85.
19. MTM, p. 106.

20. Ibid., p. 102.
21. Sebastien Chamfort, *Products of the Perfected Civilisation*, tr. W.S. Merwin, Ontario, Macmillan, 1969, p. 66.
22. MTM, p. 108.

Chapter 4: 'Nests and hotbeds of sedition and revolt'

1. He did not inherit the title until his father's death in 1785.
2. Isherwood, *Farce and Fantasy*, p. 236.
3. Colette Niclot, *The Palais-Royal*, n.d., Bibliothèque Nationale de France.
4. MTA, Albert Babeau, *Paris in 1789*.
5. Mayeur de Saint-Paul, *Le Chroniqueur désoeuvré ou L'espion du boulevard du Temple*.
6. Niclot, *Le Palais-Royal*.
7. Young, *Travels in France*, p. 105.
8. Madame Campan, *Memoirs*, Vol. 2, pp. 308–11.
9. Ibid., Vol. 2, p. 312, extract from the memoirs of the Abbé Georgel.
10. Ibid., p. 314.
11. Ibid., p. 315.
12. Mercier, *The Waiting City*, p. 46.
13. Madame Campan, *Memoirs*, Vol. 2, p. 332.
14. MTM, p. 59.
15. Madame de la Tour du Pin, *Memoirs*, p. 90.
16. Mercier, *The Waiting City*, pp. 197, 198.
17. *Ruin of a Princess*, pp. 22, 23.
18. MTM, p. 84.

19. Ibid., p. 107.
20. Ibid., pp. 47, 50.
21. Ibid., p. 80.

Chapter 5: 'Most curiously moulded in wax'

1. A. de Bersaucourt, *Opinion*, newspaper cutting, Musée de l'Arsenal Ro.17849.
2. *Artists and their Friends in England*, Whitley, London, 1928, p. 59.
3. British Library, London III, Th. Cts. 44.
4. Ibid.
5. Ibid.
6. Ibid.
7. MTM, p. 72.
8. Ibid., p. 73.
9. Ibid., p. 106.
10. *Encyclopaedia Britannica*, 9th edition, 1875, Vol. XV, p. 526.
11. Robertson, *Mémoires récréatifs*, Paris, 1831, pp. 73, 79, 81.
12. MTM, p. 196.
13. Ibid.
14. Chamfort, *Products of the Perfected Civilisation*, Aphorisms.
15. MTM, p. 128.
16. Ibid., p. 16.
17. Ibid., pp. 15, 16.
18. Derek Jarrett, *Three Faces of Revolution, Paris, London and New York in 1789*, London, George Philip, 1989, pp. 123, 124.
19. MTM, p. 108.
20. M.J. Rabaut, *Almanach historique de la revolution Françoise pour l'année 1792*, p. 100.

21. MTA, Curtius, *Services du Sieur Curtius*, 1790, tr. Doreen Hunt, p. 6.
22. MTM, p. 88.
23. A. de Bersaucourt, *Figures de Cire*, Paris, 1925 (article), Musée de l'Arsenal, Paris.
24. MTA, Curtius, *Services du Sieur Curtius*, pp. 6, 7.
25. Rabaut, *Almanach historique*
26. MTA, Curtius, *Services du Sieur Curtius*, p. 7.

Chapter 6: 'Paris in an Uproar'

1. MTM, p. 91.
2. Ibid., p. 103.
3. Simon Schama, *Citizens*.
4. Grace Elliot, *Journal of my Life during the French Revolution written at the request of George III, c. 1810*, p. 14.
5. MTA, Curtius, *Services du Sieur Curtius*.
6. MTM, p. 95.
7. Ibid., p. 93.
8. Ibid., p. 96.
9. Ibid., p. 253.
10. Ibid., p. 101.
11. Ibid., p. 100.
12. Ibid., p. 102.
13. Elliot, *Journal of my Life*, p. 15.
14. Ibid., p. 6.
15. Mildred Carnegy, *A Queen's Knight, the Life of Count Axel de Fersen*, London, 1912, p. 122.
16. Ibid., p. 124.
17. British Library, London III, Th. Cts. 44.
18. Ibid.
19. MTM, p. 110.

20. Ibid., p. 81.
21. Ibid., p. 112.
22. MTA, Curtius, *Services du Sieur Curtius*.
23. Trouncer, *Madame Elisabeth*, p. 185.
24. MTA, Curtius, *Services du Sieur Curtius*, pp. 11, 12.
25. *Ruin of a Princess*, p. 42.

Chapter 7: 'Be my brother or I will kill you'

1. Young, *Travels in France*, p. 218.
2. MTM, p. 248.
3. Madame Campan, *Memoirs*, Vol. 1, p. 95.
4. MTM, pp. 194, 197.
5. Madame Campan, from preface by J. Holland-Rose.
6. Carnegy, *Queen's Knight*, pp. 149, 150.
7. *Ruin of a Princess*, p. 50.
8. Madame de la Tour du Pin, *Memoirs*, p. 142.
9. MTM, pp. 116, 117.
10. *Ruin of a Princess*, p. 79.
11. MTM, p. 120.
12. *Ruin of a Princess*, p. 60.
13. Monseigneur de Salamon, *Papal envoy during the reign of Terror, Memoir of Monseigneur de Salamon the Internuncio at Paris during the Revolution 1790–1801*, ed. Abbe Bridier tr. Francis Jackson, Sands & Co., London, 1911, pp. 88, 89.
14. Ibid., p. 96.
15. *Ruin of a Princess*, p. 56.
16. G. Lenotre, *le Drame de Varennes*, Paris, 1921.
17. MTM, p. 136.
18. *Ruin of a Princess*, p. 228.
19. Elliot, *Journal of my Life*, p. 34.
20. MTM, p. 149.

Chapter 8: 'How bitter was the contrast!'

1. MTM, p. 145.
2. Ibid., p. 278.
3. Faucheur, *Histoire du Boulevard du Temple*, Paris, 1863, Bibliothèque Nationale de France, Paris.
4. MTM, p. 156.
5. Ibid., p. 154.
6. Ibid., p. 146.
7. Ibid., p. 176.
8. MTA.
9. *Morning Chronicle*, 25 September 1797.
10. MTM, p. 161.
11. Ibid., p. 209.
12. Ibid., p. 217.
13. *Ruin of a Princess*, p. 84.
14. MTM, p. 232.
15. Bersaucourt, *Opinion*, Bibliothèque Nationale de France.
16. MTM, p. 233.
17. Ibid., p. 238.
18. Mercier, *Picture of Paris*, p. 204.
19. Ibid.
20. Ibid., pp. 205, 206.
21. MTM, p. 247.
22. Ibid., p. 241.
23. Ibid., pp. 242, 243.
24. Ibid., p. 245.
25. MTA.
26. MTM, p. 291.

Chapter 9: 'The blood of the innocent'

1. MTM, p. 261.
2. Salamon, *Memoirs*, pp. 10–12.
3. MTM, p. 272.
4. Rose Diaries, Vol. 1, p. 170.
5. Mercier, *Picture of Paris*, p. 208.
6. MTM, p. 277.
7. Ibid., p. 303.
8. Ibid., p. 313.
9. Dr Poumiés de la Siboutie, *Recollections of a Parisian*, tr. Lady Theodora Davidson, John Murray, London, 1911, p. 42.
10. *Town and Country Magazine*, 21 January 1793.
11. Rose Diaries, Vol. 1, p. 138.
12. Elliot, *Journal of my Life*, pp. 87, 92.
13. MTM, p. 252.
14. Ibid., p. 253.
15. Mervyn Heard, Paul de Philipsthal and the Phantasmagoria in England, Scotland and Ireland, *The Magic Lantern Society Magazine*, 1996, 1997, 1998, Part 1.
16. MTM, p. 339.
17. Ibid., pp. 340–2.
18. Ibid., p. 343.
19. Citoyen Michel, *Almanach des Prisons, Conciergerie et Luxembourg*, Paris, 1794, p. 7.
20. MTM, p. 345.
21. Ibid., p. 344.
22. Ibid., p. 363.

Chapter 10: 'This cavalcade of mockery'

1. MTM, p. 369.
2. Ibid., p. 383.
3. Ibid., p. 381.
4. Ibid., p. 146.
5. Ibid., p. 405.
6. *Morning Post*, December 1793.
7. Salamon, *Memoirs*, p. 202.
8. MTM, p. 402.
9. Ibid., p. 401.
10. MTA.
11. MTM, p. 292.
12. Ibid., p. 293.
13. Ibid., p. 294.
14. Elliot, *Journal of my Life*, p. 139.
15. Ibid., p. 144.
16. MTM, pp. 285, 287.
17. Ibid., pp. 422, 423.
18. Ibid., p. 424.
19. Ibid., p. 427.
20. Ibid., p. 431.
21. Ibid., p. 441.
22. MTA.
23. Ibid.
24. Ibid.
25. Ibid.
26. MTM, pp. 355, 356.
27. Ibid., p. 435.
28. *Ruin of a Princess*, narrative of Madame Royale, pp. 286–9.
29. G. Lenotre, *Marie Thérèse Charlotte de France*, tr. J. Lewis May, Bodley Head, London, 1905.
30. MTM, p. 460.
31. Ibid., p. 464.

Chapter 11: Madame Tussaud

1. MTA.
2. *The Times*, 13 November 1795.
3. MTA.
4. Ibid., *Aris's Birmingham Gazette*, 5 September 1796.
5. Ibid., 13 February 1797.
6. Salamon, *Memoirs*, p. 194.
7. *Morning Chronicle*, 21 September 1797.
8. Ibid., 25 September 1797.
9. Ibid., 28 September 1797.
10. Revd Dawson Warren, *Journal of a British Chaplain in Paris during the Peace Negotiations of 1801–1802*, ed. A.M. Broadley, Chapman & Hall, London, 1913, pp. 32, 37, 38.
11. MTA.
12. Ibid.
13. MTM, p. 481.
14. Ibid., p. 491.
15. Ibid., p. 466.
16. Ibid., p. 495.
17. Ibid., p. 499.
18. Dawson Warren, *Journal of a British Chaplain in Paris*, George Jackson's Journal, p. 230.
19. MTM, p. 500.
20. British Library, London III, Th. Cts. 44.
21. Covent Garden Theatre Museum, Lyceum Theatre folder.
22. British Library, London III, Th. Cts. 44.
23. Ibid.
24. Ibid.
25. Nicholson, *Journal of Natural Philosophy*, February 1802, p. 33.
26. British Library, London III, Th. Cts. 44.
27. Dawson Warren, *Journal of a British Chaplain in Paris*.
28. Ibid., George Jackson's Journal, p. 251.
29. Dawson Warren, *Journal of a British Chaplain in Paris*, pp. 30, 49, 50.
30. Ibid., p. 128.

Chapter 12: 'Everyone is astonished by my figures'

1. Tussaud's 1803 catalogue.
2. British Library, London III, Th. Cts. 44.
3. Ibid.
4. Covent Garden Theatre Museum, Lyceum Theatre folder.
5. MTA, Letter, 25 April 1803.
6. MTA.
7. *Edinburgh Evening Courant*, 14 April 1803.
8. *Encyclopaedia Britannica*, 9th edition, 1875, Vol. XV, p. 208.
9. *Edinburgh Evening Courant*, 7 May 1803.
10. MTA, Letter, 11 May 1803.
11. Ibid., Letter, 26 May 1803.
12. Ibid., Letter, 29 May 1803.
13. Ibid., Letter, 9 June 1803.
14. *Edinburgh Evening Courant*, 11 June 1803.
15. MTA, Letter, July.
16. Ibid., Letter, 10 October 1803.
17. Ibid., Letter, December 1803.
18. Ibid.
19. Ibid., Letter, 18 January 1804.

Chapter 13: 'Joseph and I must go on our way'

1. MTA, Letter, 27 June 1804.
2. The original loan was made in Paris, not in Ireland.
3. MTA, Victor Tussaud, *Anecdotes*.
4. Heard, *Paul de Philipsthal*, Parts 2 and 3.
5. MTA, Letter, 27 June 1804.
6. MTA.
7. Ibid., Letter, March 1805.
8. Ibid., Letter, 20 June 1805.
9. Ibid.
10. MTA.
11. *Greenock Advertiser*, 29 July 1808.
12. MTA.
13. Land Tax records for the Parish of Lambeth Dean, 1909: Mrs Nesbitt paid 13s 6d tax for 'land & cottage'; London Metropolitan Archives LT85/1/4.
14. MTA.
15. Charles Dickens, *The Old Curiosity Shop*, Oxford Illustrated Dickens, OUP, 1998, p. 215.
16. MTA, Account book, 1811–13.
17. Ibid., Victor Tussaud, *Anecdotes*.
18. Dickens, *The Old Curiosity Shop*, p. 206.
19. Ibid., p. 211.
20. *Bath Chronicle*, December 1814.
21. Dickens, *The Old Curiosity Shop*, pp. 213, 214.
22. MTA.
23. *Encyclopaedia Britannica*, 9th edition, 1875, Vol. IV, p. 740.

Chapter 14: Tussaud & Sons

1. *Cambridge Chronicle*, November 1818.
2. Ibid., 4 November 1818.
3. Ibid., 11 December 1818.
4. Dickens, *The Old Curiosity Shop*, p. 215.
5. *Cambridge Chronicle*, 25 December 1818.
6. MTA.
7. Dickens, *The Old Curiosity Shop*, pp. 242, 243.
8. MTA, *Liverpool Mercury*, August 1821.
9. Ibid.
10. Ibid.
11. Ibid., Victor Tussaud, *Anecdotes*.
12. Ibid.
13. *Bath Chronicle*, 17 January 1824.
14. Dickens, *All the Year Round*, no. 37, 7 January 1860.
15. *Bath Chronicle*, 17 January 1824.
16. Ibid.
17. Ibid.
18. Ibid., 31 January 1824.
19. Ibid., 14 February 1824.
20. Dickens, *The Old Curiosity Shop*, p. 303.
21. *Bath Chronicle*, February 1824.
22. Ibid., 28 February 1824.
23. *Cambridge Chronicle*, 29 October 1824.

Chapter 15: 'The most unqualified approbation'

1. *Edinburgh Evening Courant*, 19 January 1828.

2. *Bath Journal*, 31 October 1831.
3. MTA.
4. *Encyclopaedia Britannica*, 9th edition, 1875, Vol. XVIII, p. 134.
5. Originally the London Horse and Carriage Repository, it opened as a Bazaar in 1829.
6. MTA.
7. Dickens, *All the Year Round*, no. 37, 7 January 1860.
8. MTA, Victor Tussaud, *Anecdotes*.
9. Ibid.
10. Joseph Nightingale, *The Bazaar, its origins, nature, and objects explained*. Letter to George Rose, 1816.
11. MTA.
12. Ibid., Victor Tussaud, *Anecdotes*.
13. Francis Hervé, *Madame Tussaud's Memoirs*, Preface, pp. ii, iii, iv, MTM.
14. Dickens, *All the Year Round*, no. 37, 7 January 1860.

Chapter 16: 'Your wife for Life'

1. MTA.
2. Brazier, *Histoire des Petits Théâtres*, 1837, p. 186.
3. MTA.
4. Ibid.
5. Ibid.
6. Ibid.
7. Ibid.
8. Ibid.

9. Ibid.
10. Ibid., Victor Tussaud, *Anecdotes*.
11. John T. Tussaud, *The Romance of Madame Tussaud's*, Odhams Press, London 1911, p. 83.
12. Dickens, *All the Year Round*, no. 37, 7 January 1860.
13. Tussaud, *The Romance of Madame Tussaud's*, p. 310.
14. Dickens, *All the Year Round*, no. 37, 7 January 1860.
15. Tussaud, *The Romance of Madame Tussaud's*, pp. 109–11.
16. MTA, Victor Tussaud, *Anecdotes*.
17. Ibid.
18. Tussaud, *The Romance of Madame Tussaud's*, p. 313.
19. MTA.
20. Ibid.
21. Ibid., Harcourt Jackson, *Sunday Chronicle*, n.d.
22. Ibid,. Victor Tussaud, *Anecdotes*.
23. Ibid.
24. Anita Leslie, Pauline Chapman, *Madame Tussaud, Waxworker Extraordinary*, Hutchinson, London, 1978.
25. Dickens, *All the Year Round*, no. 37, 7 January 1860.

Appendix

1. Illustrated catalogue of the Musée Grevin, 7th edition, Musée de l'Arsenal, Paris.

Bibliography

PRIMARY SOURCES

MANUSCRIPTS

Bibliothèque Nationale de France, François Mitterand building, Paris
  History of the Palais-Royal, sundry books and pamphlets
Bibliothèque de l'Arsenal, Paris
  History of Paris theatres including waxworks, phantasmagorias and magic lanterns
British Library
  Auckland Papers, Vol. XLVIII, Add. 34459, f. 98; Add. 34458, f. 73 – letters from Mary
  Nesbitt
  LONDON III, Playbills, Theatre Cuttings 44, 45, 46
Cambridge University Map Library
  Map of Paris, 1777
Centre historique des Archives Nationales, CHAN, Paris
  French Revolution archives
Madame Tussaud's Archives
Musée Carnavalet, Paris
  French Revolutionary history and illustrations
National Library of Scotland
  Newspapers
Theatre Museum, London
  Enthoven Collection, Lyceum Theatre cuttings

BOOKS

Almanach de Versailles, 1775, 1782, 1786–1789
Bachaumont, Louis Petit de, *Mémoires Secrètes*, John Adamson, London, 1780
Bersaucourt, *Figures de Cire*, Paris, 1925 (Bibliothèque de l'Arsenal, Paris)
Bullock, William, *A Companion to Mr Bullock's London Museum and Pantherion* (12th
  edition), 1812
——, *Descriptive Synopsis of the Roman Gallery in the Egyptian Hall, Piccadilly*, 1816
Campan, Jeanne Louise Henriette Genet (tr.), *Memoirs of the Private Life of Marie Antoinette,
  also Memoirs of Madame Campan*, Introduction by J. Holland Rose; 3 Vols (Vol. 1 with
  F. Barriere), Liverpool, Henry Young & Sons Ltd, 1917
Chamfort, Sebastien Roch Nicolas, *Products of the Perfected Civilisation*, tr. W.S. Merwin,
  Ontario, Macmillan, 1969

Bibliography

Citoyen Michel, *Almanach des Prisons, Conciergerie et Luxembourg*, Paris, Year III of the Republic (1794), 4th edition

Curtius, Guillaume Matté, *Les Services du Sieur Curtius*, tr. Doreen Hunt, Paris, 1789

De la Tour du Pin, *Mémoirs*, tr. Félice Harcourt, Harvill Press, London, 1969

Dickens, Charles, *All the Year Round*, London, Wellington Street, 1860

——, *The Old Curiosity Shop*, Oxford Illustrated Edition, OUP, 1998

Elliot, Grace Dalrymple, *Journal of my Life During the French Revolution, written at the request of George III*, c. 1801, Rodale Press, 1955

Faucheur, Théodore, *Le Boulevard du Temple depuis son origine jusqu'à sa démolition*, E. Denton, Paris, 1863

Houry, Laurent d', *Almanach Royal*, Paris, 1786

Junius, The letters of, London, printed for John Wheble in Paternoster Row, 2 Vols, 1771

Lenotre, G, *Le Drame de Varennes Juin 1791*, Perrin & Co., Paris, 1921

——, *The Daughter of Louis XVI, Marie Thérèse Charlotte de France*, tr. J. Lewis May, Bodley Head, London, 1905

The Ruin of a Princess, as told by the Duchess d'Angoulême, Madame Elisabeth, sister of Louis XVI, and Cléry the King's Valet de Chambre, tr. Katharine Prescott Wormeley, T. Werner Laurie, London, 1913

Massin, *Les célébrités de la rue*, Gallimard, Paris, 1981

Mayeur de Saint Paul, *Le Chroniqueur désoeuvré ou L'espion du Boulevard du Temple*, London, 1782

Mercier, Louis Sebastien, *The Picture of Paris, Before and After the Revolution*, tr. Wilfred and Emilie Jackson, George Routledge, London, 1929

——, *Le Tableau de Paris*, Paris, 1782–8, tr. and ed. Helen Simpson, *The Waiting City*, Harrap & Co., London, 1933

Myers, A. and S. Joseph & Co., *The Magic Lantern. Its History and Effects*, London, 1854

Niclot, Colette, *Palais-Royal*, booklet, n.d

Rabaut, M.J., *Almanach historique de la revolution Françoise pour l'année 1792*, Onfroy, Libraire, rue S. Victor no. 11, Paris, 1792

Remise, Jacques et Pascale, *Magique Lumineuse*, Ballard, Paris, 1979

Robertson, Etienne Gaspard, *Mémoires récréatifs, scientifiques et anecdotique du Physicien aeronaute E.G. Robertson*, Rignoux, 1831, Paris, 1834

Rose, Rt Hon. George, *Diaries and Correspondence*, ed. Revd Leveson Vernon Harcourt, 2 Vols, Richard Bentley, London, 1860

Salamon, Monseigneur de, *A Papal Envoy during the Reign of Terror, Memoir of Monseigneur de Salamon the Internuncio at Paris during the Revolution 1790–1801*, ed. Abbe Bridier, tr. Francis Jackson, Sands & Co., London, 1911

Salvador, *Le Boulevard du Temple et ses Célébrités, depuis soixante ans*, Massin, Paris, n.d.

Feu Seraphin, Histoire de ce Spectacle, ed. Scheuring, Lyon, 1875

Siboutie, Dr Poumiès de la, *Recollections of a Parisian*, translated by Lady Theodora Davidson, John Murray, London, 1911

Tussaud, John. T, *The Romance of Madame Tussaud's*, London, Odhams Press Ltd, 1921

Tussaud, Marie, *Memoirs and Reminiscences of France, Forming an Abridged History of the French Revolution*, ed. Francis Hervé, Saunders & Otley, London, 1838

Warren, Revd Dawson, *The Journal of a British Chaplain in Paris during the Peace Negotiations of 1801–1802*, ed. A.M. Broadley, Chapman & Hall, London, 1913

Wilson, Harriet, *Memoirs*, ed. Lesley Blanch, Century Publishing, London; first published 1825, this edition 1985

Bibliography

Young, Arthur, *Travels in France during the Years 1787, 1788, 1789*, ed. with an introduction by Jeffry Kaplow, New York, Doubleday & Company Inc., 1969

JOURNALS

Bath Chronicle, 1814, 1824, 1831
Bath Journal, 1824
Cambridge Chronicle, 1818, 1824
Edinburgh Evening Courant, 1803, 1828
Encyclopaedia Britannica, 1875, 9th edition
Greenock Advertiser, 1808
Morning Chronicle
Morning Post
Musée Grevin catalogue, 75th edition
Rochester Gazette & Weekly Advertiser, 1833
Town and Country Magazine, Vol. VII, 1775, 1793

SECONDARY SOURCES

Altick, Richard. D., *The Shows of London*, Cambridge, Mass., Harvard University Press, London, 1978
Bruce, Evangeline, *Napoleon & Josephine, An Improbable Marriage*, Phoenix, London, 1996
Carnegy, Mildred, *A Queen's Knight, the Life of Count Axel de Fersan*, Mills & Boon, London, 1912
Chapman, Pauline, Leslie, Anita, *Madame Tussaud in England, Waxworker Extraordinary*, Hutchinson, London, 1978
Chapman, Pauline, *The French Revolution as seen by Madame Tussaud, Witness Extraordinary*, Quiller, London, 1989
——, *Madame Tussaud in England, Career Woman Extraordinary*, Quiller, London, 1992
Cottrell, Leonard, *Madame Tussaud*, Evans Brothers, London, 1951
Coulter, John, *Norwood Past*, Historical Publications, London, 1996
Heard, Mervyn, *Paul de Philipsthal and the Phantasmagoria in England, Scotland and Ireland*, The Magic Lantern Society Magazine, 1996, 1997, 1998
Hibbert, Christopher, *The French Revolution*, Penguin, 1980
Holmes, M.R.J., *Augustus Hervey, A Naval Casanova*, Portland Press, Edinburgh, 1996
Isherwood, Robert M., *Farce and Fantasy, Popular Entertainment in Eighteenth Century Paris*, OUP, Oxford, 1986
Jarrett, Derek, *Three Faces of Revolution, Paris, London and New York in 1789*, George Philip, London, 1989
Schama, Simon, *Citizens, A Chronicle of the French Revolution*, Viking, London, 1989
Stuart, Dorothy Margaret, *Molly Lepell, Lady Hervey*, George Harrap & Co. Ltd, London, 1936
Trouncer, Margaret, *Madame Elisabeth*, Hutchinson, London, 1955
Wilson, J.B., *The Story of Norwood*, The Norwood Society, 1990

Index

Index

Acknowledgements

For research into the history of the French Revolution, I would like to thank the many archivists who helped me at the Centre Historique des Archives Nationale in Paris; the Bibliothèque Nationale de France, which contains the history of the Palais-Royal and the boulevard du Temple; and the archivists at the Bibliothèque de l'Arsenal, which holds the history of French artists and entertainers. The Musée Carnavalet is where I discovered the wax bust of Curtius, believed to be a self-portrait. The Carnavalet, which is a valuable source of Revolutionary material, also houses an extensive picture library and I would like to thank the curators for their help. I would also like to thank Marie-Thérèse Pipart for her hospitality and generous help while I was in Paris, and Cathy Brooks for her research assistance there.

The background knowledge of the Revolutionary period came from many sources in London and Paris, as listed in the bibliography. Some of the secondary sources included Simon Schama's *Citizens, A Chronicle of the French Revolution*, Christopher Hibbert's *The French Revolution*, and Derek Jarrett's *Three Faces of Revolution, Paris, London and New York in 1789*.

In London, the Enthoven Collection at the London Theatre Museum yielded some valuable history on the Lyceum Theatre, as did the British Library's books of Theatre Cuttings.

Madame Tussaud's generously allowed me access to their archives, where I received invaluable help from the archivists Rosy Cantor and Susanna Lamb. Theresa Ford, the librarian at the *Bath Chronicle*, gave me access to contemporary copies of the newspaper, and helped with information on Bath at the period of Madame Tussaud's visits. Barbara Jordan did useful research for me on

Madame Tussaud's visit to Rochester. I would also like to thank Jaqueline Mitchell for her welcome editorial advice.

Above all, I would like to acknowledge the wonderful work Doreen Hunt has done in deciphering and translating from the French many documents and letters, for communicating with the authorities in Paris on my behalf, for checking my manuscript for glaring mistakes, and for listening to the unfolding history with endless good humour and patience. For all that, and much more, a very special thank you.

Teresa Ransom
Cambridge, 2003